MAU MAU'S CHILDREN

AFRICA AND THE DIASPORA
History, Politics, Culture

SERIES EDITORS

Thomas Spear
David Henige
Michael Schatzberg

Mau Mau's Children

THE MAKING OF
KENYA'S POSTCOLONIAL ELITE

David P. Sandgren

THE UNIVERSITY OF WISCONSIN PRESS

The University of Wisconsin Press
1930 Monroe Street, 3rd Floor
Madison, Wisconsin 53711-2059
uwpress.wisc.edu

3 Henrietta Street
London WCE 8LU, England
eurospanbookstore.com

Printed in the United States of America

Library of Congress Cataloging-in-Publication Data
Sandgren, David P., 1941–
Mau Mau's children : the making of Kenya's postcolonial elite /
David P. Sandgren.
p.   cm.—(Africa and the diaspora: history, politics, culture)
Includes bibliographical references and index.
ISBN 978-0-299-28784-9 (pbk.: alk. paper)
ISBN 978-0-299-28783-2 (e-book)
1. Kikuyu (African people)—Kenya—Biography.
2. Kenya—History—1963—Biography.
I. Title.   II. Series: Africa and the diaspora.
DT433.582.A2S26   2012
305.896′395400922—dc23
2011042649

To

my Giakanja students

Contents

ILLUSTRATIONS

following page 55

FOREWORD

Both the Mau Mau struggle against British colonial rule in Kenya during the 1950s and the transition to independence in the 1960s have been the subject of considerable academic study and debate, but the experiences of ordinary Kenyans during and after the struggle for independence have largely passed under the academic radar. This book focuses on a group of them, from their experience as schoolboys during the struggle for independence to that as an emergent elite following it. Both of these experiences were vital to the processes of decolonization throughout Africa, but they rarely feature in the literature beyond fictional accounts from the era. Many of us seeking to teach this heady and transformative period have therefore used those fictional accounts while we sought in vain to find more historical ones.

David Sandgren was a young American teacher at a new secondary school in central Kenya during the four years immediately before and after independence in 1963. His students, all boys from rural areas, where they had grown up in the midst of Mau Mau, were often the first of their families to attend school. Following independence, they went on to postsecondary studies and careers in the public, and later private, sectors as the first generation of Kenyan Africans to assume the mantle of postcolonial society. Most had not been active in either the Mau Mau insurgency or the British counterinsurgency, though many in their families participated on one side or the other, and few participated actively in postcolonial politics. Rather, they took jobs as teachers, civil servants, technicians, and businessmen in the rapidly expanding post-colonial state, and most prospered. Sandgren subsequently returned to the United States to write and teach African history, but he returned to Kenya some thirty years later and interviewed seventy-five of his former

students and twenty-two members of their families to learn what had
become of them. These are their stories, gracefully interwoven by
Sandgren and informed by his own deep historical knowledge of colonial
and postcolonial Kenya.

Using life histories to compile a collective biography has become a
popular way to convey the experiences of women, minorities, workers,
and others not normally represented in recorded documents or news
stories. Yet life histories must represent something more than the experiences of a few individuals if they are to tell us something of broader
historical events and processes. In Sandgren's case, he was able to locate
and interview most of his former students, making his sample unusually
complete. And while a few prestigious boarding schools had catered to
elite Kenyans for decades, Sandgren's school was one of many day schools
that sprang up at the time to meet the needs of poor rural Kenyans who
sought to gain access to the fresh opportunities opening up with decolonization. It was these students, and many others like them, who became
the new Kenyan middle class recruited into the expanding professional
and administrative ranks of the newly independent nation. Yet, while
this group played a significant part in the transformation of Kenyan
society, his subjects were all young Gikuyu men, and thus not representative of women, peoples from other areas, or Kenyans as a whole.

Sandgren employed open-ended interviews that gave his subjects
free rein to express their experiences in their own terms. While individuals usually construct their own histories in ways they find pleasing
and make sense to them, there was wide unanimity in his subjects' accounts, demonstrating these were as much the memories of a generation as of diverse individuals. Yet their accounts also disclose individual
variations within wider generalities. And they reveal how his students
perceived the process of decolonization and their emergence as a new
educated elite and thus also constitute an intellectual history of how
many Kenyans thought about their history.

Mutual trust is a critical element in collecting oral histories, but while
most scholars labor for months to gain such trust, Sandgren's students
already respected him for his role in their schooling. As a result, the
interviews reveal little dissembling, though there was an obvious reluctance to talk about politics and ethnicity. Both of these were fraught
issues in postcolonial Kenya, where civil servants were enjoined from
political participation and Gikuyu, who had been favorably treated
during President Kenyatta's regime (1963–78), came under suspicion

during President Moi's (1978–2002), the period when Sandgren was conducting his interviews.

In presenting his students' accounts, Sandgren has organized them around several critical topics in Kenya's modern history. The first is colonialism and the Mau Mau struggle for independence, which tore apart local communities in their struggles to survive amid the brutal counterinsurgency campaign conducted by the British. The second is the central role of education in providing new opportunities for poor rural children while at the same time subjecting them to a highly competitive system of selective exams that guaranteed most would fail. The third topic is the formation of a new elite, as the few students who succeeded in moving into new roles in the rapidly expanding public and private sectors built new lives for themselves in the city. And the fourth is the experience of their children, raised in comparative affluence and enjoying elite secondary and university educations but facing limited opportunities as they emerged from their schooling, contrary to their fathers' experiences.

The British colonial system, predicated on the settlement of large numbers of white farmers, had displaced Africans from their lands, restricted them in reserves, and forced them to labor on white farms separated from their families. These policies were particularly destructive of Gikuyu society, and Gikuyu responded from the early 1920s by organizing a succession of political parties, all without much success, until they began to threaten to take up arms against the colonial regime in the early 1950s in what became known as Mau Mau.

From 1952 to 1956 the government responded to the threat with a brutal counterinsurgency campaign known as the Emergency, corralling men into sprawling detention camps and concentrating women and children in protected villages surrounded by barbed wire and guarded by the African Home Guard, which had been recruited by the colonial authorities. Violence became endemic in the reserves as the British tortured detainees to get them to renounce their so-called pathological behavior, the Home Guard assaulted and raped their wards, and insurgents wrecked revenge on colonial police, white settlers, and the Gikuyu Home Guard alike. The violence quickly pitted Gikuyu against one another as people struggled to survive, often by alternately appearing to support the colonial authorities by day and the insurgents by night. It was in the immediate aftermath of this wrenching conflict that Sandgren's students resumed their schooling in rudimentary rural primary and middle schools that mixed the children of former insurgents with those of the Home Guard as Kenya moved toward independence.

British colonial rule had been accompanied by the introduction of Christian missions and schools throughout central Kenya. Many Gikuyu were soon drawn to education as a means of coping with the dispossessions of colonial rule and getting jobs as teachers and low-level functionaries employed by the colonial administration, missions, and white farmers. The desire to gain an education soon became so strong that when the missions attacked Gikuyu cultural practices and drove many from their schools, Gikuyu formed their own independent churches and schools that lent further support to political movements formed earlier. Yet many Gikuyu then saw their schooling abruptly terminated during Mau Mau, as the authorities closed independent schools, resuming only with the effective defeat of Mau Mau. With independence now in the offing, the demand for education became even greater, standards were improved, and many new secondary schools, like Sandgren's, were opened.

Even so, the competition to advance was fierce, intensified by a four-tier exam system that systematically weeded out poorer students at the ends of Standard 4 (fourth grade), Standard 8, Form 4 (twelfth grade), and Form 6. Fewer than one in twelve students who entered school at Standard 1 advanced to secondary school eight years later, and even fewer proceeded on to Form 5 and then university. The pressures to succeed caused students to study into the night, repeat grades and retake exams, and pressure teachers and relatives in order to advance to the next level.

Secondary school was little different. Though the students who had made it that far already comprised an elite 1 percent of their age cohort, the secondary schools had better facilities and teachers, and the students continued to work extremely hard; still only one in four were able to advance beyond Form 4 to Form 5 and then university. Yet given the rapidly increasing opportunities in newly independent Kenya as the economy expanded and expatriates went home, completing Form 4 was all the others needed to go on to promising careers in the public and the private sectors, thus providing a reward for their hard work at last. As the number of Form 4 school-leavers and university graduates increased manyfold in the succeeding years, however, such opportunities constricted dramatically, and unemployment among school-leavers became an increasingly serious problem by the 1980s. Sandgren's students were thus uniquely placed to achieve success, and they soon joined the new Kenyan middle class.

Entering the unfamiliar world of the urban workplace, his students became part of a new urban elite, living in a style that few of them could have imagined and that dramatically eclipsed that of their less-educated rural relatives. In their first jobs, they earned much more in a month than their parents in a year, and their incomes rose rapidly thereafter. By the time Sandgren revisited them thirty years later, all lived in comfortable and well-furnished houses, dressed well, owned cars, sent their children to the best schools and universities (some abroad), and invested in agricultural land, urban real estate, and businesses for retirement. Most had also paid the school fees of their siblings and continued to support their parents and relatives as well, thus continuing to maintain older communal responsibilities while also adopting newer individualistic ones.

In contrast to their fathers, who still lived in homogenous rural areas, Sandgren's students usually lived as nuclear families in multiethnic government housing or cities away from home. Their fathers also had multiple wives and many children, whereas most of his students had only one wife and four children. And the students were more likely than their fathers to help raise their children. Yet most of the students still preferred to marry women from their home area, where they knew their families. They continued to negotiate the marriage with their future father-in-law. And they continued to name their children after their own parents, thus maintaining traditional spiritual links across the generations. In these and many other ways, they thus continued traditional beliefs and practices while simultaneously adopting new ones, a transition that is reflected in the lives of their children.

While Sandgren's students had struggled hard to escape rural poverty, their own children have been raised largely in urban affluence, with their comforts and schooling assured. Yet their job prospects are much poorer in the stalled Kenyan economy, where they may end up working for, and continuing to benefit from, their parents' successes. They have attended multiethnic and multiracial schools and move easily among schoolmates and friends from other groups but are less comfortable visiting their rural Gikuyu grandparents. They identify as Kenyans though still live largely among fellow Gikuyu. They speak assured English and Swahili but are less fluent in Gikuyu. Their individualistic aspirations outweigh their parents' commitment to establish families. In the end, while their lives have become less constrained by the bounds of kinship and ethnicity than those of their parents, they have yet to become autonomous. Nor are they likely to.

Sandgren's students and their families thus have much to teach us about the dramatic changes brought about by independence, the ways they struggled to gain an education and transform their own lives, and the nature of the changes they wrought that continue to revolutionize Kenya society. To understand their lives is to understand one of the most transformational epochs in African history.

Thomas Spear

Professor of History Emeritus
University of Wisconsin–Madison

PREFACE

Our understanding of Africa has frequently been limited to the general perceptions of our time: crisis, catastrophe, poverty, violence, and most recently the destruction brought about by HIV/AIDS. Such perceptions are occasionally balanced by the more positive images of Africa's scenic beauty and its wonderful wildlife endowment. But seldom do we know Africa as a continent of people who have struggled but also succeeded, who have made plans and brought them to fruition. Generally we know Africa only at arm's length, seldom up close and in detail. If we have followed postcolonial events on the continent, we may have concluded that the peace and prosperity anticipated after independence have gone largely unmet and that the various indices of well-being reveal not growth but decline. While these perceptions are not necessarily incorrect, they are certainly not the whole story, especially when one applies them to individual Africans.

This book does just that by following the lives of a group of Kenyan men from childhood in the late 1940s well into adulthood in the mid-1990s. We will have a close look at their childhood during the Mau Mau Rebellion, primary and secondary schooling, jobs and careers, marriage and family life, and even retirement for some. To reveal the lives of Kenya's first postcolonial elite, the book will explore significant elements of daily life for seventy-five men over a fifty-year span of time.

In the last thirty years or so, a large and growing scholarship has explored the causes of Africa's underdevelopment, including colonially constructed economies that were not well suited to benefit the African states that inherited them: hurried attempts at imposing democratic but alien political structures at the time of independence; ethnic rivalry within newly independent nations, which often culminated in civil war and the rise of military governments; foreign aid, which frequently deepened poverty and fueled corruption rather than creating the robust society it promised—and so the story goes, creating a worldwide pessimistic perspective of the continent. But the chapters that follow focus on a period of infinite optimism on the continent, when in the 1960s and 1970s newly independent Africans thought anything was possible. It was a time of "youthful liberating momentum," when high expectations and ideas of catching up with the rest of the world were considered entirely possible.[1] The very process of attaining independence through constitutional and legal means predicted that the new African states would shape their futures in positive directions. Africans were excited about their new relationship with the world, where with new national leaders and ambassadors in foreign capitals, they would take their place as equals in the world community.

Indeed these were heady times, and Kenyans fit very nicely into this paradigm of forward-looking optimism. They were on the verge of becoming free after seventy years of British colonial rule, with Jomo Kenyatta, a hero of the liberation struggle, as their new president. A new constitution had enabled them to elect their first-ever local representatives to a national parliament. Kenyans projected that, with such people now running their government, only good things would follow, such as ample employment, good prices for their crops, and a growing economy guaranteeing abundant life. They were especially sure that new schools would be built to satisfy the hunger for education and that the lives of their children would shine. Without doubt, they were entering a golden age.

Western-style education was critical in attaining this future and in the formation of new African elites. The linkage between education and elite formation began during the colonial era when missionaries first introduced Western education, mostly to African boys, as a pathway to their conversion. Because of their need for a cadre of minor officials in government and the private sector, colonial governments encouraged this education and its continuation to high school for some and even to university for a select few. But as Grace Bunyi reminds us, not only did these students receive a Western-style education, they received it in the language of the colonial power: "English, the language of the socially and politically powerful white colonial officers, white settlers, businessmen/women and missionaries became available to Africans as a means of gaining power."[2] Kenyans then had already begun to understand the connection between education and advancement in colonial society. To their peers, Africans fluent in the colonizer's language were immediately recognized as powerful and regarded with awe. Their junior positions in the colonial government eventually led to knowledge and understanding of their inferior status and inspired youth movements, trade unions, and anticolonial political developments. Eventually, members of the early elite helped to negotiate the end of colonial rule and in some cases influenced the armed struggle that fought for independence. A scholar who has written about this period, Magnus O. Bassey, observed that "almost all the political transformations that took place in Africa at this time were largely the by products of the activities of educated Africans."[3]

Finally, from the very beginning of its existence, this early elite ensured that their children would enjoy the same status by sending them to the best schools in the colony and abroad to receive a Western-style education and to become fluent in English. As a result, by the last years of colonial rule in Kenya, as in most African colonies, the educated African elite had largely become a hereditary group.[4]

But in the very last few years of colonial rule, waiting in the wings and still invisible were the makings of another group that would rise over the next decade to become the first postcolonial elite. Like their colonial predecessors, they too were the products of a Western-style education, including fluency in English. But unlike the colonial elite and its offspring, these young people were nearly always the sons of smallholder rural farmers, few of whom spoke English and had at best a year or two of education but frequently were illiterate. These young people started their education in simple neighborhood schools and moved on to nearby secondary schools. All experienced the setback of having their education sharply interrupted and even suspended during the Mau Mau Rebellion. How these young people overcame such handicaps to successfully acquire a Western-style education and enter Kenyan society, eventually to become Kenya's first postcolonial elite, is the topic explored in the rest of this book.

I have had a unique vantage point to observe and to learn about this first postcolonial generation. I went to Kenya in 1963 as a young college graduate to teach in a small, all-boys rural high school called Giakanja Secondary School. I taught four years there and then returned to the United States to attend graduate school and eventually to teach African history at Concordia College in Moorhead, Minnesota. In 1995, with the assistance of a Concordia sabbatical and a Fulbright Research Fellowship, I returned to Kenya to interview my former students and to collect their life histories. Our lives had intersected during their high school education, when I taught them history and English. For me those years were pivotal in introducing me to the colony (and then country) of Kenya, to the central highlands of that country, and to the Gikuyu people, the ethnic group from which my students came. During my later academic study of the continent, I regularly drew upon my experiences from Kenya during this time. I was a young adult eager to learn about the new and interesting place in which I found myself. For my students, however, their high school years, though interesting and certainly important, were but one epoch among many in their lives, some that had taken place before I had arrived to teach them and others unfolding long after they had left school.

The chapters that follow are the result of what I learned from their life histories. It is a story of childhood hardship and the struggle for schooling in a colonial society where educational opportunities were limited and advancement to the next level was based on successfully passing rigorous national examinations. Nevertheless, they endured the hardships and met the challenges as they became Kenya's first post-colonial generation. On a personal level it is a story of great success, especially when one compares their present lives with their humble beginnings.

The period of time when they were youngsters was dominated by their experiences during the Mau Mau Rebellion, part peasant revolt against British colonial rule and part civil war that engulfed the highlands of Kenya and centered on the very area in which my students lived. This turbulent period in their young lives is explored in chapter 1. The other topics that dominated their early lives include education, which started at about age six (and was frequently interrupted during Mau Mau) and then continued for twelve years, ending with the completion of high school at about age eighteen. My students' experiences with education are explored in chapters 2 and 3, which concern their first eight years in primary and intermediate schools and especially about their high school experiences at Giakanja. It was during this shared time together that I witnessed their development into young men who often struggled to overcome personal and financial difficulties and to excel in their studies and eventually in their school leaving exams. They were shaped by the school in their growing maturity, but as Giakanja's first students, they also helped shape this young school into a successful institution that produced talented and successful young men. Upon leaving Giakanja, these young men joined the wider world as

Kenya's first postcolonial generation. There they pursued further education and careers, married and started families, and became members of Kenya's economic and social elite. These topics are explored in chapters 4, 5, and 6. Finally in a closing chapter I reflect on the children of these elites—the next generation. How are they likely to fare in the Kenya of the twenty-first century, where the abundant jobs and economic opportunities and comfortable life of their parents' generation seem much less available?

ACKNOWLEDGMENTS

Both individuals and institutions have assisted in bringing this book to completion. Foremost among them have been my former Kenyan students who have been my primary research subjects. Of course back in 1963, I did not know how the three classes I would teach at Giakanja Secondary School would so profoundly affect the rest of my life. It was not long, however, before they began to reveal their lives of struggle and their striving for a better future. This can-do spirit inspired me and kindled my interest in African history, which I later pursued in graduate school and thereafter as a college professor. But I mark the beginning of my understanding of African cultures and peoples, especially of rural life during the era of colonial rule, to my association with these students all those years ago. I often wondered what their adult lives were like. I began to formulate a research project that would address that idea, one that eventually took me back to Kenya in 1995. Not surprisingly, they welcomed me back, introduced me to their families, gave me hospitality and friendship, and above all agreed to be interviewed. With profound gratitude, I dedicate this book to them, which could not have been written without their kindness and cooperation.

The Kenya National Archives has also been instrumental in the success of this project, especially in making available material concerning the Mau Mau Rebellion and Kenyan education. Their library also gave me access to useful government publications. I give my thanks to the staff, especially to Richard Ambani, Peterson Kithuka, Grace Esiromo, and Evanson Kiiru. Thanks also to the staff at Rhodes House Library, Oxford, U.K., for help with their manuscripts collection.

Others who gave unstintingly of their expertise include Tom Spear, who helped shape this book in large and small ways, including the contribution of an illuminating foreword, and Robert Strayer, whose assistance and encouragement enabled me to take my ideas for this book to their next level of development. I give my sincere thanks to both of them. Thanks also go to Jan Vansina and David Henige, whose advice gave direction to my earliest ideas about this project. My thanks also go to the Department of History at the University of Nairobi, especially to Dr. Henry Mutoro, the chair of the department.

I am indebted to Dr. Shirin Walji for her kind offer of a place to stay in Nairobi, which enabled me to use that city, crucial to my research, as my primary base of operations. I also wish to thank my assistants Doreen Kathure and Pauline Watene for their careful transcription of my interviews.

To my colleagues at Concordia College in Moorhead, especially those in the Department of History and Peter Hovde, whose counsel encouraged me to continue on after my first draft, I offer my sincere gratitude. Thanks also to Judith Sinclair for her careful assistance with the many tasks involved in the final preparation of the manuscript.

I also wish to thank Concordia College for awarding me sabbaticals for the researching and writing of this book and to the Fulbright Program for a research award that supported my fieldwork in Kenya.

I wish to thank the staff at the University of Wisconsin Press for their fine work in turning my manuscript into this book, especially Gwen Walker and Sheila McMahon for their guidance and patience.

Finally I wish to thank my wife, Ann, whose critical reading of my manuscript drafts has been a major influence on its improvement, together with her love, encouragement, and good humor, which have sustained me throughout.

ABBREVIATIONS

AFC	Agricultural Finance Corporation
AIPC	African Independent Pentecostal Church
CE	Cambridge Exam
CEE	Common Entrance Exam
CSC	Cambridge School Certificate
CSCE	Cambridge School Certificate Exam
DC	district commissioner
DEB	District Education Board
DO	district officer
KISA	Kikuyu Independent Schools Association
KNA	Kenya National Archives
KPE	Kenya Preliminary Exam
LNC	Local Native Council
PEO	provincial education officer
SOK	Survey of Kenya
TEA	Teachers for East Africa

MAU MAU'S CHILDREN

Introduction

My own journey to Giakanja started in February 1963, when as a senior in college I saw a poster advertising opportunities to teach in East Africa. There was a tear-off postcard that I sent in. The packet of information that came in response informed me of a shortage of high school teachers in Kenya, Tanganyika, Uganda, and Zanzibar. Though I was a history major, I never had taken a course on Africa. I was ignorant but also intrigued and curious about such an opportunity. So I sent in my application, and in March someone was sent to interview me. I later learned from relatives and my part-time employer that the FBI had checked on me as well. Then in April I received a letter—if I wanted to join Teachers for East Africa (TEA), they would accept me. I was astonished! Since I had said nothing to my parents, they were equally astonished! Years later, revealing the stereotypes of their generation, they told me that when I announced that I was going out to East Africa to teach for two years, they worried that they might not see me again.

I left Minneapolis in mid-June for two months of TEA orientation at Columbia University. There were fifty-seven of us at Columbia, and we all had a very full summer being taught such things as British English (the language of instruction in high school), Kiswahili, and the East African educational system. It had never occurred to me that the American educational system was not universal. We also studied East African history and politics, which were considered important subjects as independence approached. I was enjoying many other experiences, too: I had ridden on my first jet airplane to get to New York City, heard my first Spanish and Italian in the ethnic neighborhoods, met members of the Nation of Islam (the Black Muslims), attended my first Broadway play, and met my first Kenyan, who was a guest preacher in a Harlem church. Six months later in Kenya, as I was driving along a country road near the school where I was teaching, a motorcycle passed me. We

3

both stopped. It was Bernard Muinde, the Kenyan pastor I had met in Harlem, now back in his own country and in charge of forty-two congregations in my area. We became friends.

If the first part of my TEA adventure comprised the orientation program at Columbia University, then the second part began upon my arrival in Nairobi in early August 1963. In those days the industrial area of the city had not yet crept all the way out to the airport, so that on our ride in, we caught our first glimpses of giraffes and zebra grazing in the distance. The Ministry of Education housed us at the Norfolk, Nairobi's most elite hotel. I remember feeling a little uncomfortable, not only when I attempted to practice my elementary Swahili on the hotel staff but also when trying to puzzle out what to expect in my first five-course dinner and how to use all those forks next to my plate! Morning coffee and afternoon tea were taken on the veranda, where well-healed tourists gossiped about safaris taken or speculated about where, forty-one years earlier, white settlers had fired into the unarmed crowd of African people who had gathered to protest the detention of Kenya's first nationalist, Harry Thuku.

After breakfast each day we trooped out to the nearby university for meetings on such topics as secondary education in Kenya, staying healthy, the African schoolboy, and the peoples of Kenya. We visited some Nairobi secondary schools and most afternoons divided up to attend curriculum seminars in our disciplines.[1] I also learned that I was to be posted to Giakanja Secondary School, which was located about ten miles outside of Nyeri in the Gikuyu Reserve and somewhat inaccessible. I definitely would need a car. The classified ads in the *East African Standard* revealed that there were few cars available in my price range (about $250). However, I did find one—an old red MG sports car, which I was surprised to find in Kenya but thrilled to buy. In time, I came to understand that with its canvas top it was not a very practical car in Kenya's dust and rain. Also, it probably did not convey the image of a sensible, hardworking American that TEA liked to promote about its teachers. But I was a twenty-two-year-old American kid without such awareness yet. Three decades later, the former provincial education officer (PEO) who had welcomed me to his area could not quite recall who I was until I mentioned that I arrived at his Nyeri office in August of 1963 in a red sports car. He said he could still remember thinking at that time, somewhat uncharitably, that this was exactly what an American would do! Similarly, my students at Giakanja revealed decades later to me that they were not surprised to see the sports car because they were sure all

Americans drove one! The following year I sold it to finance the purchase of a "sensible" Volkswagen Beetle, but in the meantime, when the Nairobi orientation ended I headed off to my posting in the MG, driving through the Kenyan countryside with the top down.

I arrived at Giakanja two weeks before the start of the fall term, so there were no students or staff present. I remember that the school clerk showed me to my house, which was new and shiny but bleak, without any decoration or electricity. In the kitchen was a wood stove, and I wondered how I would ever get that going to cook a meal or heat my water. The PEO had previously introduced me to some Nyeri shop-keepers, to whom I now returned for food and other provisions. He also had offered to give me dinner, and I discovered that his wife taught at Giakanja, so we spent the evening in conversation about the school. Their kindness to me and also the friendliness of the headmaster, Robert Ndegwa, whom I met the next day, helped to ease me into my new life at the school.

Nyeri became increasingly familiar in the weeks that followed, and I grew comfortable there. I made friends with several Indian shopkeepers, was invited to their homes, and tasted my first Indian cooking. They introduced me to my first Indian movies, and several times I was invited to day-long Indian weddings. Within the first weeks of my arrival, I found a church with a service in English and met the missionary pastor, John Ridout, his wife Shirley, and their two children. They became good friends at Nyeri and have been lifelong friends ever since. The church also opened up the world of Nyeri's white-settler community to me, since a number of them also attended Sunday services. I was initially invited home to Sunday lunch and in time was asked to their parties, weddings, and funerals.

The settlers approved of my teaching at an African high school, but upon hearing that I was the only European (white person) there, they automatically assumed that I was the headmaster. They reasoned that education would save Gikuyu youth from the many shortcomings of their parents' generation, of which they had a low opinion. Many of these settlers had been members of the Kenya Regiment during the Mau Mau Rebellion and had fought against the Gikuyu. Initially my relationship with these settlers was as pupil to teacher, with their lessons tending to dwell on the great settler contributions to Kenya. In the beginning I had been prepared not to like them and had thought of them as interesting cultural specimens from Kenya's past, but in time my friendship with several families became more genuine, and there was more equality in our relationship. In the four years that I knew these settlers, I also detected a softening in their attitudes toward Kenyans; they did not always see them as a single monolithic whole, and they acknowledged the positive development of the country.

I learned more about my students' lives and culture, too, though the fact that Giakanja was a day school initially limited my contact with students outside of the classroom, in contrast to the boarding schools, where the staff had responsibilities for the supervision of student activities after hours and on weekends. But I did have some contact with them through the athletic program, in which I assisted each spring with track and field events and each summer with volleyball. Together with two Peace Corps Volunteers who arrived a year later, I introduced softball to the school, which quickly became popular. I also was the school librarian throughout my four years at Giakanja. Each of these activities provided some opportunities to know the students a little more personally. I also employed needy students to help with yard work on Saturdays. Though they were timid and rigidly formal with me in the classroom, gradually through these more informal opportunities I began to hear about their families and friends and sometimes about their hopes for the future. Of course they were as curious about my cultural background as I was about theirs, so our conversations sometimes consisted of sharing our experiences with each other.[2] At the end of my first term, I volunteered to take home two brothers who lived about twenty miles away from the school. I had envisioned just dropping them off and leaving. But obviously they had sent word ahead that they would be arriving by car and that some hospitality was in order for their teacher. Upon my arrival I was greeted by the whole neighborhood, then shepherded around their small farm, and finally seated at a table in the yard, where I alone was served lunch with the whole family and their neighbors watching. I later learned that this was the first time anyone in the family had ridden in a car or seen an American. I attempted to greet them and converse with my simple Gikuyu (my student's vernacular language) to everyone's amusement. Over time I had many opportunities to visit student homes and meet their families.

Through these encounters I learned much about Kenyan culture and grew increasingly comfortable living there. That is not to say that I did not continue to commit many cultural blunders. I remember one incident that occurred about a year after my arrival and was particularly humbling. On this occasion I gave a ride home to one of the school's laborers. On our arrival I was invited in for a cup of tea and I noticed that his wife was pregnant. I decided that it would be appropriate to buy them a gift in anticipation of the baby's birth. The next time I was at their house, I gave them a gift for the baby, which they put aside without comment. I was surprised by what seemed to be rude behavior. When I asked a teaching colleague about it, he said that it was very bad luck to acknowledge a child before its birth. Only then did I connect up what I knew: Kenya had a high infant mortality rate, and Gikuyu only welcome children into the family with a naming ceremony some months after birth. It was a humbling experience and alerted me to the fact that I should not be smug about what I had learned—there was always much more to know. I also came to understand that I had probably made many other cultural errors without knowing it.

To be sure, while my cultural ignorance set me apart, the very program that recruited me and the terms under which I served also separated me from my teaching colleagues. Teachers for East Africa prided itself in the fact that its teachers served under the same conditions as all graduate teachers in East Africa. But they did not foresee that I would be the only graduate teacher at Giakanja for most of my tenure there. Also, all expatriate teachers were automatically made education officers, an employment grade that brought additional benefits. So I was the only expatriate teacher at Giakanja and the only education officer as well. Therefore my employment contract included many features not available to my African colleagues. Among them was an overseas allowance to my salary and a 25 percent bonus at the completion of my contract. In addition, I received an outfitting allowance (a carryover I am sure from the time when one would need special clothing and supplies for living at isolated postings), an allowance to fund my (nonexistent) children's private education, a three-month paid leave, paid passages back to the United States, and air- and sea-freight shipping allowances. Finally, I was eligible for a low-interest car loan and an interest-free advance on my salary to make the down payment.[3] The most noticeable of these benefits was my car.

For much of my time, I was the only teacher at Giakanja who had a car. While I frequently gave rides to town to my colleagues and picked up people from the neighborhood who were on the road walking, still I knew that I was often identified as the "American with the car." My privileged position in the community was drawn to my attention at a political meeting I attended some months after I arrived. Tom Mboya, a popular politician in Prime Minister Jomo Kenyatta's interim government, was campaigning on behalf of the local candidate. Mboya spent a long time explaining to the crowd that when independence came, Kenya would enter an age when everyone would have what they wanted. "For instance," he said, "you will all be driving cars. In fact, copy down the license plate numbers of the cars you want and I'll make sure that you get them." I remember that everyone had laughed because they knew it was a joke. But as I walked back to the school compound with a colleague and he explained to me what Mboya had said, I became aware that the metaphor for the good life in Kenya was the car, and I was the only one in the whole neighborhood who owned one.

Five months after my arrival, Kenya became independent on 12 December 1963. This occasion marked an important period in my successful adjustment to the country and to Giakanja. From the moment of my arrival, one could not forget that independence was near. The anticipation of it was apparent each day in conversations with my teaching colleagues and students. White settlers and Asians at Nyeri were ambivalent or fearful of its arrival and expressed much skepticism about the ability of Africans to govern themselves.

As the time of independence drew closer, I remember thinking about attending the ceremonies in Nairobi. The American embassy sent all TEA teachers a letter warning us not to attend the Nairobi ceremonies or even go to any that were planned in provincial centers like Nyeri for fear of possible violence. None of my European or Asian acquaintances at Nyeri planned to attend for they too feared violence. The embassy suggested that we stay at home and watch the ceremonies on TV. Of course Giakanja had no electricity, let alone TV. That letter warning me off instead galvanized my determination to go. I was probably a little naive about the threat of violence, but I also felt affronted about being kept from witnessing a country gain its independence. How could one not attend what was perhaps the greatest historical happening of one's life? My folder of memorabilia on the Kenya independence celebrations contains two passes for attendance. I cannot remember how I got them, but they permitted a TEA friend and me to attend.

The evening I spent witnessing the ceremonies that created Kenya into a new nation independent from British colonial rule was one of my most memorable experiences ever. I remember arriving at sundown (about 6:30 p.m.) at the temporary stadium built to hold thousands of people and located just west of Nairobi on the Athi Plains. During the long wait to midnight I remember seeing displays of ethnic dancing and military and police marching bands. But two things especially stand out in my memory from that evening so many years ago. First, the conversations that were going on around me were so heartwarming and joyous. I had been apprehensive at first when I realized the size of the crowd and the fact that I could see no other white faces. But as I sat there, I began to hear what people were saying around me: such phrases as, "I never thought that I would see this day happen in my lifetime," or "I thought that only my children or grandchildren would witness this event," or "We will be alright now; our future will be golden!" People were awed by the moment, optimistic about the future, and peaceful. The second memory comes as the very moment of independence drew near. As the crowd counted off the last sixty seconds before midnight, the British Union Jack was lowered down the pole at the center of the stadium. As the very last couple of seconds ticked off, one could see the flag fall onto the ground into the dust and then all the lights went off. A moment later when the lights came back on, there was the new Kenyan flag at the top of the pole, flying for the first time ever. Not a sound could be heard in the immense stadium as the army band played the Kenyan national anthem for the first time. Tears streamed down people's cheeks as they listened, and when it was finished, a thunderous roar filled the stadium for many minutes. I too was gripped by emotions, knowing that I had witnessed a special moment in Kenya's history.

Upon my return home, I discovered that none of my friends and acquaintances at Nyeri and no one at Giakanja School had attended the independence ceremony in Nairobi. I found myself frequently describing my experience to white settlers, Asian shopkeepers, teaching colleagues, and especially to my students, who wanted to hear all the details over and over again. In a way, my witnessing of Kenya's independence celebrations became a metaphor for my entire experience in Kenya. It captured the joyous mood of optimism about the future that surrounded me in that stadium and permeated my four years of teaching and learning in Kenya. My students, their parents, and my teaching colleagues, though they sometimes struggled, also were buoyed by their conviction that the hardest times were over and the future would be better. They were convinced that their hard work would pay off and that their future would be successful. I too felt this way about them and about my own success as a teacher and a cross-cultural learner in East Africa. Just as I was privileged to witness Kenya's independence ceremonies, so I also became aware that I was witnessing the transformation of my students from struggling school boys into successful students. Of course from my perspective now, more than forty years later, I realize that I was also witnessing their entrance into becoming the first elite generation to take its place in Kenya's society after independence.

One of the joys of teaching is reconnecting with former students, but except for two brief encounters in the 1970s, I never met any of my students again after I left Giakanja in 1967. I often wondered what had become of them, and in the late 1980s I began to consider the possibility of reconnecting with them for the purpose of collecting their life histories. This became a reality in 1995, when I received a Fulbright Research Fellowship to do just that, but I left for Kenya armed only with a few contacts. One of my former Kenyan teaching colleagues from Giakanja, now retired from a long career in education, provided valuable help locating former students. I reconnected with the two Peace Corps Volunteers I had known at the school, and they had a couple of contacts for me. And then coincidentally, two weeks before I left for Kenya in September 1995, I got a letter from a former student asking if I would buy a set of Galloway Big Bertha golf clubs for him. Twenty years earlier we had briefly met in Nairobi but then had lost touch with each other. Now he had contacted me right at the time when I would be trying to find him. And that request for a set of $2,000 golf clubs—"Just send me the bill and I'll reimburse you"—tipped me off that at least some of my former students had done well for themselves.

Even though I had taught a broad range of students during my four years at Giakanja, I decided to focus on the first three classes that graduated from the school—in 1965, 1966, and 1967. These were the students with whom I had the longest contact, some for their entire four-year education at Giakanja. There were about thirty in each of these classes, for a total of ninety students. Of those, I was able to locate and interview seventy-five of them. Most of those interviews were conducted either in their homes or at my Nairobi apartment. A few were held after hours at their place of business or in my hotel room when I was interviewing outside Nairobi. Generally there were just the two of us present and the interviews were conducted in one two- to four-hour sitting. In addition to seventy-five interviews with former students, I conducted twenty-two others with their wives, grown children, and others associated with Giakanja. These interviews were useful for comparisons between my male students and their female counterparts of the same generation, as well as for comparing the experiences of their children's generation. I also learned much about courtship, family life, and parenting from them that I could compare to my students' responses on the same topics.

I started the search for my students at Nyeri, the closest town to Giakanja. It was a commercial and provincial government center of about ten thousand in the 1960s but had swelled to a quarter of a million people thirty years later. My first inquiries there led me to former students who were now in business, education, or the civil service. I soon learned from them that most of my students lived in Nairobi, Kenya's capital, and I made that city my base of operations. In time I found other students in Mombasa, Kenya's second-largest city and chief port on the Indian Ocean. Others were scattered throughout the Rift Valley, but especially in Nakuru. After a few contacts with the first students I met, my meetings with them settled into a common rhythm. Our first contacts were sometimes by phone, but many times I just showed up at their work site or their home. We reminisced about our time together at Giakanja, usually prompted by photos that I had brought, but occasionally even by photos they had taken or received from classmates. Sometimes they took me to lunch or entertained me in their home or even invited me to play golf with them on the weekend; twice I was their guest at some of Kenya's game parks. Clearly they were pleased to see me and wanted to impress me. Indeed I was impressed, even astonished, by their achievements and enjoyed these social gatherings a great deal. Eventually I was able to schedule an interview with them and after it took place, we saw each other much less. Some of them would contact me about a classmate they had found for me to interview. Others, I did not meet again. A few of them wanted to keep in touch and so occasionally throughout the year, I would receive invitations to lunch or Sunday dinner, usually in their homes, and in this way I got to know their families and even some of their friends. Two students regularly invited me to play golf with them. Consequently, I came to establish a special familiarity and rapport with about a dozen students that was not typical of the group. During these more casual social gatherings, I often learned about my students and their families and more generally about Kenyan life in the 1990s. Though not exclusively so, it was from this special group that I also chose a number of wives and children to interview as well.

The interviews themselves were the heart of this project. My intention was to simply encourage my former students to tell me about their lives, beginning with their earliest memories and continuing chronologically to the present. In this way I saw my interview producing a life history, "[a] self-voiced life story."[4] While some scholars have limited their interviews to a pool of representative informants, sometimes using elaborate schemes to achieve this end, I made no selection, hoping to interview all my former students and nearly achieving that goal.[5] An important reason for not limiting my interviews to a smaller representative number was because I was curious about what had become of all my students. I reasoned that since I had unusual access to this group (I was favorably known to all of them), I should attempt to collect as many life histories as possible. This assumption proved to be correct, because no one turned me down. Though all the place names, dates, and events are correct, I have chosen to use only the first names of those interviewed to protect their privacy. For those with the same first name, I have added a letter in their endnote citation to distinguish among them (i.e., Adam a, Adam b, Adam c, etc.).

Did they tell me the truth, and even if they intended to do so, did they accurately remember the past? These are vexing questions to life-history scholars. Though my students knew that as their former teacher I was curious about and interested in their lives, they also came to understand that I wanted to write about them. Nevertheless, they largely controlled the agenda of the interview. I might ask them for a clarification of something they said, or I might prompt them to elaborate on a topic they had brought up, but I tried not to otherwise interrupt them or to steer the interview. Clearly they told me what they wanted to, but there is great integrity in those seventy-five life histories, and they frequently discussed in similar ways the epochs of their lives, such as Mau Mau and schooling, career, and family. Of course there were certainly exaggerations and silences in their life accounts, but only a few times did I detect deliberate deception or falsehoods.

A significant silence that did emerge concerned my students' reticence to talk about their political thinking and activities. After the first few interviews, when this silence became noticeable, I began to inquire more directly about their ideas concerning President Moi's government, especially since it did not favor the Gikuyu. I could not draw them out with such questions and began to wonder if they were just not very political. In addition, those working in the Kenya civil service stated that their terms of employment did not permit any political discussion or activity.

This cohort might have been too frightened to speak openly about the political times in which they lived under the Moi government. They had been well placed ethnically during the presidency of their fellow

Gikuyu, Jomo Kenyatta. But that comfortable era ended with his death in 1978 and ushered in a long period of conflict, instability, and vicious ethnic politics under the new Kalenjin president, Daniel arap Moi. Critics of the government disappeared or were detained and sometimes brutalized. The atmosphere of paranoia that developed, with government agents thought to be listening and watching, was still present during the time of my interviews. I am sure that my former students were sufficiently intimidated and perhaps embarrassed by these circumstances and did not want to discuss politics with me. Perhaps they were even concerned about my safety if I was thought to be involved in this sensitive issue by a suspicious government. At the time, such explanations seemed to answer the question about why politics was absent from their narratives.

Though my students' life histories revealed similarities, they did not live identical lives. There was a range of experiences, decisions, and outcomes among them that also revealed the diversity of this postcolonial Kenyan generation. This book explores the full range of all their lives through an analysis of their life accounts.

My thinking about this project concerning the lives of my former students, and the decisions I have made about the collection and presentation of their life histories, have been informed by a large and growing literature on life histories. One very early example, perhaps even a pre-life-history example, is Leonard Plotnicov's 1967 publication, *Strangers to the City: Urban Man in Jos, Nigeria*. The focal point is chapter-long portraits of four men followed by shorter accounts of four others. Each man's life story is based upon multiple interviews and then told in Plotnicov's own words. A more recent example is Jean Davison's *Voices from Mutira: Change in the Lives of Rural Gikuyu Women, 1910–1995*. Like Plotnicov, the central core of Davison's book are the seven chapters, each of which portray a single woman's life, but this time each is a life history in the woman's own voice from multiple interviews edited by Davison. Finally, from outside Africa is a book on Soviet women edited by Barbara Alpern Engel and Anastasia Posadskaya-Vanderbeck, *A Revolution of Their Own: Voices of Women in Soviet History*. Eight chapter-long life histories are found in this 1998 publication, each based on a single interview and presented in the women's own words. While each of these scholars presents us with captivating and clear portraits of individual lives, it is only in the last two examples that readers learn of the power and passion of participants' lives through their own words. Furthermore, it is only with the Soviet women that we hear largely unedited

voices recounting their lives. This has been the model that I have followed, a story of postcolonial Kenyans told in their own words as much
as possible.

Some of the literature on the analysis of oral traditions has assisted
me as well, especially because it facilitated my understanding of how
members of the cohort "constructed their lives in ways that made sense
to them."[6] In particular, Leroy Vail and Landeg White's *Power and the
Praise Poem: Southern African Voices in History* is especially instructive. They
argue for understanding oral texts through their careful analysis, as well
as paying close attention to the historical context in which they were
constructed and performed. In masterful chapters, they demonstrate in
their six case studies how to historize the text to understand its meaning.
In one case, "'Paiva': The History of a Song," the process is especially
thorough. Only after examining the song's many versions and squeezing
meaning from each, together with a thorough identification and study
of the historical events the song described, followed by a close study of
the changing times in which the various singers lived and the many
interpretations previously considered, do they finally and convincingly
arrive at its ultimate meaning.[7]

Vail and White's admonition to dig deep into the text and into the
historical context of its construction can be applied to my narratives as
well. Such a process may reveal another interpretation concerning the
silence about politics. As future chapters will reveal, a common thread
running through the cohort's narratives is that hard work, careful
planning, and perseverance will eventually pay off. By the time the Moi
era had arrived, they were well established in their careers and family
life. Significant salaries accompanied their senior positions in the public
and private sector, and they were busy in their roles as husbands and
fathers. The payoff had clearly arrived. But as we have seen, it was
dangerous to openly rebuke the Moi government, so they chose to stay
politically silent but to implicitly criticize the government by their everyday actions: doing their job, raising their family, and thriving.

If we are to understand that what this cohort told me in their narratives was a construction of their lives that made sense to them, then
another issue remains for consideration, as identified by Elizabeth
Tonkin's *Narrating Our Pasts: The Social Construction of Oral History*. Her
thesis is "that representation of pastness . . . are made by persons in
interaction situated in real time and space [and] are purposeful social
actions."[8] That is to say, all narratives have not only tellers but listeners
too, and as the listeners change, so also will the narrative. The past that

the cohort narrated to me made sense to them (and to me), but it was just one past, not their only past, because its telling was situated in a particular time and place and articulated to me, their former teacher and a sympathetic listener. Did they make it up? Of course not, but as Tonkin reminds us, the narrative that I heard was a social construction tailored for me.

The literature on oral history, though helpful, was not fully appropriate to my needs since the purpose for collecting life narratives about the cohort was to develop a collective biography about the entire group, now an important segment of Kenya's civil society. In this pursuit I have found some assistance in the literature on prosopography, which Lawrence Stone defines as "the investigation of the common background characteristics of a group of actors in history by means of a collective study of their lives."[9] The emphasis in this type of investigation is on the process of amassing a collection of data about a group, "where the analysis of the sum of data about many individuals can tell us about the different connections between them."[10] Ultimately, the prosopography literature alerted me to the value of collecting data on my cohort, in addition to what might be revealed in their narratives. In several of the chapters that follow, I make comparisons among members of the cohort on such topics as Mau Mau affiliations, educational achievements, family characteristics, and levels of prosperity that would not be possible without these data. But the collective biography of this cohort is not a prosopography, because I have constructed it using a collection of individual narratives that I frequently use to illustrate characteristics of the whole cohort. In prosopography methodology, the aggregate is always more important than the individual, who may not even be known to the researcher, which explains why it is a favored method for studying pre-modern societies where individual narratives are seldom available.[11]

Finally in my search for examples of collective biography, I found Susan Geiger's discussion of women's contributions to the development of Tanganyikan nationalism. In this paper she presents a dual argument: first, women's life-history narratives reveal that their contributions and activities to Tanganyikan nationalism were fundamental to its development, and second, she states, "Without insisting that any one Tanganyika African National Union activist's life history is 'representative' of all/other women activists, I maintain in offering the narratives of some, a collective biography of many is constituted."[12] It is the second part of the argument that I am interested in, because it is there that

Geiger iterates what I intend to demonstrate in the coming chapters. That is, the life-history narratives of my former students constitute a collective biography of the entire group of these Gikuyu young men who took their place in Kenyan society as the first postcolonial generation.

How representative is my sample of seventy-five students compared with the rest of their generation? Without a doubt, they were not representative of secondary-school-leavers from the top-tier boarding schools, many of which had been established decades earlier and had given exceptional education to a small number of Kenyan boys for a long time. Such schools restricted their intake of Form 1 students to those receiving the highest Kenya Preliminary Exam (KPE) scores in the country. Half or more of these students earned the highest score on their final Cambridge Exams (Division I Certificates) and there was rarely a failure among them. Many students from these schools were the children of parents who themselves had received secondary school educations and were members of the small African elite that dated from the colonial era and later became the most senior people in government, business, and the military. My students were not representative of this group; none of them had parents with more than a couple of years of primary education, and a significant number were illiterate.

Nor was Giakanja representative of the bottom tier of secondary schools, where, ironically, the Ministry of Education predicted that it would fit. Their rationale was based on the belief that new schools, and especially day schools like Giakanja, would not perform well, perhaps with less than half of the first few classes earning Cambridge School Certificates (CSCs). This did not happen.

Rather, Giakanja was comparable with the second-tier boarding schools in Central Province and Western Kenya, dating from the late 1940s, that had subsequently matured into respected academic institutions. The annual percentage of their students earning a CSC was approximately 80–85 percent of those taking the exam. Even though this was a high rate of success, all three classes in my Giakanja study fit solidly into this range.

A confluence of factors accounted for why Giakanja students performed exceptionally and scored far above what might have been usual for their circumstances. These included not only the students' can-do attitude toward overcoming their deficits, especially those caused by the Mau Mau Rebellion and the meager day-school setting at Giakanja, but also the careful guidance of the headmaster during those years and the youthful zeal of the teaching staff. Together, all involved forged a learning community that empowered students to reach high levels of achievement and confidence.

The vast majority of young people who came of age in the decade following Kenya's independence did not attend secondary school at all. Many went to primary school and some had gone to intermediate but did not go further either because of a lack of understanding about the value of education or a failure to score high enough on their qualifying exams to continue. Giakanja students had known these young people as playmates and even as fellow students in primary school, but once in secondary school, and certainly later in their careers, they rapidly outpaced this group on their way to elite status with other members of their cohort. It is their story that this book will explore.

1

Late Colonial Childhoods

Kenya is an East African country approximately the size of Minnesota, North Dakota, and South Dakota combined. It straddles the equator and has the Indian Ocean as its eastern border. The geographic area that we now call Kenya has had a long and venerable history characterized by ancient coastal city-states and extended-family farming and herding enterprises in the interior. Vast areas of the interior consist of hot and dry plains suitable only for sparse populations of pastoralists. Most of the country's population resides in the much higher central plateau, where rainfall is regular and abundant and the soils are suitable for intensive agriculture. It is here that the Gikuyu people live, the ethnic group of these students, occupying the hills and valleys of an area approximately one hundred miles by fifty miles.

Gikuyu Society and the Colonial Experience

By the beginning of the twentieth century, Gikuyu were well established in this area, with their extended families (*mbari*) occupying neighboring homesteads. The Gikuyu were primarily farmers and pastoralists who, in addition to these pursuits, also engaged in trade with neighboring people and sometimes further afield. They hunted, smelted iron, and produced pottery. While the most common political, economic, and social institution was the mbari, which was led by family heads and functional at the neighborhood level, Gikuyu were also loosely organized into clans and age sets, which helped to knit together larger areas of people for defense and provided opportunities for the shaping of useful self-help strategies for survival. Nineteenth-century European travelers frequently reported that Gikuyu had created for themselves a vibrant and wealthy society, filled with healthy and hospitable people.[1]

It was to these people that the British turned their attention in 1895, annexing the entire region and calling it British East Africa (Kenya, after 1920). The arrival of the British and the system of colonial rule that they set in motion had disastrous consequences for Gikuyu, as well as for many other people of Kenya.[2] First, large tracts of land were seized by the state for its own purposes or sold to the incoming white settlers who eventually numbered forty thousand at the height of colonialism in the 1950s. Some Gikuyu were evicted from their land, while many others were prevented from expanding into the forests to create new *mbari* settlements. Land previously used for common seasonal grazing now lay outside the boundaries of the newly created Gikuyu Reserve.

The colonial labor system also had a negative impact on Gikuyu because it impaired their ability to remain self-sufficient in their rural homesteads. In addition to being forced to "give" their labor free on a regular basis to such colonial projects as building administrative centers and roads, the state also initiated taxes to be paid in cash to force Africans to work on settler farms or other European enterprises. For those who had lost their ancestral land to the colonial intrusion, the shift to wage labor was permanent. For the majority of Gikuyu who had access to at least some land, a period of labor each year in European employment was still necessary to earn cash to pay their taxes.

The history of Gikuyu (and other Kenyan peoples) in the first five decades of the twentieth century is an intriguing story of adapting to the new demands and realities of the colonial state.[3] Many Gikuyu who had lost their land or had it reduced were able to take up residence as squatters on European farms, exchanging their labor for access to land. Others sought the education offered by Christian missions as a strategy to enter the colonial economy as skilled laborers. In time such people used the savings from their salaries as government clerks, railroad workers, and teachers to start their own businesses. By the 1940s many Gikuyu were embedded in both the urban and rural commercial worlds of the colonial economy.[4]

In addition to coping with the colonial intrusion, Gikuyu were also involved in protesting it. Through such organizations as the Kikuyu Association, the Kikuyu Central Association, and the Kenya African Union, the first of which began in 1919, the Gikuyu continually protested against the loss of their land, unfair taxation, and onerous labor practices to the colonial government in Kenya, and eventually to the British government in London, in vain attempts to reform colonialism. But by the late 1940s all such attempts to persuade, threaten, or cajole the British into creating a more equitable colonial system had failed, and Gikuyu began to consider going to war against the colonial state to expel the British and regain their land.

My students, most of whom were born between 1946 and 1948, were just beginning to enter primary school during the early 1950s. They remember their early lives as being closely associated with home in the Gikuyu Reserve, herding family cattle and playing with friends. It was a life near their mother and siblings. About 25 percent of the boys came from polygynous households, and while they were closest to their own mothers and her children, many knew their father's other wives as mother too, and remember these early years as being harmonious. More than one of them said to me, as Peter did, "My mothers were good to me."[5] Fathers were often absent, working in Nairobi or on European settler farms. A few remember visiting their fathers who had migrated to Rift Valley, a neighboring province, where they worked or owned businesses; several even grew up in Rift Valley. Only a few fathers held professional positions as teachers or government clerks. One student came from a prosperous family who owned a general store in the Gikuyu Reserve. The rest came from peasant farming families of humble means, some even destitute, but these boys considered such a condition normal; they were like their neighbors. "We had a hard life," said Jacob, "but we were no exception and we never felt it so much because it was the kind of life everyone was facing. . . . Life was hard but that was the life of the majority."[6]

Education

The educational system available to Kenyans had grown out of two distinct traditions. First were the missionaries, who had pioneered churches and schools in Kenya from the first decades of the twentieth century. Among Gikuyu in Nyeri District, the Church of Scotland Mission and the Catholic Consulate Mission had filled the countryside with little one- or two-room schools in their effort to "capture" as many children as possible for their denominations. Mission schools provided a basic and somewhat haphazard literacy. Education from the missionary perspective was more a means for evangelism than an end in itself.[7]

As a result, the government, and later the Gikuyu themselves, sought to establish its own schools. In 1924 the government opened a vocational school at Kabate that was based on "the theories of [U.S.] Negro education developed at Hampton and Tuskegee Institutes. . . . These theories stressed the idea that education must be vitally related to the needs of the people."[8] In the same year, the government also established Local Native Councils (LNCs), which began to advocate for more local schools. After the 1934 Education Ordinance created District Education Boards (DEBs), the two groups of organizations joined forces to "push for the development of higher levels of education and the establishment [of] what were called primary schools."[9] By 1938, such schools had been so enthusiastically embraced by Gikuyu that the LNCs and DEBs had to be cautioned by the government not "to vote their [entire] revenue for local education, to the detriment of other services."[10]

At the same time, Gikuyu also sought to establish their own schools through the Kikuyu Independent Schools Association (KISA). This organization developed in the early 1930s in response to the missions' attempt to deny Gikuyu access to mission schools if they continued to practice African customs, especially female circumcision. Mission societies reasoned that since their schools were the only ones available to Gikuyu and their demand for education was high, then Gikuyu would not jeopardize their access to education by continuing to circumcise their girls, a rite the missions strongly opposed. In response Gikuyu inaugurated their own school system that by 1952, after being in operation for nearly twenty years, rivaled the missions and the DEB schools both in the quantity of schools and the quality of education.[11]

By mid-century many Gikuyu men and a few women had gained some formal education through one of these educational systems, and some had become teachers themselves. Gikuyu viewed education positively, as leading to employment and economic betterment in a colonial society. Many of my former students reported that the value of education was instilled in them at home from an early age and going to school was something that they looked forward to.

Understanding Mau Mau

As important as family and education were to these students, both were disrupted by the Mau Mau Rebellion in the 1950s, when Kenyan nationalists turned from persuasion to armed struggle. To preempt the prospective conflict, the British declared a state of emergency on 20 October 1952, and British troops began to arrive in the colony to augment local security forces. Hostilities would continue until 1960 and involve the mass detention of men thought to be involved in the rebellion and the forced removal of women and children from their farms into Emergency villages. A major division developed in Gikuyu society between people called "Mau Mau": those who were guerrilla fighters as well as supporters of the rebellion, and those labeled "loyalists," who worked against the rebellion, including members of the local Home Guard militia, informers, and many Christians. This division split families apart and set neighbor against neighbor. As we shall see, many people faced the dilemma of being caught between the opposing forces of Mau Mau and loyalist and had to appease both in order to survive, thus blurring the distinction between them.

The military phase lasted from 1952 to 1956 and consisted of bands of guerrilla fighters attacking police stations, Home Guard posts, military patrols, settler farms, and loyalist Gikuyu, all with the hope of pressuring the colonial government to leave Kenya. The security forces were hampered in their attempts to defeat the insurgents because of their ability to hide among a sympathetic rural population or to retreat to camps hidden in dense forests nearby. It was a brutal war of attack and retribution in the midst of a vulnerable rural civilian population among which my students and their families lived. Of course some of them were only youngsters of five or six when the war began, but a number were older, and all of them were quickly thrown into events that left them with vivid memories.

The literature on Mau Mau has only recently begun to explore these internal conflicts. Early scholars produced dozens of books and articles that depicted Mau Mau as a unified movement and a nationalist response to the political and economic abuses of colonialism in Kenya.[12] That view changed when John Lonsdale published an influential essay on the moral economy of Mau Mau, in which he painstakingly unpacked *Ithaka na Wiathi*, a common name for Mau Mau, setting out how Gikuyu linked land (*ithaka*) to the process of moral growth (*wiathi*).[13] Lonsdale deduced that land alienation to white settlers, residential restriction to a colonially demarcated reserve, and population increase had hindered Gikuyu moral growth and the establishment of civic virtue. As local Gikuyu communities grappled with a crescendo of questions, disputes, and dilemmas concerning the rise of land-poor and landless people, they questioned "how fathers could remain men if they had no land for their sons, or sons become men without marriage . . . [because] women could scarcely marry men of no property."[14] For Lonsdale, these questions increasingly framed Gikuyu conversations leading up to Mau Mau.

Subsequent scholarship on Mau Mau has continued to focus on internal conflicts and issues within Gikuyu society. Greet Kershaw's *Mau Mau from Below* meticulously explores the relations in land that developed among several small Gikuyu communities in Kiambu from the time of their early nineteenth-century settlement to the impact of colonial rule and land alienation in the twentieth century. Her research reveals that Mau Mau needs to be situated around the long-standing tensions and the communities' deepest rivalries concerning patron-client relationships, the availability and use of land, and their children's future well-being. Kershaw's Kiambu study, like Lonsdale's essay, is a corrective to previous scholarship since her communities would not have known Mau Mau as a unified nationalist movement driven only by anticolonial fervor, but rather as a set of local responses organically rising from issues and rivalries of long standing.[15]

Similarly, Derek Peterson explored the experience of Gikuyu in Nyeri, the district in which my students grew up.[16] Following Kershaw's dictum that community-based issues provided the context for Mau Mau, Peterson examined several episodes that occurred in the years before the war at Nyeri. One concerns the forced dipping of cattle, begun in 1945 to protect against tick fever. When local breeds began to die, rumors quickly circulated that the dipping was actually a scheme to cull their herds so that the wealthy who owned high-grade cattle could sell them at greater profit. The next year, a government report fueled further discontent when it recommended that a portion of Nyeri's population be moved off their land to ensure soil fertility. This coincided with rumors that some Nyeri people would be sterilized and others subjected to birth control as a colonial strategy to limit Gikuyu growth. Lastly, in 1949 the government issued the Beecher Report, which outlined a sharp reduction in the number of children who could attend school, especially beyond Standard 4 (Std. 4), the grade in which English was taught.[17] In a few short years, Nyeri Gikuyu felt that their land, livestock, children, and wealth—the very basis for stable families and moral order—had all been threatened. When Mau Mau began to offer oaths of commitment, people responded because of the need they felt to rebuild and reaffirm the threatened dimensions of their lives. Peterson argued that Mau Mau began at Nyeri as an initiative to solve local problems and was embraced by both Christians and Mau Mau. Christians took the oath, "not seeing any distinction between the moral goals of Christianity and Mau Mau."[18] Beyond mutual oath taking, Peterson cited instances of cooperation. Churchwomen cared for forest fighters in their homes, feeding them and treating their wounds; Mau Mau took up collections for widows and orphans and adopted abandoned children; and the Home Guard supplied information and ammunition to Mau Mau in an effort to "limit senseless violence."[19] Drawing on their comprehensive knowledge of local history, Kershaw and Peterson each came to the conclusion that Mau Mau is best understood as locally driven, conflicted, and complex, rather than as a simplistic conflict between loyalists and forest fighters.

It is on the subject of loyalists that Daniel Branch focused his recent book, a subject that he said had been neglected by scholars.[20] His argument is that while the categories of loyalist and rebel did not exist in Gikuyu society before the war, most people switched sides (sometimes more than once) to survive. Still, as the war progressed, loyalists' numbers grew and settled into a recognizable group, many as members of the Home Guard. In that capacity, the colonial government certainly identified them as allies and entrusted many with the administration of Emergency villages. After 1956, when Mau Mau was in retreat, Branch showed how loyalists were favored by government: first, in being given land confiscated from rebels during the war; second, in employment, as new jobs in local government opened up; and last, in increased access to education for their children. Though Branch's book sheds much new light on loyalists, the main critique of his thesis is that in his narrow focus on loyalists, he mistakenly confused a strategy of survival for a loyalist identity.[21] Gikuyu assumed loyalism when it would enable them to gain ends not accomplishable by other means. This nuanced behavior is corroborated in the lives of my students who experienced "on the ground" the many meanings of Mau Mau.

Growing Up with Mau Mau

Because the students were so young at the time, the beginnings of the Mau Mau era are the haziest for them, but many nevertheless associate two things with that period. First, there was a general atmosphere of secrecy, with adults whispering to each other and even small children like themselves being admonished to be careful about what they said to others. Later in the early years, Alex realized that they were not to mention to anyone the nocturnal visits by the guerrilla fighters.[22] Second, a few students associate the early years of the Mau Mau era with their parents or neighbors going to hear Jomo Kenyatta, a nationalist politician (and later Kenya's first president), address a political rally.[23] Kenyatta had long been associated with nationalist activity in Kenya, even being sent to London to deliver petitions of protest. He was also regarded as a champion of the Gikuyu with the publication of an ethnography in which he extolled their culture and criticized colonial and missionary attempts to change it.[24] More recently, he had become the president of the Kenya African Union, a multiethnic association that sought to redress Kenyans' grievances against British rule. He arrived at Nyeri as a well-known, popular figure considered to be a hero by the local people who turned out to hear him speak. James remembered that his mother told him about seeing endless streams of people returning home from the event late in the evening, singing Kenyatta's praises. She told him that soon Gikuyu would have the land back that had been stolen from them decades earlier by the British.[25] For Peter and Francis, Kenyatta's speech at Nyeri had a very special meaning because their fathers were friends with Kenyatta and they remember meeting him. One family housed Kenyatta overnight when he came to speak. They remember the excitement of the moment, and later, when they learned that Kenyatta had been imprisoned as an accomplice of Mau Mau, they relived that moment of meeting him and remember it being discussed at home.[26]

For about 10 percent of these students, the beginning of Mau Mau was associated with the forced repatriation of their family back to the Gikuyu Reserve from Rift Valley, where they had grown up as squatters on white settlers' farms.[27] Students remember the scramble to pack a few belongings and then the long journey on the back of a truck and by train to Nyeri—a journey of five or six days. They remember the excitement of the journey and finally arriving at the homestead of a grandfather, an uncle, or a more distant relative. Most families had lived for long periods of time in Rift Valley and might never have met these relatives before. Amid a widespread land shortage, their return was often not welcomed.[28] While they were squeezed in and given a roof over their heads, eventually they were on their own. The most vivid accounts of repatriation speak of the intense poverty and hunger such families experienced. Usually fathers were absent and so a mother and her small children were left to struggle for survival. They eked out a bare existence on a small piece of land; usually the poorest, least productive piece was all their relatives gave them. Mothers were often forced to work as day laborers on others' farms to supplement their own meager crops, but as David remembered, "if there was no work that day, we all slept hungry."[29]

Such families lived with the knowledge that their relatives thought of them as economic burdens. It is not surprising that each of these students returned to the Rift Valley and made it their permanent home as soon as they could after finishing secondary school.

Other students were introduced to the realities of the Emergency when a parent was detained, an experience for more than 25 percent of them. Several remember the security forces coming at night to take their fathers away. Joseph cited this incident: "I was awakened by the shouts of the askaris [police]. My father told us to stay in the house but the policemen yelled at us all to come out. They had my father tied up with his hands stretched above his head. My mother stood in front of me so that I couldn't see but I still could hear my father groan from the blows. They finally dragged him away and I didn't see him again until 1960 [seven years later]."[30] Several students had both parents detained, and they and their sisters and brothers were forced to live with relatives. One student said that as soon as his father was detained, the local Home Guard came for his mother and imprisoned her at their post for the next year, where she was forced to be their concubine. She lived through the experience but has never told her son about it. What he knows, he has learned from other sources.[31]

These fathers were whisked away into detention, not to be seen again for three or four years, and sometimes longer. If they had been working outside their home district, such as Nairobi, they just vanished, and my students and their families never knew what happened to them until they returned home years later. Some fathers and other male relatives and family friends never returned. All of them were herded into a vast system of camps, some in barren and remote places, to purge them of Mau Mau sympathies and punish them for their crime. In *Imperial Reckoning*, Caroline Elkins suggested that between 160,000 and 320,000 detainees, and perhaps many more, were spread among dozens of these camps.[32] In the warren of camps, detainees were daily worked to exhaustion, sometimes to death, and subjected to multiple forms of physical torture. According to Elkins, the goal was to make detainees "absolutely miserable" and to create an "unbearable experience" in order to force them to divulge information about Mau Mau and to confess and recant their oath of allegiance to the rebellion.[33] The colonial administration held that only through the constant application of pain would these results be realized. In time most men broke under such conditions of abuse and were eventually released, but hard-core detainees who never confessed were moved to the most severe camps, where many died from their untreated injuries and disease or were killed outright. But even for those who confessed, there were still many months and even years to be endured as they were shunted through the pipeline of camps that scrutinized the sincerity and truthfulness of their confessions. Those who eventually returned to their families frequently did so with aged and broken bodies and troubled minds.

Whereas only some of my students had fathers and other relatives detained, all of them and their families experienced the next trauma of Mau Mau: the destruction of their homesteads and forced removal to Emergency villages. By 1954 it was clear to the colonial administration that Mau Mau could not be defeated without severing the support that guerrillas received from their communities. The supply line of food, firearms, ammunition, and information had to be permanently cut between the Mau Mau rebels, who in their forest hideouts were unreachable by the government security forces, and the passive wing of sympathetic relatives and friends who farmed in the countryside. Now that there was a system for detaining the men, the colonial government also wanted to control and punish rural women, all of whom were considered to have taken the oath and to be in sympathy with the rebellion.

Many students clearly remember how this new government policy was implemented in their area. Jacob describes his experience: "As I walked home from school, I could see the smoke rising above the trees long before I realized it was coming from my home. When I arrived, all the buildings were on fire and the Home Guard who had set the thatch burning was holding my parents so they couldn't put it out."[34] Soon afterward they were marched to an open spot and told to begin building their new houses. Several hundred people, sometimes many more, camped out in the open while they constructed round, one-room houses and then erected the barbed wire fencing, guard houses, draw bridges, and spike-filled trenches that surrounded these camps. By the end of 1955, more than a million Gikuyu had been forced into such places.[35] Though young, my students remember the cramped living conditions, the disease that came with improper sanitation, and the intense hunger they often felt. At the height of the Emergency, such villages were under a twenty-three-hour curfew; people were let out for only an hour to cultivate and gather food from their gardens and only then under armed guard.[36]

Children too young to attend school themselves were herded together in the center of the village as their parents were daily led out to perform forced labor tasks elsewhere. Most of 1954–1956 was used to dig a fifty-mile trench around the perimeter of the Aberdare Forest to keep Mau Mau fighters bottled up in their strongholds. District administration documents confirm the terrible conditions under which everyone lived. From August 1955, a community development officer wrote a monthly report about the very areas in which many of the students lived in village confinement in order to "note some of the hardships suffered by some of the very young in the poorer villages. Some of these children, not more than 2–3 years old, with fathers dead, detained or working away from the area, appear to be shockingly under nourished. . . . In one particular case the father of a family of seven has been away in Nyeri since January last and has failed to send either cash or kind to his wife. Already two of his children have died. . . . Cannot some sort of *communal* soup kitchen be made compulsory in every village?"[37] But nothing appeared to have changed because the same officer wrote months later, "The comparison between the well fed resident in a Mau Mau concentration camp and some of the children in the villages, orphaned by possibly bosom companions of these same inmates, is appalling."[38] Each village had a burial ground for those who died under such conditions. Many of my students lost brothers and sisters to disease, malnutrition, and neglect during their confinement.

The threat of death through disease, starvation, or the exhaustion of forced labor was not the only terror experienced in Emergency villages. Daily beatings were administered for lateness to roll call, for failure to meet work quotas, for illness, or for no reason at all. Similarly, women were repeatedly interrogated about their involvement in Mau Mau and oath taking. Beatings, rape, and torture were systemically used to induce confessions and to punish those considered guilty. Such activities were frequently held in the village square, where all were forced to watch and to anticipate their turn. My students would have frequently witnessed this violence and experienced some of it, too. Etched in their memories would also have been the recognition that some of the persons administering such pain would have been their former neighbors, now comfortably housed as loyalists in the Home Guard post located at each Emergency village.[39] Other students, as sons of loyalist parents, lived in the Home Guard posts and undoubtedly knew about the brutality of Emergency village life.

Another memory of my students dating from this time concerned going to school. Though earlier generations of Gikuyu had only a very rudimentary education available to them through the missions or Gikuyu independent schools, perhaps the equivalent of first and second grade, most Gikuyu valued education highly and they wanted their children to attend school. But schooling also became entangled in the trauma of the Mau Mau Rebellion. For many the rebellion disrupted their education. None of the students who were repatriated with their families from the white-settler farming areas were able to immediately start or continue their education. Schools in the neighborhood were often full, and a place had to be found first where they could be squeezed in. Their education in the Rift Valley had usually been inferior to that of their new classmates, and so they were dropped back a grade, where they were with younger children. Sometimes repatriated children had to wait more than a year. David missed three years of primary school and had to start over in the first grade at age fifteen; when I first met him as a ninth grader he was twenty-three years old.[40] Newton was so delayed by the Mau Mau Rebellion that, even though he passed his Std. 4 leaving exam with a high grade, his way to the fifth grade was barred because he was seventeen years old. The European schools supervisor said to him, "You're too old [for fifth grade]; go and get married!"[41] Helped by his uncle who was a teacher, he lied about his age and enrolled in a distant school where no one knew him. For others who had attended schools that were under Gikuyu leadership and administered by KISA, their education abruptly stopped in 1952 when the colonial government closed all KISA schools. Such schools were accused of being used after hours as centers where the Mau Mau oath of unity had been administered to elicit Gikuyu cooperation and sympathy for the rebellion. The government also doubted the loyalty of KISA school committees and teachers.[42]

Although it was likely that at least some KISA schools had been involved in oath-taking activities, they also delivered a good education to large numbers of Gikuyu children. The government had for more than fifteen years considered them an asset to the colony, as this 1940 memo from the Advisory Committee on Education in the Colonies states: "[The] Government of Kenya has changed its mind about Gikuyu Independent Schools. It no longer considered them largely political, anti-missionary or anti-Government, but now to be primarily educational institutions. The Government . . . could close schools that were not up to the educational standards set by the Ministry of Education, but it no longer closed such schools merely because they existed."[43] The KISA school at Gachatha was an excellent example of such an independent school. In 1952 at the outbreak of the Emergency, it provided primary education to about five hundred children, three of whom would become students at Giakanja Secondary School.[44] In the previous two years, the local government chief had made allegations that oathing was taking place there, but the district administration had insufficient proof and Gachatha was not closed until 14 November 1952, when all 161 KISA schools in the colony were shut down.[45] The appeal made by parents to the governor of Kenya pointed out that the people of Gachatha area and the parents of the school children had built and supported this school at their own expense for nearly two decades; in 1951 alone 11,600 shillings (approximately $1,600) was raised locally to support the school. Now the five hundred Gachatha students were without a school, and the government would not pay compensation for the loss of buildings, equipment, materials, and land.[46] Furthermore, the parents informed the governor that they themselves had denounced Mau Mau and had disassociated their school from any Mau Mau activities:

> For some time, as declared in the press, persons claiming to be leaders of Mau Mau have been posting letters at some of the African Independent Schools, which have been closed down calling on parents not to allow their children to attend these schools and making threats against the parents and children. "We the parents of children who were attending the African Independent Schools and other persons who were concerned, with their ownership and management, repudiate and condemn these letters and threats! We have nothing whatever to do with them. The persons who are writing these letters are the Mau Mau and not the owners of the schools nor responsible for them, and their activities. [They] can only cause ill-will between Government and the Missions on the one side and owners of the closed schools and parents and children on the other." We most earnestly appeal to our African brothers to denounce Mau Mau, to have nothing to do with it, "Mau Mau is evil, the enemy of ourselves and dangerous to [*sic*] progress of our children." If we approach Government in a peaceful and constitutional way, we hope we shall be able to undue it to open our schools once more under our own managements, but that will not come if we allow ourselves to be influenced or frightened by Mau Mau.[47]

The powerful language of this appeal notwithstanding, Gachatha and all other KISA schools were closed for good, and the three future Giakanja students there, as well as several from other KISA schools, were among the 161,000 that had their education abruptly halted. Though the Nyeri administration declared that "there are ample facilities for primary education in the district" and that students from closed KISA schools could be easily absorbed by nearby schools,[48] that was not the experience of these students, who all missed more than a year of education before they found places at other schools.[49] The three students at Gachatha had to wait nearly two years until the DEB built a school nearby to absorb the Gachatha students. The delay in construction was caused by the unavailability of Mau Mau detainee labor.[50] The irony is that some of the detainees were the fathers of the very students who had attended Gachatha. The fathers had previously contributed toward the education program of Gachatha, even donating their labor at the construction of the independent school, and now as detained persons suspected or convicted of being Mau Mau rebels, they were being forced to build another school for their children.[51]

Furthermore, Gachatha reveals the divisions in Kenyan society to be more complex than a simple dichotomy between colonial occupiers and African nationalists. KISA schools had been initiated as a protest against missionary-directed education. They were built and nurtured at the grassroots level and became the pride and joy of their communities. But when Mau Mau began a campaign to close them as agencies of the colonial government, local communities like Gachatha rebelled and denounced Mau Mau. At first glance this was a surprising action because the origins of independent schools (and their related churches) were decidedly anticolonial. Their availability as centers for after-hours oath taking was congruent with this nationalist position. But threatened with the loss of their school through Mau Mau intimidation, the Gachatha community vigorously denounced the insurgency. Ironically, the colonial government doubted their loyalty and ultimately closed Gachatha and all other independent schools.

With the advent of the Mau Mau Rebellion, even those students who were able to continue their educations did so at great risk because they all lived in a war zone. In the first two years of the rebellion, both students and parents were exposed to interrogation by Mau Mau, who wanted to close down all schools because of their association with the colonial government through state supervised curricula, staffing, and teacher education. Many schools received Mau Mau letters advising them to close down or else, and Mau Mau acted on these threats, burning schools down and shooting teachers. In Nyeri District, Mau Mau had destroyed a total of sixty-four schools by 1954. For the local area in which many of my students lived, this government memorandum sent a chilling message: "As every inflammable school in the location has already been burnt by Mau Mau, it is quite likely that attacks on school

teachers and pupils will [now] take place."[52] The students remember
that by 1953 they were being escorted to and from school by armed
Home Guard. Home Guard posts were sometimes sited near schools for
protection, too. These students remember that many of their teachers
came to school armed, and occasionally Mau Mau fighters shot through
classroom walls while the students were inside.[53] Sometimes they would
be dismissed late from school if a Mau Mau gang was spotted in the
area, and Francis remembers his whole school being kept overnight for
fear of attack on the way home.[54] For others it was far worse: the *East
African Standard* reported on 18 May 1954 that two teachers had been
murdered in Nyeri District: "Two teachers were shot in front of their
classes when a gang attacked a CCM [Catholic Consulate Mission]
school at Githunguri. In the same district, one of his pupils was in a
gang, which murdered the headmaster of Kiamwangi Intermediate
School."[55] Schooling was thus associated not only with education and
learning but also with intimidation and fear of death.

As the 1950s continued, many students also dropped out for lack of
school fees and, more generally, because of their poverty. A 1957 Community Development Report for Nyeri District noted the following:
"There are 600 empty seats in primary schools in the District. . . . The
sole reason for these vacancies is poverty. The existence of thousands of
vacancies in the schools and thousands of children unable to fill them
because of poverty, would not be tolerated in most civilized states and
no argument in my opinion, should be permitted to keep those seats
vacant."[56] Others who managed to stay in school found that their academic performance declined over time. A number of students reported
that they did not do well on the Std. 4 Common Entrance Exam (CEE),[57]
which was vital for gaining admission to the next four years in intermediate school.

The experience of students in the 1950s was even more profound
than the delays in their education, poor academic performance, and semi-
imprisonment in Emergency villages. As Ben Kipkorir noted in his study
of Alliance High School (AHS) students: "For AHS boys in the 1950s
Mau Mau served the same purpose as had the Second World War to an
earlier generation. It opened their minds and widened their horizons."[58]
For many their experiences would be imprinted on their minds forever.
At the beginning of the Emergency, when most of them were very
young, the idea of Mau Mau freedom fighters battling the colonial
government for the return of lost Gikuyu lands was intriguing and noble.
Even being marched to school under the protection of Home Guards,

seeing their teachers' guns in the classroom, and hearing shots in the night was exciting to many of them. But soon there were dead bodies to be seen and people they knew were being tortured. Stanley reported that the cruel realities against the Mau Mau finally dawned on him when he saw a heap of dead bodies at the Giakanja chief's camp. He and his friends had taken their families' cows to the neighborhood cattle dip as they had done each week, but this time they saw a lorry dumping dozens of dead bodies as they passed the local administrative center. The student and his friends noticed that some of the corpses' hands had been cut off, and later when he asked his father about this, he was told that rather than send the bodies all the way to Nyeri to check their finger-prints, they only sent the hands. He heard further that a bounty was paid for the body or just the hands of known Mau Mau freedom fighters. On subsequent trips to the cattle dip, he frequently saw bodies at the chief's camp or sometimes just a pile of hands. These sights gave him bad dreams for a long time.[59]

As killings became a normal event, students frequently heard about and witnessed them. James said that he and his age mates often saw the local European district officer (DO) driving around the area with his rifle pointed out the window of his Land Rover. Such was his reputation for shooting people indiscriminately that they dived for cover whenever they saw him coming. One day after returning from school, James was informed that the DO had killed his uncle who lived next door.[60] Harun also noted that it was common in his area for the Home Guard simply to kill those young men who had been repatriated home from working in Nairobi, on the assumption that they were all Mau Mau. "They did so openly. They pulled them from their houses, took them to an open field and shot them. I saw the bodies; some were even my relatives."[61] Two other students lost "their other mothers" (their father's second wives) to the wrath of local Home Guards. In both cases these students said that their fathers were known Mau Mau fighters who had avoided capture. Jonas also commented: "For revenge, they [Home Guard] shot her while she worked in the garden. She bled to death before we found her."[62] Another woman, Dickson said, was "hacked to pieces by Home Guards because they knew that she was my father's favorite."[63]

Four students' fathers, one of whom was Joseph's, were killed during the Emergency. Joseph said that his father was working on a European farm at the beginning of the Emergency. He was accused of being a Mau Mau oath giver, roughly interrogated on the farm by his settler boss and the police, and died from injuries received during interrogation.

"I consider him to be a hero."[64] Two others had fathers who were subchiefs, the lowest administrative post in the district administration. Both students said that Mau Mau assassinated their fathers because they were loyal to the government and that their deaths were in the line of duty.[65] But others have reported to me that the local people did not greatly mourn the deaths of these men because they had abused their power as Home Guards.[66]

James's father's death at the hands of Mau Mau prompted much mourning and sadness across a wide area because so many people loved him. He was the headmaster of the local primary school and an elder in the Presbyterian Church, a respected and talented educator and devout Christian who had refused to take the Mau Mau oath in support of the insurgency. Although he was thus known as a loyalist, he was widely revered throughout the area. James related the story to me of how his father was killed. The attack was not observed by anyone, but it is thought that he had been riding his bicycle home from school in the early evening when Mau Mau ambushed him along the road. When his father failed to come home that night, the alarm was raised, and early in the morning searchers found his bicycle lying in the weeds where the attack had taken place. "I went to look the next morning; I can still clearly see in my mind the spot where he was killed, the blood stains on the grass. These memories have not left my mind, even to this day."[67]

But the body was not found, only the evidence of an ambush. The whole community was shocked and frightened. But within ten days several Mau Mau suspects had been taken into custody. The son has no memory of the aftermath of their capture but Wilson, one of his father's primary school students and later a student at Giakanja, vividly remembers what happened next:

> They brought the Mau Mau and they had been tortured. Some were brought through the school-yard, which was near the Home Guard post. Some were naked and bleeding, others had been shot and were being dragged along by others. . . . I think people turned completely bloodthirsty. Do you know that when I think of [the genocide in] Rwanda now, I think of the Mau Mau time; people become completely abnormal. They had a thirst for blood. Once you kill, you just want to go on killing. . . . I thought it was the end of the world. I thought that these bad things that were happening would happen to me.[68]

They confessed to the killing and led the authorities to the body. Joseph witnessed all of this, including the funeral that followed:

The body was found near the falls, that's where they put it into a sack and dumped it there with some stone weights. Some of the pieces were missing, especially the head. During the burial, all the schools in the location were closed so all could attend. . . . The people were crying and he was given some kind of military honor [gun salute]. So many people came to the burial; he was a much-loved man. I was there and the body was decaying; the stench was too much for me. I couldn't believe that when someone dies, they stink so much. It was my first experience with a rotten body. It was very bad for me because I knew him well [as my teacher] and now I could see that he's there and rotten. I had nightmares for a long time because all I could remember was the rotten body and the soldiers.[69]

The victims of the Emergency were thus numerous; regardless of the sympathies and position of the students' families, they were caught between competing loyalties to Mau Mau and to the local colonial administration represented by the Home Guards. Both groups insisted on loyalty, and both were prepared to coerce people to receive it. Students remembered their homes being visited at night by Mau Mau who came for food and information. They were often relatives, and one never refused their requests. But the next morning, the Home Guard would appear saying they had heard about the night visitors. Their parents would then be interrogated for information, sometimes quite brutally. The reverse process might happen just as easily. David said that after the Home Guard had visited his home and taken his uncle away as a suspected Mau Mau sympathizer, his Mau Mau contacts soon appeared to threaten his mother. They wanted to make sure that food and supplies would continue to be available and that she would not betray them to the Home Guard.[70] Likewise, if the Mau Mau attacked a police post or security patrol, the Home Guard would immediately begin to harass the local population, claiming that they must have assisted the Mau Mau in the attack. Or if local Mau Mau had suffered losses from a police or army ambush, they would retaliate against the local population, claiming that they should have been warned. One student said that the Mau Mau attacked the Emergency village that he and his family were being forced to live in, burning down most of the houses. Immediately the next day, the local Home Guard burned down the peoples' homesteads that they had previously vacated in their move to the village.[71] It was tit for tat.

The parents and other relatives and friends of these students were left in a terrible quandary regardless of whether their sympathies were pro Mau Mau or not. To survive they had to convincingly appear to support both sides as the need arose. Nahashan was made aware of these accommodations in a most graphic way. One day as his uncle and mother were cultivating their land, they witnessed a Mau Mau gang being ambushed by a Home Guard patrol. Afterward the Home Guard ordered the two to help them carry away the Mau Mau bodies. When they both refused, they were severely beaten before they finally relented and agreed to the task. Traumatized, Nahashan later confronted his mother, asking her why she hadn't simply obeyed the order straightaway and escaped the beating. Her answer startled him: "If I too readily obeyed, I would have been taken for a loyalist. The Mau Mau are always watching. They would have come and beat me too, or worse!"[72]

Simply trying to survive the Emergency thus often blurred the lines between supporters of the rebellion and the auxiliary Home Guard. Peter told me how his father was driven to take a job supporting the colonial government. Though he had a long history of anticolonial activity, especially in his life-long leadership of the African Independent Pentecostal Church (AIPC), which critiqued the work of Western missionaries, he nevertheless became a government subchief during the Emergency. In that position he and his family could sleep each night within the safety of a Home Guard post. He accommodated himself to the colonial administration to protect his family, but because he was not a Home Guard zealot who abused his power, the Mau Mau left him alone.[73]

Quite a few students insisted that Mau Mau fighters and Home Guard soldiers even collaborated with each other. As Jacob recalled, "The Mau Mau came to my house for food; they were expected because my mother had sent them word. Before they left, the Home Guard arrived to talk to them; they were double dealing."[74]

Dickson said that Mau Mau were able to sneak into villages at night only with the assistance of the Home Guard.[75] He and others maintained that many Home Guard assisted Mau Mau in attacks on police posts by providing information about arms and ammunition inside and about the best time for an assault. Whether such stories are to be believed or not, they support the idea that the students were well aware of the tenuous circumstances under which they lived.[76] Joseph, the son of a subchief who had met his death at the hands of Mau Mau, said, "Both sides suffered during Mau Mau and it was just luck as to which side you might be on."[77] It was like walking a tightrope between both sides. As Dickson noted, "You have to live on this side [Home Guard] and be accepted there, while on the other side you must also be accepted. If you were against the [colonial] administration, they would put you in jail. If it was the Mau Mau, then they would kill you."[78]

Some people also exploited these dilemmas. Michael said that many fathers were falsely accused as Mau Mau and unfairly detained as a result. "Detained people had their land and businesses confiscated. My father suspected that it was his business partners who turned him into the authorities because when he was released, they were the ones who now owned the business entirely among themselves."[79]

But the saddest story about things not being as they seemed goes back to the brutal killing of James's father, the headmaster and church elder. James said that after the Emergency ended, during the time when he was a student at Giakanja, he began to hear rumors that the Mau Mau had not killed his father because he was a loyalist but because they had been paid by his brothers to do so. "I confronted them [my uncles] when I was a teenager. I said that I knew that they wanted my father's land, his inheritance, and they had him killed for it. They said nothing, but I could tell they were guilty. Years later they admitted it to me; I told them that I forgave them."[80]

What conclusions can be drawn from the young lives of these students who grew up during Mau Mau? One reality that frequently appears in their testimony is that support of the Mau Mau rebels or loyalty to the colonial government were not static positions held unwaveringly through-out the rebellion; rather, they shifted along a continuum of allegiances as circumstances dictated. The parents of children at Gachatha and other KISA independent schools denounced Mau Mau in order to save their schools from government closure, even though such action ran counter to the long KISA history of anticolonial sentiment, including the recent support of Mau Mau oathing. Other students' parents departed from previously held support of Mau Mau or loyalty to the government by seeking positions of safety in the colonial administration or in supporting roles that helped the rebels. Some families simultaneously helped both sides of the insurgency as a bold strategy for survival.

Another conclusion concerns the interpretation of the rebellion itself and the nature of the nationalist movement in Kenya. The experiences of these students lends credence to the position that Mau Mau was more than a struggle of Kenyans who took up arms to rid their land of colonial occupation. It was even more than a struggle between Kenyans who resisted the colonial penetration and those who collaborated. Such interpretations of Mau Mau leave out the people who found themselves caught in the middle, like many of the parents of these students. While such people may have shared with their neighbors a general enthusiasm for self-determination and may have even gone to hear Kenyatta speak about a future Kenya without colonial occupation, they understood Mau Mau best as it took place on the ground in their immediate communities. The drama of the insurgency played out for many people in the harsh and enduring poverty and disease associated with forced residence in the enclosed Emergency villages, the physical and psychological shock that accompanied the violent deaths of people in their communities and even in their own families, and the endemic climate of fear and uncertainty in which they lived.

As the end of the Emergency approached and the internment villages were disbanded, the students returned home with a heavy awareness of the many members of their extended families and friends who had died or been killed. Added to this awareness were the emotionally charged scenes of fathers, uncles, brothers, and neighbors who returned from detention to find similar losses. These family reunifications, while initially joyous, in time became troublesome as both husbands and wives remained silent about the traumas they had experienced. Students reported their fathers to be emotionally distant and humiliated by the constant surveillance of the local chief to whom they had to regularly report.[81] Further stress was present when both Mau Mau adherents and loyalist Home Guards settled back into the same areas as neighbors.[82] Awkwardness, shame, and anger rippled through such communities as it became apparent that many of the children born during the Emergency were the products of rape by these very loyalists.[83] How did the students cope with the knowledge and experience of these tragedies in their adolescence and later as adults? There are few answers to be found in my interviews with them years later. Perhaps these young people simply lacked the vocabulary to describe the horrors they experienced, or their silence about the impact of Mau Mau on their lives mirrored their parents' silence, which was itself a way of coping.

Finally, how did these experiences during Mau Mau shape the sensibilities of my students? While this is a difficult question to answer precisely, as subsequent chapters will reveal, the overwhelming evidence of their lives demonstrates that growing up during Mau Mau did not hold them back from future achievement. While Mau Mau slowed, and for some even temporarily stopped, educational progress, it did not extinguish the idea that education was the pathway to a better life. Perhaps Mau Mau brought the realization that eventually when my students' fates were in their own hands, they must seize the initiative and strive for success, first, in their educations, and then in their professional and family lives. The zeal with which they approached their educations, as well as the subsequent professional and personal areas of their lives, and the high degree of success they achieved suggest that they were compensating for the Mau Mau period of poverty, fear, and subjection to the control of others.

2

Entering Secondary Education

By the late 1950s the rigors of the Mau Mau Rebellion were nearly over. Most people had been permitted to leave the Emergency villages and return to their own land. Diet and health improved, and while many families still had some relatives detained, life was more normal than it had been. All of the students report that it was during this time that they began to concentrate on their education. But just what kind of educational system were they entering and what were the particular problems and issues facing Kenyan education during the period that they would be students?

To start with, the educational context in which schooling began in the late 1950s and early 1960s had been established ten years earlier, just prior to the Mau Mau Rebellion, by the Beecher Commission, which had been appointed by the colonial government. The commission had reformed the fragmented educational system that had haphazardly developed around the mission, government, and Gikuyu independent schools. A centralized Ministry of Education now instituted a standardized curriculum, minimum teacher qualifications, and a 4:4:4 system of grades. All students who could find a school and pay the necessary fees could enter at age seven in the primary grades (1–4), but only some could move on to the intermediate (5–8), and fewer still to secondary (9–12) sections by successfully passing (on the first attempt only) difficult qualifying exams.[1] The outcome of this reorganization caused problems for both parents and students. Many neighborhood schools taught only the first four grades, so moving on to the next level frequently meant joining a school further from home. Moreover, passing school-leaving exams favored the wealthier households, which could start their children promptly at age seven and keep them continuously enrolled throughout the eight-year elementary school program, increasing their chances of passing their leaving exams the mandatory first time. Clearly the

40

Beecher Commission wished to limit education to the primary grades for all but a few, thinking that would be appropriate for Africans living in a colonial society. They gave little attention to secondary education and totally missed the demand for it that would shortly develop, including the Harambee schools movement.[2]

The first to pay attention to secondary education was the Ominde Commission, which had been appointed by Kenya's new independent government. In their 1964 report, they recommended not only the expansion of secondary education but also its equitable distribution throughout the country.[3] The report was the first official recognition that the educational needs of Kenya's population were being met better in some areas than in others.

In a 1972 paper, Jerry Olson, an educator, assessed the progress made in creating more secondary schools and where they were being built. He stated that in 1961, just two years before Kenya's independence, only about 2 percent of the age group was in secondary schools — 6,400 students. Furthermore, although the percentage of young people in secondary school was pitifully small, two-thirds (4,225) came from just three ethnic groups: the Luo, Luyia, and Gikuyu, with the last capturing more than half of the places (2,240). Seven years later, in 1968, with Kenya's first African government well in place, the number of secondary students had jumped to 51,000 — an eightfold increase. But this significant growth was marred by the fact that the same three ethnic groups occupied the majority of the secondary school places in the country, with the Gikuyu in the lead at 37 percent. The underrepresented areas of the country still remained so, with some even having lost ground.[4]

This failure to implement the Ominde Commission's recommendation for an equitable distribution of new schools was trumped by the immediate manpower needs of the country. The government based its decision on a simple argument: it needed a steady stream of secondary-school-leavers to fill the jobs of the departing civil service and private sector expatriates, together with the new positions created by Kenya's growing economy. The areas of the country with the most schools and hence the most students would most quickly be able to do this. All of these conditions were best met among the overrepresented ethnic groups like the Gikuyu, whose elementary and secondary schools were filled with students pressing to move ahead to the next level, to take their exams, and to compete for jobs in the new Kenya. However, the underrepresented groups had the fewest schools with the fewest students, sometimes not even filling the available places.[5] The government deemed such groups to be the least able to quickly produce school-leavers to fill the country's labor requirements and thus were largely skipped over in its 1960s building program.

Coupled with the government-financed expansion of secondary education was the parallel development of Harambee secondary schools. Although the runaway development of Harambee secondary schools was not fully visible until the late 1960s, its roots lie earlier in the decade, with the first schools being built in 1961–62, just before Kenya's independence. Indeed, Giakanja Secondary School, which my students attended, would have become a Harambee school had local funding efforts not failed and other resources become available. By the mid-1970s the Harambee movement was extraordinarily large, having built 1,200 secondary schools throughout the country via a combination of local fundraising and government sponsorship. Although the schools were frequently substandard and its school-leavers seldom able to find employment, the public continued to clamor for even more Harambee schools and was prepared to raise the funds to build them.[6] My former students, employed and doing well by this time, contributed to such efforts in their home areas.

But government's initial embrace of the Harambee schools movement as a complement to its own expansion program could not be sustained; too many school-leavers were not finding jobs, and the national budget had an astonishing one-third of its revenue tied to supporting education. As a result, starting in the 1970s the government slowly switched its enthusiasm for Harambee schools from an economic rationale— children need to be educated to fill the rising labor needs of the country— to a more general political rationale—send children to school so that they can secure the benefits of independence.[7] But local communities continued to build: in 1969 50 percent of all secondary schools in Kenya were under Harambee management; just three years later they accounted for 62 percent.[8]

Although Harambee schools are located in all Kenyan provinces, they are not contributing to a more equitable distribution of secondary school education in the country. Since these are fundamentally self-help ventures, the poorer provinces have the fewest resources to build and maintain schools. It should not be surprising then to learn that the greatest number of schools with the best facilities, the most experienced teachers, and the most successful school-leavers are to be found in the wealthiest provinces, which, coincidently, already have the greatest number of government schools. The Gikuyu of Central Province have frequently led the country in both categories.[9]

But in spite of these regional disparities, Kenya has been remarkably successful in using education—both Harambee and government schools—as a safety valve for discontent.[10] By expanding the number of government secondary schools and encouraging local communities to build their own, the government has convincingly projected the notion that educational opportunity is widely available. The corollary to this idea, however, was that any future mobility achieved (or not) through this opportunity would be determined by merit. So if one did not manage to get into a good school,[11] or earn a good score on the Cambridge School Certificate Exam (CSCE), or obtain a good job, then that was the product (or lack) of one's own ability. Nevertheless, a significant number of young people, including my students, thought they could beat the odds against them: "Every year enough children from impoverished homes, poor schools and deprived areas join the academic mainstream to sustain the faith of the Kenyan Dream."[12]

Finally, my students' education was affected by attempts to alter the secondary school curriculum in the early independence era, which has attracted scholarly comment, particularly because so little change seems to have taken place. In a revealing paper, Daniel Sifuna noted that by the early 1970s, fewer secondary-school-leavers with academic educations were finding urban white-collar employment. The government tried to solve the problem by expanding the school curriculum to include vocational skills that met rural needs, especially by introducing agriculture and technology as new areas of study. After nearly a decade's experiments with, pilot studies on, and abortive attempts at curriculum expansion, the government made a dramatic move in 1981 by instructing all secondary schools to offer "applied education" in addition to their regular academic program. This shift involved a tremendous curriculum expansion to include the previous attempts with agriculture and technology plus business education, bookkeeping, commerce, typing, office practice, home science, clothing and textiles, food and nutrition, and art and music.[13] In a less-than-surprising conclusion, Sifuna noted that diversifying the curriculum largely failed because all of these new areas were woefully undersubscribed. Although the students acknowledged a heightened sensitivity to the problems of post-secondary employment, their educational and occupational aspirations remained the same—they wanted an academic education and white-collar jobs.[14]

My students were sojourners during these times of transition and change, having begun their educations under colonial rule and ended them as citizens of an independent Kenya. As Gikuyu they came from one of the privileged areas of the country, although, as their narratives reveal, they would have been skeptical of their comparative advantage. As they took up their education after Mau Mau, there was still a great deal of chaos and arbitrariness in the system. The oldest students were in intermediate school and beginning to prepare for their eighth-grade leaving examinations—the gateway to secondary education. Younger students were preparing for the fourth-grade leaving exam and a desired place in intermediate school. In both cases the condition of the schools and the system of education in Kenya was against them. The schools were of the most rudimentary nature, usually consisting of mud walls and floors, thatched roofs, and open windows. It was not uncommon for there to be fifty students squeezed into a classroom, many without adequate chairs, tables, and blackboards. With trained teachers in short supply, many classrooms had only untrained teachers. Ministry of Education inspection reports document these inadequacies and reveal that schools were barely able to keep up with the local demand for education. The frequent interruptions caused by the Emergency during the previous half decade also meant that a great range of ages occupied each classroom. It was not uncommon for mature fifteen- and sixteen-year-olds to be in primary classrooms with much younger children, and even twenty-year-olds grouped with children half their age in intermediate classrooms. Nyeri District in 1956 had approximately 26,000 children in primary and intermediate schools under these conditions.[15] Two years later the number had grown to 35,700.[16]

The Meaning of Secondary Education

Children and their parents hungered for education regardless of the conditions in the schools. Unfortunately what these statistics do not reveal is that promotion from primary to intermediate school, even with very good exam results, was problematic. There were 122 primary schools in the district but only 39 intermediate schools, providing room for only one-third of the students to advance. Pass marks on the fourth-grade leaving exam had to be set very high to ensure that only one in three students passed. The movement from intermediate to secondary school was similarly restricted by a lack of adequate places. In 1961, the year in which Giakanja's first class was chosen, there were only ninety first-year places to accommodate the district's more than seven hundred students who passed the qualifying KPE.[17]

Many of my students spoke about doing well on their exams, but not well enough to advance on their first attempt. A number repeated both the CEE for admittance to Std. 5 and the KPE to qualify for secondary school. Under Education Department regulations, such repetitions were not permitted, so a student had to go to extraordinary lengths to deceive the authorities, switching to a different school, enrolling under another name, or seeking out a sympathetic intermediate-school headmaster who would turn a blind eye to a repeater.[18]

Several others mention that they did not know the value of education so that when they failed the Std. 4 CEE or the Std. 8 KPE, they were not motivated to try again. One student related, "I was ready to go back to herding cows because I really didn't know about education and my future; it wasn't until I got to secondary school that I realized that I was smart."[19] In this case, his mother pushed him to try again, and he finally got to secondary school as a result. Stanley said that though his fondest dream was to get a secondary education, even when he passed his KPE well enough to secure a place, his parents opposed it: "My parents were old and did not want me to go to secondary school but to stay home and care for them and work on our little farm. It was my brother who persuaded them to let me go, but I had to return home every weekend to work. My mother took up all the rest of the farm work. She eventually realized that education was more important than sheep and goats."[20]

For many other young people, the struggle to get into school and stay there did not work out. The balance between the value of an education and the need for their labor at home worked against them, and they stayed at home. A number of students reported that even though their KPE results were excellent and their peers with lower scores had secured places in secondary schools, they were not invited to join any school. No one knew why they had not gotten in. Then after the next term had begun, a letter arrived announcing their acceptance at Giakanja. "I was so excited," Joseph said, "that my feet didn't seem to touch the ground for a month!"[21] Such anomalies were common and might even involve some corruption, as revealed in the story of David. He had passed his KPE with high marks but later discovered that his headmaster had given his letter of acceptance to secondary school to the other David in his class, a boy who had just barely passed. "The headmaster had probably done it on purpose after being paid something by the parents."[22]

After he had figured out this "mistake," David retrieved the letter and came to Giakanja, as he should have been able to do several weeks earlier.

Many students did not fare as well. The files of the Ministry of Education contain hundreds of letters of application written by students seeking secondary school places in the early 1960s. These letters were filled with hard-luck stories about how they had been prevented from doing well in school by illness, interrupted educations, poor teaching, lack of school fees, or being orphaned. And while the replies were gently and sensitively written, all these students were turned down (154 rejection letters for Nyeri District in 1961) because they were too old, they could not be added late, or their KPE scores were not high enough.[23]

Beyond the individual rejections was the more comprehensive problem that there were simply very few secondary school places available for primary-school-leavers to occupy. This situation was not unique to Kenya, being found in much of sub-Saharan Africa, where the occupying colonial regimes considered a very limited number of secondary schools to be appropriate for the few trained Africans that were needed in their colonies. For instance, in 1950 approximately 26 percent of Kenya's primary-age children were in school, but only 2 percent were enrolled in secondary schools. By the end of the decade, not much had changed.[24]

The Making of a School

While young Gikuyu were laboring in their intermediate schools, hoping to eventually secure a place in a secondary school, events were taking place at Nyeri and in Nairobi that would eventually bring a new school into being—Giakanja. In Nyeri District, even as people were recovering from the deprivations of the Emergency, they were looking to their children's education. Many children were steadily coming up to their Std. 8 KPEs, passing well but not being selected for admission to secondary school. Even attaining a very high pass well within the range for selection did not guarantee a place in a secondary school. The two Nyeri-area secondary schools could not absorb all these qualified students, and even more were anticipated for future exams since those who had their education delayed by the Emergency were now back in school, too. It was in this emotionally charged atmosphere of seeing so many truly qualified students unable to continue their education that parents began to consider raising money for their own secondary school. Central

Kenya, including Nyeri District, had a long history of privately financed schools dating back to the KISA, which started in the 1930s.[25] These schools had all been closed during the Emergency, including the KISA primary school at Gachatha in Nyeri District. Parents had experience then in funding their own schools, though doing so at the secondary level was to be a new experience.

People who lived in the Thigingi area of Nyeri District remembered both an Education Department schools supervisor and an assistant to Senior Chief Muhoya as promoting the building of a locally funded secondary school. Their widows told me that there were many months of discussion in 1960 planning for such a school.[26]

The senior DO at Nyeri, who was also acting district commissioner (DC) for much of 1960, also promoted these plans. He had worried that independence would probably come sooner than people expected and that they would not be prepared to administer their own country. He remembered warning people at public meetings late in 1960 to prepare themselves to take over running the government and that education would be important in this regard. He also hoped that the intense ill feeling between those who supported the Mau Mau Rebellion and the loyalists would dissipate as people pulled together in a common effort such as building schools.[27] He told me many years later that he believed that "joining together to build schools might well prevent a civil war."[28] But people soon discovered that funding a secondary school at the local level was impossible. Even when the four chiefs of Tetu Division met in May 1961 to explore building a school supported by the whole division, they raised less than 10,000 shillings, only a token amount compared with the cost of such a school.[29] It was only when the DO approached the U.S. government development agency in Nairobi that the possibility of actually building a secondary school in Nyeri District became a reality.[30]

The DO found that in the early 1960s the U.S. government had plans to build eleven secondary day schools in Kenya, day schools being a radical departure from the Kenyan model of boarding schools. He encouraged them to consider a site in Nyeri District. His success in this venture was confirmed in a 1961 letter to Kenya's Ministry of Education in which the United States announced its plans for the day-school construction: "It is my pleasure to confirm to you the final signing of the documents under which our Government is to finance the construction of day secondary schools at Giakanja and Amakura. It is our hope that the day secondaries will be fully as effective as the boarding schools."[31]

Interestingly, interoffice memos within the Ministry of Education reveal that the building of day schools was thought to be misguided; Kenya would rather have had U.S. educational aid spent on enlarging the existing boarding schools and building new ones.[32] Nevertheless, Giakanja, named after the local area in Nyeri District, and Amakura, located in Western Kenya, were built. The earlier plans to build eleven schools had collapsed into building only two—aid dollars had been diverted elsewhere.[33]

The four chiefs of Tetu Division had settled on Giakanja as the site most central to all Tetu locations. The school was to be situated on vacated land formerly occupied by (1) the Giakanja Primary and Intermediate School, which had been relocated to the adjacent site of a former Emergency village (2) an abandoned AIPC cemetery, and (3) part of an area formerly occupied by an Emergency Police post, a Home Guard post, and the burial ground for persons who had died in their custody. These areas were now cobbled together to form a roughly rectangular twenty-five-acre plot for the new secondary school.[34]

Construction of the school buildings began in late 1961. Julius, a local resident, remembered securing a job from the building contractor about that time. He had hoped to obtain a secondary education himself, but his KPE results were not high enough to qualify, so he needed a job. He still was employed at Giakanja when I interviewed him, now as the supervisor of all buildings and grounds at the school, thirty-seven years after he had helped to build the school. He told me that delays in the arrival of building materials prevented the school from being completely built and ready for the first class to enter in January 1962. Times were tense as the contractor scrambled to prepare the site and get at least one classroom built. Further delays took place when crews constructing the foundations for staff houses unearthed a number of human skeletons. These were determined to be the remains of former Mau Mau forest fighters or their supporters who had died while under interrogation at the police post and Home Guard post. All were taken away and reburied, but Julius remembered that their discovery reopened emotional wounds for many people in the area.[35] Because of these delays, some discussion apparently took place about postponing the opening by a year, but the headmaster argued that the intake of the first class must go forward. He said that too many talented young people had not secured secondary school places in the past, and the school must open regardless of the conditions.[36]

The intake of the first class was delayed but not cancelled; they arrived in late February 1962 to find only one classroom ready for their occupation. Construction of the science lab and the administrative offices had not yet begun. The foundations for two staff houses had been completed, but nothing else, except for one temporary mud-and-wattle house hastily built for the headmaster, which he shared with the one other teacher. Convicts from Nyeri Prison and their armed guards were scattered about, clearing the compound and planting trees. There were no lavatories built yet and no running water at the school.[37] It was not a scene that inspired confidence among the new Form 1 arrivals.

Finally, by 13 May the school had been put in sufficient order to be officially opened, even though the first class had begun their studies two months earlier. Julius, having now shifted his employment from the building contractor to the school, was present for the opening and remembered the occasion very well. First, he said the official opening of the school was a great community event. Hundreds of people came from all over Tetu Division but especially from Giakanja, the area around the school. These people especially considered Giakanja to be their school. Julius remembers hearing lots of joyful singing the previous night as he stayed up to guard the school and all the preparations that had been made. To many local people, the opening of Giakanja was a tremendous event, and they turned out to celebrate the fact that the inspiration for the school and the drive to see it located in their area had come from them. They also rejoiced throughout the day by singing the headmaster's praise, perhaps the first African secondary school head-master in the entire country.[38] Julius whispered to me after my interview with him that when I came to Giakanja one year later, the local people were sure that I would be taking over as headmaster. My arrival was thought to be confirmation of the rumors that had circulated during the school's construction that both the headmaster and his assistant would be white since their staff houses were larger than the others and contained European style toilets.

A large number of European officials present at the ceremony also marked the occasion. Julius remembered representatives from the Ministry of Education, including the minister himself, the provincial education officer, the district commissioner, and his chief district officer. There was a contingent of officials from the American embassy and C. Mennon Williams, undersecretary of state for African affairs, who had come from Washington, D.C. especially for the Giakanja opening ceremony. In addition there were the four African chiefs of Tetu Division, including Senior Chief Muhoya, now retired and recently appointed the chairman of Giakanja's first board of governors. There were also other senior members of government and the army, administrators from the district and provincial offices at Nyeri, and police and other retainers.

This huge group proceeded to be marched around the school compound by the headmaster, who showed off the classrooms, the lavatories, the two staff houses that were finished, and the pump and water systems. Julius said that they also spent a great deal of time viewing the sites of the soon-to-be-constructed administration building, science laboratory, additional staff houses, and sports fields. Hundreds of local people followed in their wake, viewing the same things. Following this inspection tour, all assembled in the open area in front of the classrooms to hear speeches and to cut the ribbon officially opening the school. The most memorable words of the afternoon, especially for the students, were spoken by Williams, who said that the United States was most happy to finance the building of Giakanja School. To mark the occasion, the United States was offering scholarships to American universities to the four top students in the first class when they graduated at the end of 1965, four years hence. Everyone was impressed with this American largesse; the students all had visions of themselves attending universities abroad. Unfortunately these scholarships never materialized for Giakanja students. Julius heard later that each of the four chiefs claimed one for a son of theirs, none of whom were students at Giakanja.

The day ended with a reception, to which all the guests and the community were invited. Sodas donated by the Asian business community at Nyeri were served, as were cream cakes specially catered from a Nairobi bakery and served by the local chapter of the national women's rights organization, Maendeleo ya Wanawake. It was a day long remembered by local people because it officially launched the school they had hoped to build but for which they had been unable to raise the funds. But many saw it even in larger terms as a positive sign for the future. The day had provided evidence that indeed the restrictions on their movement, common during the Mau Mau Rebellion, were now lifted and they could freely associate with each other as well as government ministers and foreign dignitaries. Even months later, Julius frequently encountered local people remarking to each other about that day. Prominently featured in these conversations were the cream cakes and sodas they had consumed at the reception. Soft drinks were considered reserved for the colonial elites, both European and Asian, and were not usually available in the racially segregated shopping areas frequented by Kenyans before independence. No local people had ever seen cream cakes before, and some mistakenly ate the paper in which the pastry was wrapped. Somehow this new food and drink became a metaphor for a better future. Would not this unusual food become standard fare for their children and Giakanja Secondary School graduates? And would not those who had sacrificed themselves during the Mau Mau Rebellion for a better future, some of whom were in graves beneath their very feet at the reception, be proud of these new educational and social developments? Everyone was sure that the answer to both questions was an enthusiastic yes![39]

The First Classes at Giakanja

Surprisingly, Giakanja's first class of students was not pleased to be there. When asked to identify and rank their secondary school choices the previous November, they had all chosen prestigious boarding schools in the area or even those with national reputations elsewhere. No one had chosen Giakanja; it was unknown as a new school, and once the students arrived, they were immediately disappointed. "It was a bush school," said Samuel. "There was no water, no electricity, and only one classroom."[40] In fact, they missed the whole first term because the school had not been completed. Two students took one look at the place and left, never to return. Later it was discovered that they had found places elsewhere. No one else was as fortunate.

During the term, the reality of Giakanja sunk in. The school continued to be built around them, and the noise of construction made it difficult to concentrate. A second teacher joined the headmaster, but the students complained that as former primary-school teachers, they were neither qualified nor able to adequately teach them secondary-level subjects. The laboratory was the last building to be finished and that caused a delay during the entire first year in learning science subjects. In addition, neither of the two teachers could instruct them in mathematics.

The greatest shock was that Giakanja was a day school—no boarding facilities were available. Only a few students lived within walking distance of the school. This meant that all the others had to hire rooms among neighborhood families or rent them from nearby shopkeepers. In addition they had to haul water from a nearby river for bathing, clothes washing, and food preparation. Each week they had to return home for food supplies and the charcoal fuel for cooking it. Because mothers and sisters did the food preparation at home, these boys had neither the skills nor the cultural inclination to cook for themselves. Stanley said, "In a boarding school all you have to do is study; at Giakanja we had to do everything to look after ourselves—nothing was provided."[41] But the ultimate humiliation came on school breaks, when they returned home and were scorned by their former classmates who were now students at boarding schools. "They called us cooks and said that we smelled of smoke because we cooked our own food," Johnson said. "We were ridiculed at village dances in front of girls!"[42] Dickson said, "We did not look smart [well-dressed] either, because we had only one uniform and it showed its wear from frequent hand washings and no ironing."[43]

The first group of students entered Giakanja under difficult conditions. Samuel said, "We had been prepared for a boarding school so we were not psychologically able to shift to day school education; we started on a very low note."[44] Facilities were only just being constructed as they took up their studies, and sometimes classes were suspended so that students could assist in the preparation of the compound for the new buildings. Many times they had to also clean up after the workers. In addition, they considered the instruction inferior and the general atmosphere created by the headmaster and a succession of young, unqualified teachers not up to the level they had expected. Twice, student delegations made representations at the Provincial Education Office to voice their complaints. But although unhappy with their conditions, they persevered. "We were very strong characters," Samuel said. "The school may have been substandard, but we weren't!"[45]

The next year, the first group of students was promoted to Form 2 and another group of first-year students was admitted. Their response to the school was quite different. When they arrived in January 1963, the school was fully built, with four classrooms, an administrative building, a science laboratory, and staff houses spread over the twenty-five-acre compound. The new arrivals found these facilities stunning, in marked contrast to the construction site that met the first class a year earlier. To many of the newcomers, their first experiences were magical. They were issued proper uniforms with jackets, oriented to the new flush toilets, which were the first some had ever seen in their lives, and given a tour of the campus by the older students at the school. The new stone buildings, pristine lawns, and sports fields all alerted them to the fact that they had entered a new period in their lives. As James stated, "Once you go to high school, the world is a little more opened."[46] These were students who had also embraced an academic education. In this regard, Giakanja did not disappoint them either. On the second day they were all issued their textbooks and were excited to have their own copies. "Now we could learn on our own for the first time and not be tied only to the knowledge presented in the classroom."[47] They were also introduced to lab sciences for the first time: biology, chemistry, and physics. They were thrilled to think that soon they would be conducting experiments.[48] When they returned home at the weekend, they showed off their new uniforms, explained the wonders of using flush toilets, and told parents and siblings how they had entered paradise!

For this new group and the subsequent one that arrived in January 1964, Giakanja had been transformed into a "proper school." Members of the new incoming classes often knew one or two of the older students, and sometimes they had even chosen Giakanja over the more prestigious boarding schools. It was nearer home for most students, and that was a distinct advantage for those who needed to help widowed mothers and young brothers and sisters. It was also cheaper. The fees were only one-third those of a boarding school; that was clearly a consideration for poor families. They were also welcomed and made to feel at home by the older students. All of the newcomers reported that they soon knew everyone's name at the school and generally found a friendly atmosphere. The hazing of new students, typical of boarding schools, did not occur at Giakanja. Older students assumed a paternal role over the younger ones, assisting them in finding rooms to hire and instructing them in how to cook for themselves. A little later in the second year, the sports fields were leveled and laid out, first for football (soccer) and then for volleyball, and track-and-field events. A period of time each afternoon was soon set aside for sports activities and everyone played. By the end of the term, a varsity football team was chosen and a match scheduled against Kagumo High School, a neighboring boarding school and the first choice of many students now attending Giakanja. "We trashed them 8–2; they only sent their second team, confident in an easy victory," said James.[49] Giakanja celebrated their victory for a week and could not wait until they could tell their friends at home during the school holidays that the mighty Kagumo had fallen to the new and small Giakanja; it had been a real David and Goliath contest and it left the winners feeling like champions.

It was in academics that the biggest changes took place between the first and second year. What had angered and disappointed the first class the most was that Giakanja was not up to secondary school standards. All that changed in the second year, perhaps as a result of their complaints. First, a new headmaster arrived, a recent economics graduate of Makerere, the most prestigious university in East Africa. Although he was not a trained teacher and left two terms later to join a commercial firm in Nairobi as their chief economist, he quickly instilled the school with an academic atmosphere and treated the boys respectfully as secondary school students. All students, especially the older ones in the first class, breathed a sigh of relief. One of these students later confided in me, "As secondary students, you expected to be treated like adults. The first headmaster beat us like we were primary school children—that was hard to tolerate! With the arrival of a new headmaster, the school got serious."[50]

The trend in professionalizing the school continued with the arrival of the next headmaster at the end of 1963. He was in his mid-forties and one of the first Kenyans to be educated through high school twenty-five years earlier. In fact, his last two years of high school had to be finished in Uganda since no school that included the last two years was available in Kenya at the time. He taught for a time in primary schools and then secured a place in South Africa for a teacher-training course and followed by taking a degree at Ft. Hare College in Cape Province, where he overlapped for several years with Nelson Mandela, the future president of South Africa. When he returned to Kenya in 1952, he was posted as a math teacher to Kangaru, one of the country's leading boarding schools, where he stayed until 1963, the last year of which he was acting headmaster.[51] As the eldest son of a Nyeri area senior chief, everyone knew him, including the students at Giakanja. Students there, especially those in the first class, date the turnaround of the school with this distinguished educator's arrival. The fact that he had to seek his education outside the country gives further testimony not only to the scarcity of secondary schools but also to the unavailability of higher education in most colonies as well. It was not until after World War II that universities began to be built in much of sub-Saharan Africa, and Kenya's first university was the last to be established in East Africa in 1962.[52]

The new headmaster immediately instituted a more regimented schedule, with the day beginning promptly at 8:00 a.m. with a required morning assembly, where he alternately harangued them to study hard and complemented them on their achievements. He finished outfitting the science lab with equipment, bought uniforms for the soccer team, and put together a roster of games with all the big schools in the region.

He also instituted an annual excursion to Nairobi for each class to see plays at the Kenya National Theatre, to attend the National Agricultural Fair, and to visit museums. As the school's first trained math and physics teacher, he also provided accelerated instruction that in one year brought the students up to where they should have been on the national syllabus. David said, "[He] put things right; he gave us confidence that we could do well at this day school even in the midst of so many difficulties with room and board."[53] He was firm but fair as headmaster and a dedicated and enthusiastic teacher. The students loved him. He served at Giakanja for seven years and then went to a senior position in Mombasa as PEO. He retired in 1983 to the Nyeri area, where thirteen years later I found him farming his ancestral land.

A number of other teachers were posted to the school either just before or concurrent with the headmaster's arrival. A new chemistry and biology teacher came with his wife and baby daughter. He had completed two years of junior college as well as a teacher-training program, and I came to depend upon him a great deal to help me acculturate to Kenya and its school system. He left after two years to pursue a degree at the American University in Beirut. A new geography teacher came for several years before he became director of extra mural studies at the University of Nairobi. A French teacher of Pakistani heritage who had grown up in Kenya taught for several years too. Not only was Giakanja a stepping-stone to future success for students but also for the staff, who all went on to better things. The country was hungry for talented professionals, and career mobility was high with the increasing departure of the expatriate community.

I arrived at Giakanja in mid-1963. I was twenty-two years old and had received my BA in history only two months earlier. I was an inexperienced, though trained, teacher, and Giakanja was my first teaching position. My first impressions were how very beautiful the school was, nestled into the surrounding hills of this Gikuyu farming community, and how very polite the schoolboys were to me, even deferential. I immediately understood such politeness as a legacy of the still-intact British colonial system in Kenya. But I came to realize that, although I was the only white teacher at the school, all teachers received the same politeness. Nevertheless, it did take some time for me to get used to all the students jumping to their feet and greeting me with a "good morning, sir" or "good afternoon, sir" when I entered their classrooms.

Gikuyu countryside near Giakanja Secondary School, 1960s

Gikuyu homestead, 1960s

Boys going to pick tea after school; primary school in background

Abandoned Emergency village near Giakanja Secondary School, 1965

Gikuyu market near Giakanja Secondary School, 1960s

Class I (1962–65), fall 1963

Class II (1963–66), fall 1963

Class III (1964–67), fall 1966

Morning break at Giakanja

Morning assembly at Giakanja, 1964: students listening to headmaster; teachers standing behind

Afternoon athletics; school buildings and staff houses in background

Author outside his Giakanja house, 1964

3

Confronting the Cambridge Exams

The Cambridge School Certificate (CSC) was the ultimate credential: mandatory for getting a good job or entrance to higher education and the focus of all Kenyan secondary school students, especially in their last two years. Earning a good school certificate was a prerequisite to a good life and Kenyans had known this for a long time. It was a legacy from the colonial era, when the recipients had been mostly the children of European settlers and other expatriates whose education in the colonies had to be certified by the Cambridge Overseas Examination Board. After independence, Kenyans kept this inherited tradition as evidence that their education was equal to what Kenya's European children had received but that had previously been denied to all but a very few of the Kenyans themselves . This may also account for the slowness to Africanize the secondary school curriculum once Kenya became independent. An abortive attempt was made in the mid-1970s, when the Literature Faculty at the University of Nairobi proposed that the European books on the literature syllabus be replaced with those of Afrocentric content. The government rejected the proposal, saying that it sought "to change the curriculum status quo."[1] Moving the content away from the long-established European model was clearly understood by government to threaten the legitimacy and integrity of the exam. But the most important reason for continuing to keep the Cambridge Exam (CE) program intact was its reputation as a fair and impartial standard for all—a crucial factor in a pluralistic society like Kenya's, which had significant educational disparities among different areas of the country. One educator surmised that "the very name and distance [of the exam] are suggestive of impartiality."[2] Certainly one would tamper with such a powerful symbol only at one's peril.

While the government was seeking to maintain continuity in the examination system for its own reasons, a massive study conducted among secondary school students in the mid-1960s can help us to understand how they thought about themselves and their future as they approached the time of their Cambridge Exams. At the outset, the authors noted that just by being secondary school students, this group had received an education which 99 percent of all other Kenyans lacked; but that the elite nature of this cohort was based on their educational attainment and not for being children of an upper class. Indeed, their parents were mostly peasants with only a few years of schooling at best, as was the case for my students. Not surprisingly, the answers to the study's questionnaire revealed that the students continued to have an awareness of their humble origins and feelings of egalitarianism toward those less fortunate.[3] They did not see themselves as elite, as set apart from their communities and entitled to special privileges.

In another section of the study, the authors explored students' attitudes about the efficacy and purpose of hard work. They noted that nearly three-quarters of the students believed "that the individual has the capacity to deal with his surroundings and to alter them in his favour." They overwhelmingly answered that hard work was the best road to success and that "work pays off."[4] And like my students (see chapter 4), they had a fundamental belief in the links between personal achievement, hard work, and success. They may have had a growing understanding of their position in relation to the rest of society, but that is not what would enable them to pass well on their CSCE. Rather it would be their sustained hard work that would earn them this distinction.

It was in this frame of mind during the last year of secondary school that students experienced a combination of confidence and terror as they prepared for their exams. They felt confident because they had twice already taken national exams at the end of Std. 4 to move from primary to intermediate school and at the end of Std. 8 to gain access to a secondary school. They rightfully took some confidence from having passed these exams at a very high standard. All of them had also successfully adapted to the fact that Giakanja was a day school where they had to provide their own room and board, as well as develop an academic routine to meet the demands of their studies. In fact, they had created a community where the older students mentored the younger ones as they arrived each year—scared, lonely, and without the skills or experience to easily solve room-and-board problems. There was no hazing of the new arrivals, a common practice in Kenyan boarding schools. In reflecting on the general mood among students at Giakanja, David said, "We felt toward each other like we were brothers."[5]

But their confidence and sense of achievement was tempered by the fact that their futures were inextricably tied to the results of these upcoming exams. In Harrison's words, "To pass meant access to a good life; to fail was economic death."[6] It was not just one's own economic future that was at risk either. Often the students had parents who expected their sons to care for them in old age. The O-level CSCE results were linked to the future quality of life for students' aging parents and frequently to that of younger siblings, whose school fees would be guaranteed by a successful older brother. There was also no anonymity to passing or failing, as Kihumba revealed: "Not only the family but the whole village followed one's progress. You might be the only boy to have gone to secondary school from your village. Taking the CSCE was serious business because the whole village would know the results. They bought the paper on that day (when exam results were published); even those who did not read wanted to see your name."[7] As the end of the year approached, students alternated between visions of glorious post-exam futures and a sense of terror about failing their exams.

There was also a link between Christianity and educational success, though not only a direct one. Many of the primary schools in the areas where they grew up were affiliated with either the Presbyterian Church of East Africa or the Catholic Church. As with missionary schools earlier in the century, some elements of proselytizing took place at school: headmasters and teachers were screened by the church, a local pastor might have given religious lessons leading to baptism and confirmation, and scripture and prayer were daily features at morning assembly. There was probably some expectation that students attend Sunday services of the church denomination with which their school was affiliated. I know that there was some loyalty to "being Presbyterian," because several students said that they were conflicted when they considered switching to a Catholic-affiliated intermediate school because of its better academic reputation.[8] And some students had grown up in Christian households. Amos and James's parents were church elders. Esau said that he "got serious about Christianity" when his mother was threatened by Mau Mau, though neither of his parents were Christians.[9]

Colonial officials considered Christians to be loyalists during the Emergency because of their refusal to take the Mau Mau oath of unity. This rejection of Mau Mau earned Christians the ire of their neighbors, especially because of the special treatment given to them. For instance, as loyalists they were not required to live in Emergency villages and were excused from forced labor. Christians had been set apart from the general public during the Emergency and had enjoyed privileges not available to others.

When the students came to Giakanja Secondary School, their connection with Christianity continued. Religion was a required CSC subject, and while some of their studies encompassed comparative religion, the majority was spent on Christianity, an emphasis reflected in the exam. Each morning assembly also opened with scripture and prayer, and there was a local chapter of the Student Christian Union Association at Giakanja. This student-led club occasionally held Bible study and prayer meetings, and they organized an annual Christmas service, to which all students were invited. Yet my impression was that the club was composed of the dozen or so students who came to Giakanja as Christians, perhaps with a few more added during their education there. But overall the club attracted only a portion of the 120 students present.

One factor that may explain why Christianity was not more popular at Giakanja is that it was still associated with loyalists and their opposition to Mau Mau during the Emergency. Such ill feeling was compounded at Giakanja because of the high number of students in the first two classes whose fathers and other family members had been detained as supporters of Mau Mau. As Simon explained, "Giakanja had become the last resort for children of Mau Mau, because other schools discriminated against them and would not take them." Simon, who had passed first in his class at intermediate school, experienced this discrimination firsthand when he was rejected by all of the secondary schools in the area except Giakanja.[10] Christianity carried this stigma for several years at Giakanja and dampened its appeal to students. As a result, students gave little indication that Christianity helped them through the traumas of acquiring an education or weathering the stress of preparing for their exams. Instead, they focused on their own abilities, such as working hard, setting goals, never giving up, and putting difficult times or failures behind them, as explanations of their achievements.

Preparing for the Exam

In interviews, students tended to quickly pass over their preparations for the exams. Only patient probing brought forth the details of the serious and time-consuming nature of their studies prior to the exams. A long-awaited field trip to Nairobi and occasional athletic competitions were the only interruptions to the punishing routine of study that developed during their last year. The school day, from 8:00 a.m. until 5:00 p.m., consisted of eight class sessions, morning and lunch breaks, and an hour of athletics. At 5:00 p.m. students would rush to their hired rooms to make supper for themselves and then return to evening study in the electricity-lit classrooms. At 10:00 p.m. the lights were turned off and they went home, where they tried to study by candlelight in their meager rooms for another hour or two. To keep from falling asleep, some resorted to putting their feet into pails of cold water.[11] Many struggled to wake up early to squeeze a few more hours of study in their rooms before the school day began, but the combination of fatigue and weak candlelight often enticed them to doze off.

Sometime during the initial months of 1965, when the first Form 4 class was struggling with their studies, they talked the night watchman into opening the school library for them in the early hours of the morning; soon this room was used Monday through Friday from 3:00 a.m. to 6:30 a.m. as a Form 4 study room. I remember waking early one morning to see the library light on. Since I was the master on duty that week, I walked down to the school to investigate. Imagine my surprise when I opened the door to find this room packed with students, all with their noses in textbooks or notebooks. The night watchman took me aside to explain the arrangements the students had made with him. He said that he had agreed to the students' request because he wanted them to pass their exams so that they could succeed in life. I never told anyone, and the practice continued for the rest of the year. The following year, when I was acting headmaster, my previous silence was taken by the night watchman to be tacit agreement, and the library was opened during the middle of the night for the next Form 4 class as well. Thirty years later when I interviewed the headmaster, he said that he had also known of the practice but had done nothing about it. It seems that we both had wondered at the time if students were getting enough sleep to sustain themselves for their studies, but neither of us wanted to say no to such serious and determined efforts.[12]

For the Form 4 students, the congenial atmosphere that had characterized their earlier years at Giakanja began to change during their last year as well. Now a more intense competition developed, at least among the very best students. Whereas before, students helped each other with their studies by enthusiastically sharing knowledge, books, and notes, now hesitancy developed as students vied to achieve the best results and to be at the top of their class. The competitive atmosphere intensified as each student tried to keep track of how much others were studying and then to sabotage those efforts. Joseph expressed it this way: "People would visit you on the weekend to prevent you from studying and some would not loan you a book, so you had to get a friend of theirs to ask for it and then get it that way."[13] David, who had to work with his father on a white-settler farm during the school holiday to pay his school fees, remembers well that experience. "Even the other laborers knew that I should be studying. They frequently said, 'This boy is not going to pass. He comes to do manual labor like his father.' What they didn't know was that I was studying every night and only sleeping three to four hours; I couldn't let my classmates get ahead of me."[14]

The class of 1965, the first students to sit for the CE at Giakanja, had special circumstances that might have prevented them from scoring well. They were the pioneer class with no older students to mentor them. There were no previous results that could have developed into a supportive tradition to encourage them. The legacy of their first two years, when much of their time was spent working at the school rather than learning, haunted them too. "The first year we spent a lot of time doing manual labor," Stanley said, "for about half a year there was no school at all, we just planted the hedges [for fences] and leveled the playing field."[15] Several students wanted to transfer to other schools, and two contemplated switching to teacher-training institutions.[16] For the entire first year of school, there was just the headmaster and one other teacher, both with only primary school experience. They could not teach all the subjects in the curriculum and the students in this first class felt they had been held back. "Even now," Stanley said, "I don't want to see him [the first Headmaster] . . . he wasted a lot of our time and we hated him. He was running our school like it was a primary school."[17]

A Colonial Curriculum in Independent Kenya

The other concern of the first class was the nature of the CE itself. The students knew that there were not many opportunities for additional education. There were few Form 5 seats available and securing a place in a senior secondary school and obtaining a good exam result after Form 6 were necessary prerequisites for admittance to the university. These conditions paralleled what they had already been through for the KPE at the end of primary school. There was a common perception among students about that exam, as Titus noted: "The purpose of the

Kenya Preliminary Exam was to make you fail [because there were so few secondary school places available]." So they reasoned, was this the case for the CE too?[18]

The staff found that teaching the Form 4 class was intense as well, especially in 1965, when we were preparing the first Form 4 for their CE. Each of the eight subjects taught at Giakanja was guided by a national, though not yet Africanized, curriculum, which outlined all areas of study and identified where in the four-year secondary program they were to be taught.[19] Ideally one was to have finished the whole syllabus by the end of the first term of Form 4 so that the remaining two terms could be entirely devoted to revision.[20] For both teacher and student, the focus now narrowed to trying to anticipate what questions were most likely to be asked on the exam and then to practice preparing answers to them.[21] At the end of the second term, students would take a trial exam that sought to duplicate the conditions of the actual CE they would take at the end of the next term. The results of this mock exam would indicate to both students and staff the areas of strength and weakness and thus guide the review during the last term. The volume of material to be mastered for these eight subjects was daunting. Both the trial exam and the actual CE were composed of eighteen different papers (exams), totaling thirty-four and a half hours over ten days.

When I had arrived in Kenya eighteen months earlier, I brought a liberal arts notion that education was aimed at preparing one for life and not just for work. I tried to convey to students a love of learning and an interest in the human condition in its broadest levels. But by the end of my first term at Giakanja, my American philosophy of education collided with the exam-oriented nature of Kenyan education. I did attempt to convey my love of literature, language, and history in broader terms than simply character and plot (literature), grammar and sentence structure (English), and acts and facts (history), but I encountered considerable resistance from the students.

In the introduction to a history handbook that I helped prepare for newly arrived Peace Corps teachers in Kenya, we encouraged them to interest students broadly in history: "Facts put down correctly on an exam will mean nothing to them later on in life, but an understanding of their history, and its ongoing development and evolution, will remain forever."[22] But in the final year of their secondary school education, when students were completely focused on their CE, this philosophy of education broke down, and teachers who did not give sufficient time to exam preparation did so at their peril. In his book *Growing up in East*

Africa, E. B. Castle explored the reasons students went on strike: "They know that failure to pass examinations closes doors to a bright future. Consequently, any defect in school organization, such as inadequate equipment, unsuitable textbooks, but especially what in their judgment is ineffective teaching, arouses anxieties which may explode in strong criticism of an individual member of staff and not infrequently in a demand for his dismissal."[23] Castle went on to say that since no headmaster can give in to such a demand, a clash often occurred that eventually led to students boycotting classes—striking.[24]

While there was never a strike during my years at Giakanja, there definitely were tensions between students and staff over being adequately taught, especially in the Form 4 class. I remember being surprised during a Form 4 history lesson when a student asked, "Will this be on the [Cambridge] exam?" After this happened a number of times in subsequent weeks, I came to understand that they were gently but firmly telling me that their expectation was that we now concentrate exclusively on exam preparation. One teacher at Giakanja did not respond to this question. A former student in his class vividly remembers what happened:

> Mr. X was our English master during the term before our Exams. He enthusiastically announced one day that we would be spending thirty minutes [out of a forty-minute class period] each class for the next week or two on speech drills. There was a lot of talk among us after class that this was wasting too much time and that we would have no time for exam preparation.[25] The next day before we started speech drills, we said that we were not going to have it any more. The next day after morning assembly, the headmaster told all Form 4s to remain behind. He questioned us, "Why don't you want to learn?" We said nothing. Mr. X was there and told us, "You cannot dictate what to be taught." Finally, the headmaster turned to me and asked, "M. can you tell me what is wrong?"[26]

Apparently with this question the dam burst, and the entire class explained their grievances to the headmaster. The student went on to say that when English class began the next day, Mr. X announced that speech drills would continue, but no more than ten minutes each day; the rest of the time would be spent in preparing for their upcoming exams. Thus students, who normally respected their teachers and contented themselves with the instruction they received, would nevertheless react boldly if they felt thwarted in exam preparation. In this case, the headmaster prevented this incident from escalating by quickly working out a compromise by which everyone could abide. As we shall see, though, there was no reaction to the colonial content of the curriculum.

My own responsibilities for the class of 1965 and the Form 4 classes in the two subsequent years were to prepare them in English language, English literature, and history—a total of four CE papers. By far the most important of these subjects, and indeed of all of the others, was English language because if one failed this subject, he could not receive a school certificate. Furthermore, the centrality of mastering English was essential in all the other areas of a student's education since all subjects were taught and examined in English. As Gordon D. Morgan noted, A student with weak English language and reading skills will be hampered from passing in all other areas: "It seems that a major task of secondary schooling is to get the African student to master English. . . . The better the student is in English the better his possibilities for doing well on the Cambridge [Exam]."[27]

By the time my students had reached Form 4, they had been taught in English for seven years and had accomplished much with the language, including passing (often with distinction) the compulsory English-language-based KPE, which had given them entrance to Giakanja in the first place. Since Form 1, eight out of their forty weekly class periods had been devoted to English-language instruction. Such topics as grammar, vocabulary, reading comprehension, and essay and summary writing occupied these class sessions right through to Form 4. Yet English remained a third language for many of the students; few spoke it outside the classroom, and all struggled with the language on a daily basis.

In the last year, specific attention turned to the two English-language papers. In paper one, students were asked to write an essay from a list of topics for one and a half hours. Some of the topics listed in the previous year's exam (and available to all teachers) included: the value of a hobby, legends of my country, helping mother, and an account of the chief industry of my country. Paper two asked students to answer three questions. In question one, students had to summarize a passage in approximately one-third of the original words "using a continuous connection of ideas." Question two asked students to read a three- to four-paragraph passage and then answer questions about it. Question three tested the students' ability to manipulate the language of a sentence without changing the meaning. Here are some examples:

1. "He likes being idle better than working for his living." Rewrite by beginning, "He would rather . . ."
2. "*Tom Jones* can be seen next week at the Odeon Cinema. It is one of the great films from the early sixties. It is being shown at the Odeon for the second time." Join into one sentence using *which* and *where*.
3. "The second cake she baked was even less successful, when it came out of the oven, than the first." Finish . . . *as the first.*

These examples demonstrate the difficulty of the English papers and give credence to the fact that passing this exam was an enormous hurdle for students. For the entire last year, I remember giving students rigorous practice in timed essays, summarizing, reading comprehension, and sentence construction. Gradually most of them were able to complete these assignments within the time limits at a passing standard. Nevertheless, a total of eight students failed English in the first three classes and did not earn a CSC as a result.

A single literature paper of two and a half hours tested their comprehension of four set books. For the 1965 class they were Shakespeare's *Macbeth*; *My Family and Other Animals,* by Gerald Durrell; George Eliot's *The Mill on the Floss*; and Robert Bolt's play *A Man for All Seasons.* Generally students began their study of English literature with shorter and simpler books in Forms 1 and 2, only starting the set books in Form 3 and then reading one each term for the next four terms. This schedule of study enabled the teacher to slowly introduce literature and gauge the class's ability. With this information, the literature teacher would then choose the set books from among those offered by the Cambridge Examiners.

When I arrived in August 1963, three of the set books had already been purchased: *The Mill on the Floss, Macbeth,* and *My Family and Other Animals.* I would not have chosen George Eliot's 650-page novel about nineteenth-century rural English manners. Although students could master the plot—of love lost and found and grievances settled—they were frequently confused by the sometimes-archaic language and a setting beyond their visual experience. It was the most difficult book for them. I spent a great deal of time explaining the language and interpreting the locale; rural nineteenth-century England was another planet. A far easier book was *My Family and Other Animals,* Durrell's account of growing up on the Greek island of Corfu. This humorous book is filled with vivid details set out in direct language that the students could comprehend. It was their favorite, and the entire class thought that after a term of study they had mastered it. They also liked the two plays, *Macbeth* and *A Man for All Seasons,* though they did not love them like *My Family.* A

Shakespearean play was compulsory, and *Macbeth* was a good choice because it is short and has a simple plot. Neither was the case two years later, when students had to read the much longer and more complex *Julius Caesar*. I was surprised to find that the students had less trouble with the Elizabethan English of Shakespeare than with George Eliot's use of the language. They memorized and could translate and explain key passages with greater ease than I would have expected. The Form 4 class in the next year also had *Macbeth* as a set book. That year the Kenya National Theatre in Nairobi offered a production that we took the students to see, and it greatly enhanced their interest and comprehension. *A Man for All Seasons* was the only set book that I chose. It was the last read and the quickest one to be completed, perhaps because both the students and I were now so familiar with our literature routine: master the plot, learn new vocabulary and idioms, identify the meaning of key passages, and write essays on interpretation. The students also found Bolt's main character, Sir Thomas, most compelling as he strived to do the right thing, even at the cost of his own life.

Like literature, there was also a single history paper of two hours; students were to answer a total of five essay questions from three sections. The title of the paper, "The Development of Tropical Africa," was somewhat misleading because two out of the three sections had little or nothing to do with the continent. The first section contained questions about early European empires in Latin America and the Caribbean, North America, and the Far East. Occasionally questions concerning Africa appeared, but usually in relationship to larger questions concerning trade or exploration. For instance, this question appeared in the 1964 examination: "Why did the Portuguese begin and persevere with the exploration of the coast of Africa?" Section two was concerned with the workings of the British government. Here are a few typical questions: "Show the stages through which a government-sponsored public bill (*not* a finance bill) passes in the United Kingdom Parliament before it becomes a law." "What are the duties of the British Prime Minister with regard to (a) the Sovereign, (b) the House of Commons, and (c) the cabinet?" "Show how the House of Commons in the United Kingdom controls (a) taxation, and (b) government spending." Only in section three were there direct questions concerning Africa, though the central focus was on British colonialism on the continent. Questions such as the following were found in the history papers during the early to mid-1960s: "Who were the Pioneers, and what is their place in the history of Rhodesia?" "How and why did Zanzibar come under British rule?" "What is meant

by 'indirect rule'? When, where and how was it operated in *either* West
Africa *or* East Africa?"

In reflecting on preparing Form 4 classes for the CE, two problems
come easily to mind. The first concerns the difficulty in trying to teach
students to carefully read the questions in their practice exams and then
craft their essays to answer those questions. Students wanted to identify
from past exams those questions that were most likely to be found on
their examination and then to memorize their essay answers to them.
Though they had prodigious memories for this activity, it only worked if
the questions were the very ones for which they had memorized answers.
If the question was only slightly different, their answer would not fit
well.[28] The very nature of the CE reinforced the tendency for students
to favor learning by rote and memorizing information to be set out on
their exams, rather than understanding the subject and building their
essay answers around the evidence for that subject. Morgan reminds us
that this is what we should expect to happen when "students have very
limited working English vocabularies and where their social mobility
[and financial future] depends upon their doing well on the tests."[29] They
became exceptional exam takers but not broadly educated individuals.

The second problem follows on the first one and concerns relevance.
The literature and history curricula were designed around set books and
subjects that were not integral to the lives of these students. On the eve
of Kenya's independence and the years immediately following, their
history studies included no content about their own country and very
little on their region. The same comment could be made for literature.
Although their set books could be considered classics, all took up other
times and places; none were about Africans or by African authors. One
can speculate as to why such a colonially based curriculum continued
beyond colonial rule. Perhaps there had not been enough time to change
the curriculum before Kenya's independence. The pace had been quite
brisk leading up to the negotiated ending of British rule, and I remember
some Kenyans telling me at the time that they were surprised at how
quickly the day of independence had arrived. The colonial curriculum
may also have lingered on into the postcolonial era because there was
no outcry for change. Perhaps because lack of an outcry was the ultimate
byproduct of the colonial curriculum, it muted protest by subtly com-
municating a message of inferiority. These students learned that history
and literature were about other peoples, principally Europeans, and not
about themselves.

Even more powerfully negative was the related idea that Africans like themselves had no history or literature. The ultimate message of the curriculum and the exam that reinforced it was one of inferiority. The superiority of European or white culture was proclaimed loudly and widely in Kenya during the colonial era. This superiority was sharply brought home to me upon my arrival at Giakanja. Both the community and the students greeted my arrival as the first white teacher as a sign that academic standards would rise. As one former student told me thirty years later, "The Mzungu [white man] at the time had quality; he was a man in command of this country and though the country was in transition from the white man to the Blackman, we felt that the Mzungu still had quality to deliver. . . . Psychologically, we had a lot of hope in you as our expatriate member of staff."[30] I would have been astonished to hear this while teaching there since I came as an inexperienced teacher into a foreign culture and frequently sought help from my experienced African colleagues. However, in the minds of my students and perhaps their parents, who frequently and deferentially welcomed me into their homes, I instilled confidence in them as they pursued their education. This attitude might have been rational had it been limited to me being their English teacher, since I was the only native speaker of English at the school during my first year,[31] but they were thinking in larger terms—a white teacher meant a superior teacher. Such thinking was the natural and devastating heritage of white rule with its attendant colonial curriculum and examining power.[32]

Waiting for Results

Eventually the day arrived in late November each year when the Form 4 class took their examinations. They might have drawn confidence from the trial exams they had taken three months earlier in August, when they came away with the experience of what it was like to take one paper after another for two weeks straight. The trial exam also gave them a clearer idea of their strengths and weaknesses. I was not present at the school during the time when my Form 4 students took the CE since I was made responsible for administering the exams at another school.[33] There I witnessed the stress and tension that students brought to each exam when the stakes were so high. Many times I told students to take deep breaths to try to relax before starting an exam. I am sure that such an atmosphere was also present at Giakanja. When the exams ended at Giakanja, the Form 4 students unceremoniously left the school. There were no celebrations to mark the occasion or speeches of good cheer to send them on their way. Because I was busy finishing up my invigilation duties at another school each year, I usually missed saying goodbye to many of them. It was very anticlimactic. Students with whom I had worked very closely for two or more years were gone, and with only a few exceptions, we did not meet again for more than thirty years.

In the 1960s, CE results were published in the newspaper sometime in mid-February. All the students vividly recall what they were doing when they heard the news. Michael remembers well how he learned about his results:

> People liked me in my village and they were always telling me "you must pass, you have to pass." So after we finished the examination, I didn't go home; I kind of hid away from them until the results came out. . . . I went to Nairobi and stayed with my friends there, waiting. I remember very well the day the results came out because I was not working but staying at a friend's house. They had a telephone in the house and it rang about 9:00 a.m. I picked up the telephone and this friend of mine told me, "You know what, the results are out and you are in Division I." I couldn't even believe what I was hearing. I was so happy, so overjoyed because I had been wondering how shall I go and tell people at home if I don't do well. I asked my friend, "Do you mean it?" and he said, "Yes, I have the paper here and I'm reading the names." I said, "Can you read my name?" And he read me the name from the newspaper and that's how I got the result.[34]

David reveals the anxiety that accompanied his hearing that the results were out:

> I was at home and I told my mother that I was going to go look for the results. I set off on foot because I could not afford to go by any vehicle. I reached a place called Gachatha, near to Giakanja School, and there I met someone with an *East African Standard* [newspaper] who I had known in primary school. . . . He said that I didn't have to search for the results any further, that he had seen them and that Giakanja had done very badly. I told him that it doesn't matter; one can repeat or even do the exam again privately next year. He said that he was sorry to have to tell me that I had done especially badly. I told him to let me see the newspaper, because I was thinking that maybe I should turn around and go

back home. Then I saw that he was laughing and that he was just playing a joke on me. He shook my hand and said that I had in fact done marvelously well. I shed tears when I looked at the paper and saw that I was in Division I.[35]

After receiving such good news, David walked on to Giakanja School to check the official results posted there. He met the headmaster, who congratulated him: "You were one of my best students." When he raised the issue of getting a letter of recommendation for his application to Kenya Railways, the headmaster said, "Don't get a job now; that is part of Kenya's past. You must go on for more education and I have already made arrangements for you to attend Nakuru High School for your A levels."[36] Reflecting on this conversation with the headmaster, David said that continuing his education was the key to his current position in a large European-owned company. Giakanja had launched him, and his advanced studies later continued him along: "You know, you start climbing trees at the bottom not the top. . . . And you know the bottom is very slippery, but the minute you reach the first branch, then at least you know that eventually you are going to reach the fruit at the top."[37]

Learning of one's results was not always such a joyous occasion. Daniel relates that he was already working in Nairobi when the results were published:

> I had been checking the newspaper regularly and on that day, I was checking again. I felt that when I found my name, then I would really be somebody. But when I looked, I didn't see my name in the first instance so I went back and checked again and I didn't find it.[38] I finally knew that I was not there. . . . Everybody would be proud to say, "You see, this is my name" but when you didn't have anything to say about yourself and yet my friends knew that I was waiting for the results, I just went into isolation.[39]

The next week he traveled to Giakanja hoping to find that an error had been made. The headmaster gently told him that he had just missed getting a Division III score. "For the lack of two points, I was labeled a failure."[40] The headmaster counseled him to try again the next year as a private candidate, which he did and successfully passed. He also took his A-level exams as a private candidate and passed them too. But from the tone of his voice, I could tell that these accomplishments did not fully compensate for initially failing his CE. Not finding his name in the paper left a wound that had never healed.

Although there were failures in each of the first three classes, the overall results for these years were remarkably good.[41] Giakanja competed very well against other schools like itself, and its results even rivaled some of the older schools with national reputations. In reflecting on those early years, the headmaster claimed that Giakanja students were as good as any that he had taught at Kangaru.[42] The students themselves were so pleased. They had been the butt of many jokes by those in boarding schools. As Harun exalted, "We were not equal to those who went to boarding schools until the results came out; the exam results equalized everyone."[43] William said, "Boarding school boys always boasted of their schools and made fun of us . . . but when the results came out, everyone could see that we had done better than many of those Kagumo boasters."[44]

Their enthusiasm over the results was warranted. Each of the first three classes did better than the previous one, both in the overall pass rate and in the number of Division I or Division II passes. Each class also had a higher percentage of their number passing each year than was the national average.[45] Peter, a student in the class of 1967, achieved the best single score of anyone in the first three classes. This score was also one of the best in the whole country, and it has remained the best score ever achieved by a Giakanja student.[46] Peter's high Cambridge score passed into the collective memory of these three classes—they can all cite his achievement—as well as the initial failure and eventual success of Ephantus, a student in the class of 1966 who was the only failure that year. He retook the exams as a private student the following year and passed, then passed his A levels in 1969 and entered Uganda's Makerere University (the most prestigious in East Africa) earning a BA in 1975 and an MA in public administration from the University of Pittsburgh in 1979. Since then he has risen to positions of responsibility, first as the clerk of the Nyeri County Council and more recently achieving the same position at Embu.[47] This was an enormous achievement for one who left secondary school having failed his exams.[48]

For some the CSCE was the pinnacle of their schooling experience; almost all of them entered the fraternity of those who passed, an achievement that still brought them pleasure and confidence thirty years later. Some wished that they had done better, even complaining that they had repeatedly done better on all end-of-term exams and the trial exam, only to be eclipsed in the Cambridge by classmates whom they had previously bested.[49] Some moved on to further education, but all eventually entered the workforce to become part of Kenya's postcolonial elite.

4

Making a Career

As students were finishing up their secondary schooling, waiting for their exam results, or trying out their first attempts at employment, what were their educational and occupational aspirations and how had their education influenced these aspirations? A questionnaire administered in 1969 by a group of Nairobi educators to a sample of Form 4 students sought to answer these questions and uncovered some surprising results. It seems that the better the student as measured by CSCE results and better the school (in a hierarchy of national, local, Harambee), the lower the student aspiration to continue their studies to Forms 5 and 6 and university and the greater their interest in immediately joining the workforce. The reverse was true as well: students from the least good schools with the poorest CSCE results had the highest expectations to continue their educations and the least interest in immediately starting their working careers. These results seem to be counterintuitive. Surely it would be more accurate to say that the better the school and student, the higher the aspiration to continue one's education. But the analysis of the data reveals a more nuanced interpretation. In the words of the author, H. C. A. Somerset, "Realism in setting aspirations has two components: firstly, adjusting to the facts of the labour market and secondly, adjusting to the facts of one's own intellectual strengths and weaknesses."[1] The national schools had sufficient staff to give their students careful career guidance, as well as to alert them to the highly competitive admission to Form 5. Such schools also had alumni able to give guidance about specific careers and more generally to equip students with a realistic appraisal of the job market. This information, the author hypothesized, led to a downward setting of expectations for those hoping to go on to Form 5 or land their "dream job." Students from the larger number of local catchment schools like Giakanja seldom had the benefit of career advisement or counsel about the rigors of admission to higher education.

Their knowledge was most often limited only to their academic standing at their own school, and they were largely ignorant of the job market altogether. Although they were seeking to make rational decisions about the future, their range of knowledge was narrow, and they did not realize that their aspirations were unrealistically high.[2] Each group used the information available to them in making decisions about their educational and employment futures. As a result, students from the selective national schools, made over-cautious decisions, even to the extent of undervaluing their very able abilities, whereas students from good but local catchment schools had only their class rank and personal academic assessment to draw upon. As a result, this group frequently had an inflated sense of their future.

In an essay from the same collection as the research cited above, economist Emil Rado shifts from the aspirations of Form 4 students to their actual placement in the workforce, particularly focusing on what guided them in their choice of job, at least at the beginning of their career path. He sets out a series of hypotheses suggesting that although job seekers often do not know what jobs are available or what such jobs actually entail, they compensate for this ignorance by having a broad knowledge of salaries, which becomes their primary criterion for job selection. Thus Rado's first hypothesis is that "it is not education *per se* which influences aspirations, but the income opportunities which education provides." They often do not know much about the jobs for which they apply, "but are well informed about a wide range of pay prospects." While salary, promotion, and security are the primary considerations for job choice, if something better is found they easily leave their current position, if only for slightly better compensation. Very few will choose to be unemployed; if they have not found a job within three months, they will take any job. Secondary-school-leavers consider their education to have prepared them for a wide range of jobs. They do not generally have aspirations for a particular position; rather, they will consider almost any job, anywhere, so long as the salary offered fits their understanding of competitive compensation.[3]

Finally, a study by Peter Kinyanjui tracked what happened to Form 4 Kenya school-leavers between 1965 and 1968, a period when this cohort had grown from 5,878 to 19,317.[4] First, in each of the years, approximately 24 percent of the school-leavers joined Form 5, with the vast majority continuing to Form 6 and then to university. About the same number went to training for careers in the public and private sector, such as teacher education, medical, agricultural, and secretarial areas.

Employment in the public and private sectors absorbed 25 percent and 14 percent, respectively; last, about 10 percent of school-leavers secured positions as untrained teachers in Harambee schools. All percentages reflect choices made in the first year after secondary school, with many of the best CSCE scores (the top 20 percent) earned by those going to Form 5.[5]

The study also issued a note of caution about unemployment. While some unemployment was most probably present during each year of the study, it was masked by those persons who took jobs of last resort as untrained teachers. But by 1968 even those positions could not absorb all secondary-school-leavers who could not find jobs elsewhere. This new condition was most dramatically seen in the bottom 20 percent of CSCE scores—unemployment for this group rose from 2.3 percent in 1967 to 35.3 percent in 1968. Quite prophetically, Kinyangui calls attention to this transition in the Kenyan economy: "A secondary Cambridge School Certificate is no longer the passport to paid employment that it was in the past."[6] In the 1960s, secondary-school-leavers like my students began to fill many of the available jobs and would continue to occupy them for the next thirty years or so, thus making the labor market increasingly selective and eventually closing it by the 1980s to many future school-leavers, especially those with poor CSCE results.

But when Giakanja students in the classes of 1965, 1966, and 1967 entered employment, this bleak future was still a decade or more in the future. Until then, jobs were abundant and Kenya's economy was strong. Its rate of economic growth in the fifteen years following independence was among the highest in Africa. Until about 1980 the economy grew annually at approximately 6.8 percent, with the industrial sector reaching an annual average of nearly 10 percent. Such growth generated many employment opportunities, first in government, which expanded to manage this growth and to provide services funded from the increasing revenue of a robust economy. The private sector also grew rapidly since the government encouraged private enterprise in industry, commerce, and foreign investment, although the state itself did participate in some economic enterprises. Kenya's economic expansion in the years after independence created a demand for workers that was often hard to fill. In 1964 a government survey of manpower needs for 1964–70 projected major shortages, especially in the categories of (1) professional occupations such as secondary teachers, engineers, surveyors, and pharmacists and (2) skilled technicians and clerical workers, especially bookkeepers and cashiers.[7] Even though the number of Form 4 leavers grew each

year (1965—5,878; 1966—6,455; and 1967—9,230),[8] the government
survey projected shortfalls in category (1) of 3,000 and category (2) of
25,000 workers.[9] Clearly the demand was greater than the supply; as a
result these students were in an ideal position to be employed.

Government initiatives to Kenyanize the labor force after independence also created opportunities for school-leavers like those from
Giakanja. First announced in 1965 in Sessional Paper No. 10, *African
Socialism and its Application to Planning in Kenya,* and then set out in more
detail two years later in *Kenyanization of Personnel in the Private Sector,* this
initiative sought "to ensure that the continued employment of non-
citizens does not deprive competent Kenyans of opportunities to fill
vacancies and new jobs and to replace non-citizens at all levels in private
and public enterprises."[10] According to the memorandum, by 1967 less
than four years after independence, the civil service had been successfully Kenyanized and now it was time for the private sector to do the
same. The document chided private employers by saying, "To date the
record of the private sector in Kenyanizing employment . . . has not
been so impressive as the achievement of the public sector."[11] The
government further implied that it would no longer accept the excuse
that no qualified Kenyans existed for positions in the private sector and
stated that it expected private enterprise to establish such initiatives as
in-service training, sponsorship of students to training institutions and
technical colleges, and trial promotions to actively facilitate the employment of Kenyans in managerial, administrative, and other positions of
importance in private companies. The memorandum warned that
should these measures not be taken, applications for work permits to
noncitizens would not be granted.[12] Secondary-school-leavers entering
the job market at this time had not only the advantage of a growing
economy with many new jobs available but also government policy
hastening the availability of positions previously held by Europeans.[13]

Choosing a Path

But even though jobs were abundant, when students were asked years
later, Why did you choose the job that you did?, many of them noted
they were ill-equipped to make good decisions about job choice as they
ventured into white-collar employment where few before them had
gone. Perhaps Churchill expressed it best: "At Giakanja there was
general optimism about the 'New Kenya,' but as to thinking specifically
about one's life, I did not know enough about what was possible. I had

no role models. No one in my family had achieved such a life, nor any relatives or even neighbors. I was a pioneer, on my own."[14] Students also noted that Giakanja staff gave little attention to career advice. As a result, the government produced an instructional pamphlet about choosing a career. The pamphlet opened with this observation: "Most probably, whenever you have thought about which career you would like, you have become confused by the large variety of jobs at which people work. You may have thought that when choosing a career, you were expected to pick, at first go, one particular job out of the hundreds that exist."[15] Rather, the pamphlet instructs that one must have a plan, and then it suggested one with four stages:

1. Select a type of work.
2. Choose a group of jobs that fall within this type.
3. From this group, select your first job.
4. From the experience of your first job, make the necessary adjustments in the type of work area that suits your interests and abilities.[16]

Students at Giakanja would have found this advice useful and comforting as they made the transition from academic student to job seeker. Unfortunately, neither my former students nor I remember ever seeing this pamphlet at Giakanja, although it was published in time for use by the first Form 4 class. A few students recall a bank manager from Nyeri coming out to the school to discuss careers in banking.[17] Perhaps such a visit was in response to the Kenyanization of the private sector, but no one remembers any other representatives from business, industry, or government visiting the school. Philip said that an army recruiter came to the school and in fact signed him up even before he took his CSCE, but apparently this happened only once.[18] Most students say that they received no career advice at all while at Giakanja and that rings true with my own memory. Teachers were focused on their goal to turn these young people into good students able to think logically, to speak and write Standard English, to master the content of their subject area, and most especially, to teach them to pass their CSCE.

The universe for teachers was composed almost entirely of getting students successfully through their four years of secondary school at Giakanja; little regard was given to their life after Giakanja, a failing of which the staff was not even aware since they had little experience beyond school themselves. Of course the daily assembly with its scripture reading and prayers was aimed at guiding moral development, as were the rules and disciplinary procedures of the school. We teachers were aware that we should act as positive role models for our students as well. But I do not even recall thinking about giving career advice, and as a recent arrival in Kenya with almost no career experiences to draw upon myself, I would have been ill-equipped to provide any useful advice.[19]

In the absence of any guidance from school, many students set out to seek their future careers as best as they could. Some had preferences that they acted upon. "I always wanted to be a pilot so I applied to the Kenya Air Force," David recalled. "But they said I wasn't even qualified for an interview."[20] Kihumba was attracted to becoming a policeman (inspector): "My father argued against my choice, saying that he did not want to have a policeman in the family because he had to fight them during the Emergency."[21] Other students were able to act on their first choices. Several told me that they had always wanted to be teachers. They had many teacher role models during their lives, and they were attracted to learning and knowledge and also the respect that the community gave teachers.[22] They generally had satisfying careers, although one is now taking early retirement because he says that people have lost respect for teachers: "They harass us about giving their children low grades, even when they are deserved." He confided to me that he might even have chosen the wrong profession.[23] Some students tried several jobs until they found a good fit. Joseph said that he always thought that he wanted to work in an office, but he discovered that, after working in a government ministry office as a clerk for six months, he hated it. "I'd rather be out in the field," he concluded, and so he joined the Survey of Kenya (SOK).[24] David stated, "I started with a job in a bank but then shifted to what I thought might be a better job with Kenya Railroads as a computer trainee." He said that he was convinced that he had made a good choice when they sent him twice to England for a year's training each time. But when a position opened in a large foreign-owned company, he immediately shifted there and remained for many years until retirement. He surprised me, however, by concluding that he should have stayed with his first choice—the bank—because several of his classmates with long careers in banking had ultimately done better than him in salary and benefits.[25]

Perhaps the most interesting account of settling into a career came from Jacob, who had not done particularly well on his CSCE, having received the lowest Division III result awarded to his class of 1966. He took a job at a small Nyeri retail business, where he started at the bottom doing menial jobs, including taking the day's receipts across the street to the bank. One day while doing the banking, the manager called him into his office and said to him, "I've been watching you for several months and have been impressed with how conscientious an employee you are. Would you like to work in a bank—I'm offering you a job." Jacob was astounded because he had no idea that he had come to the notice of the (European) bank manager. "I immediately accepted the offer, and I've worked for this banking corporation ever since." When I interviewed Jacob thirty years after he first started with the bank, he was a manager himself, of a large Nairobi branch of the same bank.[26]

Many others tell a different story of landing their first job. James said, "I had no clear plan about how to get a job. I went to Nairobi with two classmates and we just roamed the streets, dropping into various places of business to inquire about jobs, to apply, and to interview. It was very haphazard."[27] Robert told me that he had been "tarmacking" for a job for six months, until he heard from a friend who was from his home village and working in Mombasa that the customs department was hiring.[28] "I went immediately to Mombasa, got an interview and was hired. Now I've been there for twenty-eight years."[29] Alex said that his sister who worked in the Provincial Administration at Nyeri helped him get his first job. "I was a conservative fellow," he reported to me twenty-eight years later, "and I've stayed in government throughout my career."[30] Being helped to find that first job by a relative, friend, or "someone from my village" was a common answer to the question, Why did you choose the job/career that you did? So although career advice was absent at Giakanja, students could count on help from a combination of family, friends, and fellow Gikuyu, as they themselves would provide to their family and relatives in the future.

Salary also was a factor in the jobs that students accepted. Titus started out to be a teacher, and upon leaving Giakanja, he enrolled in the S1 (secondary school) course at Kenyatta College. Upon completion in three years, his S1 salary would have been approximately 970 shillings a month.[31] He stated that during his very first school holiday, he "interviewed at Barclays [Bank], Nyeri because they were offering 660 shillings and with overtime, 1,000 shillings a month salary I could not resist because I needed money now to educate my brothers and sisters."[32] Joseph tells a similar story. After taking his CSCE, he secured a position with the Kenya Post Office, which sent him on a three-year course for further training at Kenya Polytechnic. He was at first thrilled to be receiving a free technical education and being paid 270 shillings as well. But when he also learned that Barclays Bank was offering a starting salary of 660 shillings, he joined the bank: "I needed to support my [widowed] mother and sister."[33] Joseph's father and a brother had tragically died even before he left Giakanja, and his mother was destitute.

Kihumba also had to alter his career plans because of obligations to his parents and siblings. "I did not go to Form 5 because I had to get a job to earn for the family. My uncle had helped pay my school fees at Giakanja, and I was now expected to pay for my [five] younger brothers and sisters." Because of his good CE results, Kihumba immediately obtained a job with Standard Bank. Reflecting on his beginning in 1967 he said, "I can remember receiving my very first paycheck; it was about 600 shillings, which I thought was a fortune. I bought blankets and clothes for the whole family and enough food for a huge feast."[34] He might have calculated that if his uncle had paid out the equivalent of three years' school fees at Giakanja, it would have come to about 600 shillings total; now he had earned a comparable amount in his first month at the bank. Over the years, his hard work and continuing education brought many promotions. By 1987 he had risen to become chief accountant for Standard Bank's thirty-nine Kenyan branches. He paid the school fees for his younger brothers and a sister and has continued to assist his family financially ever since.[35]

Education beyond Giakanja

Students with the easiest and most straightforward decisions to make were those who had scored exceptionally well on their CSCE, obtaining either a Division I or a very good Division II certificate (distinctions or top credits in each subject). Such scores made them eligible to continue their education at senior secondary schools for two more years (Forms 5 and 6), which was the gateway to university entrance. Instead of taking eight subjects as they had in secondary school, they now specialized in three, usually choosing between the arts and sciences areas. Classes were small and full of the very brightest students in the country. Studies were rigorous, and both teachers and students had high expectations about what was to be accomplished. These students also discovered that their education was free, since the government had cancelled all fees starting in 1966, and all their other needs were cared for as well. They ate the best food of their life in the dining halls, their laundry was done for them, and there were many sports and recreational opportunities available—all free of charge. All they had to do was study. However, these gifted students often found that while they could devote themselves entirely to their studies, a condition that they had longed for at

Giakanja, they now wished for the companionship with their peers that had been forged through adversity in secondary school. In contrast, their schooling now seemed sterile and even monotonous. Jonas confided to me that the absence of hardship at his senior secondary school initially was exhilarating but later caused him not to be as serious about his studies as he should have been. He found that he had to draw fully on what he had learned about himself at Giakanja—he could achieve academic excellence if he strived for it, even under unfavorable circumstances. In time and after much struggle, he was able to pull himself back on track to being a serious and high-achieving student.[36]

A significant number of students who went to Forms 5 and 6 scored well enough on their Higher School Certificate Exams to go on to university. From the three Giakanja classes under study, twenty-five out of ninety students went to Forms 5 and 6 and of these, nineteen continued on to the university. University education was also free, and that made the decision to continue very easy, although a few students seriously considered ending with Form 6 even though they had been accepted at the university. Erastus realized that his father had never recovered from his Mau Mau detention experience, and as Erastus was the oldest of ten children, he really needed to start helping his family. But the headmaster refused to give him a reference for employment, saying that if he left school now he would never be more than a clerk. Erastus went on to Makerere University and though he was tempted to take up the course in medicine, he chose the BS course in agriculture instead because it took just three years to complete. "I needed to finish in the shortest time possible so that I could take over my father's responsibility for the family."[37]

Charles had a similar experience when he received an offer of employment from Barclays Bank. The headmaster urged him to go on to the university, saying that he would always regret not getting his university degree.[38] Samuel intended to stop his education at the end of Form 6 because he was tired of school. But after only six months as a junior employee at East African Power and Light, Kenya's large utility company, he became disillusioned with work. "They never took seriously anything that I said because of my junior status."[39] Without difficulty he was able to take up the place at Makerere University that he had vacated. Richard actually did work for a whole year between finishing Form 6 and beginning his studies at the university, but he regretted his decision. "I only wanted to get money for myself; it was a wasted year."[40] Later at the university, his experience of having an income caused him to search for ways to earn during the school holidays, even when the work was not related to his studies. "I never considered the pocket money given us at the university enough because I had become used to having more."[41]

For the most part, however, the students enjoyed their lives at the university. The classes were small and the work was rigorous but very stimulating. There was a great deal of reading, more than they ever had experienced, but also many opportunities to discuss the theories of their disciplines. Among the nineteen students, they could begin to envision what their careers would be like because of practical (field) dimensions of their studies, especially among those in engineering (3), agriculture (4), accounting (2), and education (2). Makerere University in Uganda, the oldest and most prestigious in East Africa, was an especially intellectually stimulating place in the late 1960s. All the students who attended commented on the serious atmosphere, which was idyllic for maturing and learning. "It was a great place to study and learn. . . . We all felt that we were seeking truth," Samuel remarked. Not all learning took place in the classroom either. "On Friday nights we had prominent speakers come to talk to us; some of them were even famous like Mwalimu Nyerere [president of Tanzania] and Milton Obote [president of Uganda]. They would speak for a while and then we could ask questions." Such interchange also enabled them to hear perspectives on issues and ideas from Tanzanian and Ugandan students, as well as from other Kenyans. Samuel said that after his first year, when he felt more relaxed and confident about his own studies, he took advantage of the wonderful opportunity to develop friendships across ethnic and national lines. He discovered that they shared the common goal of being eager to enter the modern world and to make a contribution.[42]

It was also during this time that Idi Amin overthrew the Ugandan government in a military coup. Charles was in his last year of studies, as were two other former Giakanja students, Dickson and Erastus. They all worried that their degree programs might be interrupted. Each had struggled to get to that point in their educations and they were anxious to finish the last year on time. They all noted that Amin's spies often were on campus posing as students and feared especially for their Ugandan friends, but as Charles noted, "Soon after the coup, things seemed to settle down and Amin was heralded in Uganda as a savior."[43] But some time after the coup, Dickson was out on teaching practice in Tororo, a town some distance from Makerere, where he began to hear stories that people were beginning to disappear. Upon his return to Makerere, he heard similar news about other places.[44] In this way the students gradually got to know the brutality of the Amin regime. "At first we really didn't know much about him. But as it turned out, he was a butcher," Charles concluded. "There was a sense of danger in the air and I didn't want to stay in Uganda any longer than I had to. As soon as my degree exams were over, I left. Amin had made himself the chancellor of the university and I didn't want to receive my diploma from him. I was really happy when my bus crossed the border and I was back in Kenya."[45] After these Giakanja students finished their educations, no others went to Makerere.

Two students studied abroad for their first degrees. John, who had earned an S1 teaching diploma at Kenyatta College and then gone on to become a secondary school teacher for eight years, received a British Council scholarship in 1979 to Exeter University in the United Kingdom. The other, Francis, went to the Soviet Union. His Division III Cambridge Certificate would not have given him eligibility to East African universities, so when he saw scholarships advertised for the Soviet Union, he applied and was accepted in 1967. He said that he was curious about Russia. "I could have applied to go to the U.S. but Russia was a closed society and I wanted to see what that was like."[46] He was excited and pleased to have been accepted.

"We landed at Moscow International Airport and then flew on to Kiev, where our first two preparatory years were located at Kiev State University." There he learned Russian and studied mathematics and science. It was academically equivalent to Forms 5 and 6, but culturally and linguistically it was an immersion experience. "At first if I wanted something in a shop, I would just go and do a little pantomime, pointing and gesturing at what I wanted."[47] After two years, he sat for and passed his language exam and then was sent to the Soviet republic of Belarus to study engineering. To supplement his stipend, during part of each summer he worked in a car factory, the largest in the Soviet Union. He also traveled to other parts of the Soviet Union and to Europe, even going to Berlin and Munich, and he vacationed on the Black Sea. He was impressed by Soviet industrialization, the electrification of the rural areas, and the commitment of the people to what they were doing. "If we [Kenyans] had set our minds on industrialization and if our people were as committed, then we would have achieved something in our country and not be where we are today." Though he said that he had gone primarily to study, still he observed many aspects of Soviet society. "I could not have stayed like a horse, which looks at just what is in front.

I had to look for something which would be of use to our people or to our country."

But there were other aspects of Soviet society that did not meet with Francis's approval. He learned that he could not make comparisons between Europe and the Soviet Union that called into question the doctrines of the Soviet state. There were informers in all his classes, so he shared his ideas only with his most trusted friends. Also, those connected most closely to the Communist Party reaped the biggest rewards in Soviet society: "If you are close to the ruling party, you have access to almost anything . . . the way we have it now [in Kenya]. But most people are left with little." As a Christian, he also did not like the official state commitment to atheism; to him it was a very misguided way of thinking. Finally, he encountered a great deal of racism. Francis sometimes attributed this to ignorance, as in the case of a woman he met on a train who told him he was dirty and should wash when he got home. But he also had racist remarks directed to him by educated and well-traveled Russians who simply thought of Africans as inferior. The racism practiced by such people troubled Francis the most, and his only solace was to concentrate on his studies.

After five years in the Soviet Union, he returned to Kenya in 1972 as a newly minted mechanical engineer only to find that he was discriminated against in employment. People called him an atheist or a communist, and his Russian education was not valued as highly as the education of those who had studied engineering in East Africa or in Western countries. It took him six months before he found employment and then, first in the private sector and later at the Ministry of Works, he had to start at a level far below his qualifications. Only after he received an eight-month scholarship to the United Kingdom to study British technical programs in hospital management, and his subsequent employment as technical advisor for the redesign and rebuilding of Kenyatta Hospital (the government's flagship medical institution in Nairobi), did he feel that his career was successful. In summing up his experiences, Francis said that while he did receive a good education for free in the Soviet Union, the society as a whole did not live up to his expectations. He admitted that the government had brought improvement to peoples' lives, but they also controlled everything through restrictions and propaganda. In the United Kingdom, however, he had been accepted as an equal, permitted to travel anywhere he wanted, and he was totally at ease. Because the United Kingdom was Kenya's former colonial ruler, he had expected not to like it and was surprised that the opposite was the case. He was sure that the openness of society contributed to its success: "Things seem to work as planned, unlike what we have here or what actually was the case in Russia."

The Public Sector and Private Business

Unlike Francis, other university graduates started their careers at an advanced level and in almost every case were employed by the government.[48] This was not because they necessarily preferred government employment, but because the government required their services for two or three years in return for their state-financed university educations. Several graduates stated that government ministries offered excellent and broad experience and even sometimes further training. Charles was taken into the Agricultural Finance Corporation (AFC), a statuary board in a section of the Ministry of Finance. "It was a great place to work, they had many resources, and it was excellent money before the oil crisis hit us with inflation and higher prices." Charles's monthly salary was 2,140 shillings plus a good housing allowance. He began as an assistant manager in the Nakuru branch, and a year later he was manager in Nairobi. Other promotions followed, and in 1975, only four years after starting, AFC sent him to the United States for his master's degree in agribusiness finance and agricultural economics.[49]

Similarly, after graduating from Makerere, Erastus joined the Ministry of Agriculture as the crops officer in Kisumu District. Less than a year later he was promoted to district agricultural officer. Two years later, in 1974, the government sent him to the University of Dar-es-Salaam in Tanzania to pursue a master's degree in economics and farm management. Upon his return to Kenya in 1976, he was promoted to the super scale in salary and became a senior agricultural officer. "I was the youngest person at that level in the Ministry of Agriculture." Each year brought new promotions, until by 1985 his position was the equivalent of director of agriculture. In thirteen years he had reached the highest position in his ministry.[50]

When Harrison graduated from the university in 1970, one year earlier than was normal,[51] he was employed as an accountant by the Kenya Meat Commission. He stayed with the commission until 1975, studying privately and becoming a chartered accountant along the way, when he decided that he would never be able to become director. Instead he opened his own accounting firm, eventually employing three hundred accountants. Then in a bold move, he sold the accounting firm and now spends his time advising a small group of clients on investments, as well as working on his own investment projects. "I got bored with the accounting, and I was having to work too hard. Now I work when I want to and it's much more satisfying."[52] Charles also made the shift from the public to the private sector. When he graduated as an electrical engineer, he was posted to the Voice of Kenya, the government radio and television station, but within the year he had moved to Kenya Cooperative Creameries. In 1975, Sigma Engineering hired him away from the government and paid the 6,000 shillings left on his government bond. Both salary and benefits were better than government, but Charles wanted to start his own company, which he did in 1982.[53]

These brief career biographies are representative of almost all the university graduates who in the 1970s and 1980s shifted their employment to the private sector or went into business for themselves. Within ten to twelve years and occasionally sooner, all but two had left the government and both of them had senior positions that satisfied their career expectations. During the same period a number of other non-degree students made the same move as well.[54] The monetary rewards in the private sector were simply too great to pass up. Salaries were significantly higher and the benefits or perks could be lavish. There were frequently housing and car allowances, private health insurance, memberships in sports clubs, and an educational allowance that enabled their children to attend good schools. One senior executive in a food-processing company added up his monthly benefits, which included all of the above plus the salaries of his household staff, as well as his household utilities and insurance. The total came to 138,000 shillings ($2,300) per month. When he added in his salary, the total monthly package was 400,000 shillings ($6,666).[55] When the government discontinued many of the perks of the senior civil service in the late 1970s for economic reasons, the private sector looked even more attractive.[56]

While I was usually not privy to the financial status of most of the students, from observation and an analysis of their general comments about finances, I would estimate that about 15–20 percent of them fit into the above financial profile. Those who owned their own businesses probably earned even more. But even for those who were not at the top of their profession, the private sector enabled them to financially prosper to a greater extent than their former schoolmates employed by government. One student who had worked for a bank in no more than a mid-level position said that his friend who had a very senior government administrative position as chief provincial engineer for the Ministry of Works earned only about one-sixth of his salary.[57]

The students' participation in the Kenyan economy during the fifteen years following independence in 1963 parallels the shifts taking place between the public and private sectors during that time. David Himbara, a scholar of Kenya, argued that, in the 1960s, the Kenyan state helped to foster a growing economy with public sector participation equal to private sector business.[58] The state invested in economic infrastructure and attracted talented secondary-school-leavers and university graduates to be state employees. Working for the government was considered an exciting and well-paid career; one had a sense of doing meaningful work for the good of the country. But by the late 1970s, the participation of the state had diminished and the dynamism of the economy had shifted to the private sector. As Himbara noted, "The role of the State was to decline, when during the post-colonial period, it became highly personalized, autocratic [and] failed to provide policy mechanisms to utilize available technical skills and resources."[59] In another publication, Himbara further recorded the decline of government as a dynamic force in the economy: "The public service businessman in the national ministries and state agencies . . . virtually 'colonized' these administrative units for their own aggrandizement."[60] As a result, many left government employment, including a number of my students who also sensed a change in workplace environment and the growing salary differential between the public and private sectors.

But regardless of the disparities between the public and private sectors, all of my students found employment. Though they were not especially skilled in finding employment or even in evaluating the employment that they found, they were all earning a salary within a few months after leaving Giakanja. Almost half of them found employment in the capital city, thus fulfilling their dream of "getting a desk job in Nairobi."[61] Among other things, these jobs enabled them to fulfill their financial obligations to their families, especially in educating their siblings. Some students also expressed a sense of patriotism about their work, especially if it was with the government. Charles commented, "I felt good on getting my first job, I was serving my country."[62] Amos expressed similar sentiments by stating that he did not want to go to the private sector for employment: "I wanted to do something for my country, and government workers are patriotic."[63] Of course, some students avoided private-sector employment for other reasons, stating that it was too risky. Jesse bluntly stated, "You could get sacked."[64] The unspoken idea was that being fired from a government position was less likely to happen.

Even those students with mediocre results on their CSCE found jobs and accomplished much. Amos admitted that he did not deserve more than the Division III Certificate that he received (though he earned a distinction on his literature paper) because he did not apply himself in secondary school as he should have. He became acutely aware of this condition when he tried to complete the first test papers in the trial exam at Giakanja. He was so nervous and anxious that he was unable to continue.[65] I feared that he would fail his CSCE later that year, but he passed, studied privately, passed his A-level exams two years later, and entered government in public administration. There he rose through the ranks to become a senior DO, then a district magistrate, a personal assistant to a district commissioner, a senior assistant secretary and deputy secretary in the Ministry of Agriculture. Only one other student rose so high in the civil service, and he had been at the top of his class, had earned a Division I Certificate, and had received a university education.

Alex also earned only a Division III Certificate but entered government as a cashier right after leaving Giakanja. He diligently took all the courses offered to improve his credentials and rose in rank, especially after passing his first-level accounting exam. In 1979 he was posted to Kenya's embassy in Ottawa as the mission's accountant, where he stayed for six years. Upon his return, he became senior chief accountant in the Ministry of Water.[66]

Nicholas earned a Division III Certificate as well. After studying and taking his Higher School Certificate Exam privately, while he was teaching for three and a half years, he was admitted to the University of Nairobi for a three-year BA education option. After receiving his degree he returned to secondary school teaching, in time becoming a deputy headmaster (even spending a year at Giakanja in that position) and finally headmaster in 1979.[67]

Even students who failed their CSCE went on to life-long careers of significance. Richard failed his English Language Exam and did not earn a credit in any of his other exams, so he failed to get any certificate at all.[68] Nevertheless, after working as an untrained primary school teacher for a term, he saved enough money to go to Nairobi to look for a job. He lived with a cousin, who advised him to apply to several government businesses, including the post office and the railways, from which he received offers. He chose the post office, where he has remained throughout his career, having been promoted four times in the accounts department.[69]

Samuel also failed his exams but still had a satisfying career teaching modern agriculture to farmers. Though he would have liked to enter the Forestry Department, when that was not available he was accepted for the two-year agriculture course at the Embu Institute of Agriculture and subsequently received a position as an agricultural extension agent in his home area. Ephantus and Daniel also failed their exams but each retook them privately, as well as their A-level exams. Both went on to further education, Daniel to the Kenya Institute of Administration and later to the United Kingdom for a thirteen-month course in criminology and probation. Ephantus attended university, first in Nairobi for a BA, and later in the United States, where he earned an MA in public administration. Both have subsequently had long, successful careers of professional enrichment.[70]

How was it that even though some Giakanja students did poorly or even failed, they still found satisfying employment and rose to advanced positions? Perhaps it was due to the availability of plentiful employment opportunities, especially in government, where there was an explosion of jobs. Perhaps exam scores were not good predictors of future achievement, though it clearly seems to have been the case for the Giakanja students who scored especially well on their exams. Another consideration is that Giakanja students were used to struggling against the distractions that society placed before them. As their narratives reveal, their struggles actually began long before they became students at Giakanja. They had endured the poverty and deprivations of the late colonial period and the Mau Mau Rebellion, as well as the competition for places in primary and intermediate school. Each of them brought an understanding of hard work and a sense of accomplishment to Giakanja, which they applied to their studies there as well as to the sphere of employment and careers in the years beyond their secondary education. They considered themselves to be exceptional. In the words of one student, "The Giakanja go-getters did well in their careers."[71] But having said that, there is still a sense of awe among many of them for what they accomplished. Joseph told me that early in his career he attended a meeting at the head office in Nairobi and looked in the office of the managing director. "Some day I'm going to be sitting in that chair," he whispered to himself half seriously. When I interviewed him many years later, he was in that chair, the first Kenyan to occupy the position in the history of the company. From the tone of his voice, he still seemed to hardly believe it.[72] Titus, reflecting on having achieved a senior position in business, commented, "My initial dream for my future was to go to Egerton [agricultural college] and become a good farmer, but as it turned out, it was too small a dream."[73]

But there is one other major factor that helps explain the success of these students, and that is being Gikuyu at a time in Kenya's history when that ethnic group was favored. Following the completion of their education, these students entered the workforce during the presidency of Jomo Kenyatta, a Gikuyu nationalist hero, and his Gikuyu-dominated government. While Kenyatta was head of state, Gikuyu had disproportionate access to civil service and white-collar jobs, as well as to industrial and commercial loans with which to start businesses.[74] Though Kenya's economy grew remarkably throughout the Kenyatta years of the 1960s and 1970s and other peoples of Kenya prospered too, being Gikuyu enabled this cohort to draw upon more than their fine education and commitment to hard work: they also had available to them the endowment of their ethnicity. While I found no specific evidence of favoritism, being alerted to new and better jobs by Gikuyu relatives and friends and being promoted by Gikuyu supervisors undoubtedly took place. Among all other factors, these students gained an initial foothold in the economy, were promoted, found investment opportunities, and prospered.

Following the death of Kenyatta in 1978, things changed with the election to the presidency of his successor, Daniel Arap Moi. Though Moi, a non-Gikuyu, moved slowly at first, it was increasingly apparent in the 1980s and 1990s that he was seeking to restructure ethnic power in the country. Potential Gikuyu rivals to the presidency, like Charles Njonjo, were purged from public life. Gikuyu no longer dominated the cabinet as they had under Kenyatta, as Moi brought in other ethnic groups for ministerial positions including Kalenjin, his own group, and halved Gikuyu representation. Government funds and projects were shifted away from Gikuyu areas and directed to other ethnic groups. One example of this change was the deterioration of the 100-mile-long Nairobi-Nyeri main road. This commercial and public transport lifeline from the Gikuyu heartland to the nation's capital had been meticulously maintained during the Kenyatta years but was now allowed to deteriorate under the Moi presidency. The one-and-a-half- to two-hour journey was increased to three to four hours of bone-jarring discomfort and, occasionally during the rainy season, became impassable. Similarly, government jobs formerly available to Gikuyu were blocked, and advancement and promotions slowed for those Gikuyu already in government.[75]

While being able to draw upon ethnic favoritism undoubtedly helped this cohort rise to middle- and upper-class positions of wealth and prestige, the withdrawal of their ethnic advantage has not lead to a reversal of fortune for them. By the 1990s many of those who had stayed in government had achieved senior positions, those who had moved to the private sector had achieved the same, and those who owned their own businesses were prospering as well. Their seniority in the civil service or private sector protected them from removal, and income earned from previous investments or entrepreneurial ventures cushioned them further. Only two students stated that their economic life under Moi had deteriorated. One owned land in the Rift Valley that had been taken over by Kalenjin squatters, who the government refused to remove, and another revealed that his building supply company was no longer permitted to compete for government contracts.[76]

The loss of ethnic favoritism did harm young Gikuyu entering the workforce for the first time in the 1980s and 1990s, when they had to compete with other ethnic groups and were even passed over as punishment for the former dominance of the Gikuyu. However, there were fewer jobs available too, as Kenya's economic growth significantly declined or was even stagnant in comparison with the 1960s and 1970s. Now, too many job seekers chasing too few jobs created high unemployment and a sense of hopelessness quite unlike the conditions thirty years earlier, when students at Giakanja had first sought employment.

5

Entering an Economic Elite

The postcolonial elite that emerged in the 1960s was not Kenya's first. Historically, a small cadre of Kenyans from two earlier generations had composed an emergent elite during the colonial era that anticipated, at least in part, the pathway to economic prosperity that opened up to my students and others of their cohort as they began their careers. In its earliest iteration, that elite began with the attainment of literacy through mission schools, which supplied the only education available. These *Athomi* (readers) hoped to use their education and their association with missionaries to negotiate with colonial authorities an exemption from taxation and forced labor but especially to gain access to mission land or to open spaces not yet cultivated in newly demarcated reserves.[1] At Nyeri, the Gikuyu Athomi also called themselves *Baragu* (wealthy men): "It signaled young converts' hopes that their labors at the mission would entitle them to the prominence that wealth would bring."[2] The first initiative that Athomi pursued was to secure land at a time when missions, government, and white settlers were expropriating it for their own use. For the landless and the land poor, from which many of the first Athomi were drawn, this was imperative for the continuation of subsistence farming and "to achieve the old Gikuyu goal of respectable adulthood."[3]

However, Athomi also looked beyond land for wealth and prosperity. The colonial economy had introduced wages, and with the Athomis' new competence in literacy, they took up employment in such new occupations as teachers, interpreters, clerks, and other government positions. As David K. Leonard pointed out, this gave them an excellent "drought-free, steady and easily tradable income."[4] At the beginning of the colonial era and, for many Kenyans, continuing for its entire duration, wage labor was a burden. Peasant farmers were driven annually to become migrant wage laborers in Kenyan towns or on white-settler farms in order to earn the cash necessary to pay their yearly tax. Wages were low and their small farms frequently had to subsidize them with food and other basic essentials of life while they were away filling their labor contract. Clearly the purpose of this system was to create a reservoir of cheap labor for the colonial economy rather than to provide Kenyans with wealth-creating opportunities. But the positions now taken by Athomi were different: they earned professional salaries, and promotions and advancement to even better jobs were possible. In a reversal of the direction to what had taken place among migrant laborers, their wages flowed back to their farms, providing income for such innovations as improving their herds with the introduction of grade cattle, expanding their farming acreage, and introducing cash crops.

The emerging elite often entered the commercial sphere as well. Gavin Kitching captured this new economic direction well in the case studies he presented in *Class and Economic Change in Kenya*. In the eighteen cases he cited, a significant number fit the following pattern: after finishing school and entering professional employment, Athomi also became businessmen in such areas as marketing garden crops, transport, and contract tractor plowing. Frequently they also opened shops in their communities, selling everyday household items where none had previously been available. Kitching demonstrated in these case studies how this Athomi-based African elite built their growing prosperity in several sectors of the economy: small-farm agriculture, wages, and commerce. Profits and savings in one area helped to capitalize other areas, each being sustained or expanded by a web of contacts and economic information gleaned from their government employment.[5]

By the 1930s and 1940s a number of Athomi had reached a significant level of economic success and prosperity. Though they may have had connections to city life through commercial activities or government employment, their base was most often in their rural community, where they most likely enjoyed some prominence. One other element characterized their lives and that was the ability to pass on their elite status to their children, who had the advantage of growing up in educated households, frequently with both parents literate. These parents sent the children to school at an early age and were able to keep them there by having the funds to pay their school fees systemically. Such diligence enabled these children to concentrate on their studies (when many of their classmates had frequent interruptions or had to drop out for lack of school fees), to pass the school-leaving exams, and for the most able, to be admitted to one of Kenya's few secondary schools; some went on to the university as well. By the 1950s this Athomi progeny, now adults, were among that small group of Kenyan civil servants who at independence occupied the most senior positions in central government ministries or provincial administration. This was the elite in place when my students and others of their cohort started their careers and entered postcolonial elite status themselves. As this and succeeding chapters will reveal, their adult lives bear some resemblance to the earlier Athomi elite, including the ability to pass elite status on to their children.

Almost all of my students came from families of humble means; many were quite poor and some, especially those families that had been repatriated from the Rift Valley at the outset of the Emergency, were destitute. Some came to school without shoes and in school uniforms grown thin with much washing and that were several sizes too small by the time the students reached the upper forms and had grown into young men. Few had sweaters or jackets to warm themselves against the cold damp weather of the April–June rainy season. Years later at a party given for me and my wife by some former students, one turned to my wife and said that a favorite memory of secondary school was the time I had given him my jacket to keep him warm when he came to school soaked by a cold morning rain. While I do not recall this incident, I do have vivid memories of teeth-chattering coldness in our unheated class-rooms during every wet season.

Imagine, then, all of them professionally dressed, driving cars, and living in their own houses, all vestiges of their former meager existence gone only a few short years later. That transition from poverty to relative wealth was typical for every one of my former students, and their financial and material security continued to increase each year. Although the first moment they began to earn a monthly salary (usually several times their family's annual income and frequently even more) was decades ago, all still remember those early days well. Joseph captured the rapture many felt when he related this experience: "In the second year after I began working for the Survey of Kenya, I received a raise retroactive to the beginning of the year. When my check arrived, it was for 1,880 shillings. It was like winning the lottery. When I cashed it at the Central Bank, I wondered if they would give me so much money. I bought a motorcycle with it and gave a lot to my parents."[6]

The generosity toward family that Joseph noted was frequently mentioned by other students as well. Surprisingly, none of them ever seemed to be discouraged by demands on their income from near and distant relatives; rather, they spoke of helping family as a normal duty and obligation. However, I do remember a senior education administrator telling me that he and his wife had finally cut themselves off from their extended family after long years of appeals for money, jobs, and general handouts. Might these students have felt that way too? It certainly does not appear to have been the case, at least with their immediate families. Not only the flush of income from first salaries was shared, but in time larger commitments were made to pay school fees for brothers and sisters as well. As their incomes rose, so also did assistance to their parents grow proportionately. Several students proudly showed me the houses they built for their parents, and many others mentioned this level of generosity—even to their wife's family. But it does seem reasonable that over time they became less charitable to the appeals of more distant relatives. However, none of my students ever volunteered that they were driven to cut themselves off completely from their families, as had the education administrator and his wife.

Postcolonial Economic Development

For some time in the first two decades after independence, many African economies did grow and develop.[7] Individual living standards rose, and the dream of life without poverty for entire societies appeared to be taking place. For instance, the rise in average annual incomes between 1960 and 1980 in some countries was quite dramatic: Botswana rose from $254 to $1,247 (expressed in U.S. dollars); Côte d'Ivoire, from $532 to $945; Gabon, from $1,658 to $4,698; Nigeria, from $291 to $409; and Zimbabwe, from $430 to $562. Even the entire continent grew by 2 percent per year.[8] People witnessed schools and medical clinics being built in their midst, and new all-weather roads linked them to markets in neighboring regions and to capital cities. In some countries large-scale projects appeared, such as new international airports, four-lane highways, dams, and factories. Foreign aid and loans financed some of this building, but the African states also took responsibility for managing their own development since the private economy was often weak, with little capital available to invest in development.[9] This development activity was based on the assumption that African economies would eventually take off, having reached the stage of self-sustaining growth. Such growth had happened in industrial countries, and by copying them the African states would soon reach their level of development, or so it was thought.

Now more than forty years later, we know that sustained economic development has not taken place and a continent without poverty is still a dream. The theorists of development economics, a new subdiscipline of economics, had prescribed one remedy after another to heal the slow growth of Africa's economies. Initially in the 1980s they recommended infusions of capital to build economic infrastructure, but when that did not produce growth and a rise in living standards, investing was switched to such basic areas as education and health. More recently, development economists have focused on the policies of Africa's state-controlled economies. Governments are now advised to divest themselves of their state-owned industries and services and to slim down their large bureaucracies of state employees on the assumption that when the economy is in private hands and the market, and not the state, makes economic decisions, then growth will take place. Yet none of these strategies have worked continent-wide to produce sustained economic growth. For the entire decade of the 1980s, average incomes declined more than 1 percent per year; in the 1990s there was some modest improvement, but each year average incomes still declined. More than half the continent was poorer in 2000 than it was in 1970. Such statistics reveal how little we actually know about how to generate economic growth and what a sense of hopelessness and frustration this admission bodes for Africa.

Perhaps out of this frustration, some scholars have formulated the theory of dependency, the most radical explanation of why economic development has failed to take place on the continent. Its fundamental premise is that the previous subordinate relationship between the African colonies and their European metropoles has been transformed in the postcolonial era into a general subordination between Africa and the developed world. As a result, self-sustained economic growth did not take place, and African governments were unable to autonomously determine the course of their national development. Simply stated, the explanation for African political instability and economic decline was that African leaders and economic elites were doing the bidding of outsiders. Though these elites were rewarded, the wealth created in such dependent economies largely flowed to developed-world destinations and not to the African masses.[10] One can understand the appeal of blaming outsiders for the lack of Africa's economic development. While there is no denying the interconnectedness of African economies and those of the developed world, the advice of dependency school advocates, that African countries should distance themselves from world markets, is now understood as just one more example of a flawed development strategy.

Kenya's economic development broadly fits the pattern sketched above for the continent as a whole: first a period of growth followed by stagnation. Initial economic activity in land and agriculture continued into the independence period under a stable and pragmatic African government, and by the 1970s, African entrepreneurs had extended their activity into trade, urban real estate, and road transport, all of which were now in African hands. By 1986 Kenyan businessmen had taken control of the U.S. Firestone Tire Company in Kenya, as well as a controlling interest in Mobil Oil, renaming it Kobil Oil Ltd. Kenyan citizens also owned subsidiaries of several multinational corporations by the 1980s, among them Barclays Bank, Twentieth Century Fox Theatres, and three foreign car assembly plants. All of this activity led to robust economic growth that averaged 5.4 percent annually from 1963 to 1986.[11] My students and their cohort started their careers at a time when Kenya was about to enjoy twenty-five years of sustained economic growth, largely without the dependence upon former colonizers that shackled many other African states. But even this remarkable period of economic development did not last; rapid population growth, a bloated civil service, and an aging infrastructure among other problems reduced annual economic growth to zero by the 1990s.[12] Unemployment climbed as the economy generated fewer jobs; Kenyans no longer anticipated bright futures for themselves as they once had, and development planners were humbled by their inability to design economies that would grow to meet their optimistic forecasts.

This cohort, however, had encountered very different conditions when they entered adulthood thirty years earlier. During their youth, education was considered the pathway to employment and the good life, and they also enjoyed the advantage of coming from Central Province, one of Kenya's four most favored educational regions. Though these students came overwhelmingly from poor families who struggled to send their children to school, being born in Central Province ensured many that there was a school available for them to attend. Many of the first schools built by missionaries were located in this region, and in the later colonial period and especially after independence, the largest number and highest percentage per capita of government-aided secondary schools were to be found there as well. Furthermore, the largest numbers of trained teachers were also found in this province.[13] Even the little day secondary school of Giakanja, which these students attended, illustrates the quality of education in Central Province: (1) it was government aided, (2) it had new, first-class facilities, (3) all teachers were trained and most were degree holders, and (4) all students experienced being taught by me, a native speaker of English, at least part of the time. This was a great advantage since English was the language they had to master in order to pass their school-leaving exams well enough to obtain a good credential for employment or further education.

The Making of an Economic Elite

Though I did not feel comfortable directly inquiring about their wealth, a number of my former students volunteered financial information about themselves and occasionally about their classmates. For many of them, I also had opportunities to observe their houses and cars, their places of business, and even the clubs they joined for social and recreational purposes. From these informal, often indirect methods, some patterns of wealth accumulation emerge. In the first category were those who remained close to their home areas around Nyeri, usually working as teachers or in low-level municipal or government positions. They concentrated their financial investments on purchasing a rural plot or enlarging an inherited one on which they lived with their families. When they were occasionally posted away from home, they returned only on weekends or even less frequently, but their families were permanent residents throughout the year. These students were enormously proud of their homesteads, and any visitor was taken around the typical five- to seven-acre property to see the cropland (sometimes including cash crops like tea and coffee), the animals and barns, the stone house, and the water storage tanks. The family's food came almost entirely from their farm, and if they planted commercial crops like coffee, tea, tobacco, or pyrethrum, they earned some income too.

But while such land materially sustained these families, owning land contributed to people's sense of security as well. Stanley noted: "I love being at home with my family and animals. I only go to town to collect my [teacher's] salary. In our tribe, soil is very important because it is the foundation of the family."[14] Not surprisingly, these ideas of land and family well-being were also expressed by students who lived in Nairobi or elsewhere away from the Gikuyu heartland when later in life they built a country home at Nyeri or bought a hobby farm or ranch. A number have done this or have expressed their desire to do so after retirement.[15] Such purchases made good financial sense because land was quickly appreciating, but I think that the return to Nyeri for a number of students also came from deep emotional ties to the ancestral land.[16]

In the second category of ascending wealth are those former students who live outside the Gikuyu heartland in the Rift Valley and at the coast in Mombasa. They relocated to these places usually because of work but later put down roots and remained there, though not without some longing to return "up country." One such student was Joseph, who was posted to Mombasa by the SOK, a government department where he held responsible positions for more than a decade. When it became apparent that the SOK would not be posting him nearer to his home area in Central Kenya, he accepted a similar though better-paying position with the Municipal Council of Mombasa. He settled in Kilifi, a community near Mombasa where he bought a house and several undeveloped plots of land, having earlier purchased other plots in Kajiado District when he had worked there for more than a decade.[17] Robert, who worked for the Customs Services Department in Mombasa for his entire career, also invested in both rural and urban land at the coast, though he had not developed it except for building a house for himself on one plot. Both men were holding the land until their retirement, at which time they would either develop or sell it, taking advantage of its appreciated value.

Those students who moved to the Rift Valley, especially the Nakuru area, also invested in real estate financed with savings from their salaries. Jesse started his investments by buying a small grocery shop, which his wife operated. He used the profits and other savings to purchase two building plots in Nakuru, one in 1978 and another a decade later. Most recently he acquired five acres of agricultural land on which he hoped to raise vegetables to sell in town.[18] Chris's investments were also connected to land, the biggest of which were ten acres of irrigated farmland located at Molo, where he raised maize, which he processed for flour at his Nakuru mill. Unfortunately he was forced to vacate this land when squatters took it over during a period of "tribal clashes" in the 1990s. He continued to process others' maize, however, so the mill remained profitable. Chris had also purchased a plot in Nakuru, which he uses as a car wash and car repair shop. He rents out the large area around this building as a taxi station. He also has a two-acre piece of undeveloped urban land in Nakuru that he is holding for future sale or development.[19] Unlike those former students in rural Nyeri who invested in land to farm for their own subsistence, and perhaps to maintain historic connections to the soil, those living at the coast or in the Rift Valley have been entrepreneurial, frequently buying plots for use or future development. Their focus on land as the preferred investment reflected a shrewd calculation of its rising value or the consistent income that it would produce. Of course, both at Nyeri and in outside areas there were exceptions to this pattern by cohort members who owned their own businesses. At Nyeri and Nakuru two of them have purchased their own pharmacies.[20] Similarly at Nyeri, one owns a transport business, another a veterinary supply company, and a third a hardware, building supply, and construction company.[21] All these businesses appear to be financially stable and profitable.

It was in Nairobi, however, that ex-students and their cohort prospered most spectacularly. In part this happened because employment there had created the most opportunity for promotions and large salaries. It was in Nairobi in the various government ministries and in the private sector that the largest number of expatriates had been employed and whose positions were then being filled by Kenyans. A number of these students were the first Kenyans to occupy their positions and to collect super-scale salaries in the civil service or expatriate-scale salaries and benefits in the private sector.[22] As their salaries rose, so did the discretionary income they could draw upon for investment. One such person is Erastus, who as an employee of the Ministry of Agriculture had always depended upon government housing, even after his return to Nairobi as assistant director of agriculture. Erastus credits his Giakanja classmate William with opening his eyes to investment opportunities: "William would invite me and my family to Nyeri to stay at his guesthouse for a weekend. During these gatherings, he began to challenge me to do something for myself, not just to be content with government [housing]. He kept on trying to get me to think with a broader financial perspective. I was slow to understand what he was driving at. But even when I knew what he was telling me, I was reluctant to act on it." Finally, Erastus related how William sent a load of cement to a small house that Erastus had built in the Rift Valley and dumped it there, filling the house with bags of cement. "Now do something with it, build something; create something," William instructed him.

From that time forward, Erastus stated, he began to look for property in Nairobi to rent out, and eventually he bought ten acres for his own house at Ngong, a small dusty town twenty miles from Nairobi's city center. "People thought that I was crazy to build so far out, but now ten years later, Ngong is considered a suburb of Nairobi and my property bought for thousands is [now] worth several million shillings."[23] His house was in a magnificent setting, perched near the top of one of the Ngong hills with the Rift Valley stretching away in one direction and Nairobi visible on the plains below in the other.

While not many students had the means or the opportunity to create the wealth Erastus did, a number of others have purchased land and built homes at Ngong, some even speculating on the appreciation of this land over the last twenty years.[24] But it was Charles who was able to use the specialized knowledge gained through advanced training and employment to invest on a large scale. Earning the second-best score in his class on his CSCE (17 pts.), Charles could easily have gone to Forms 5 and 6 and on to university. But as the only child of his widowed mother, he knew that he must find work to support her. "I chose to seek employment at a ministry [that was] in the hands of expatriates who would soon be leaving Kenya." This ministry was also offering a two-year training course with salary starting in February 1966, so he took it and soon excelled in his studies. Because I had written a letter of reference, the ministry sent me quarterly progress reports that indicated Charles's exam scores were two and even three times better than the next best student. The tone of the director's comments about Charles's progress was pleasure that he was doing so well, mixed with amazement that an African could learn so readily. Charles focused his course on land valuation, and in 1973, upon returning from a two-year course in London, he became a chartered surveyor and eventually Kenya's head valuer. When he hosted a party for a group of American students that I brought to Kenya in 1976, he and his wife and two children were living in a beautiful new townhouse on a Nairobi golf course. When I interviewed him twenty years later, he told me that he had also purchased a seven-acre plot in Karen, Nairobi's underdeveloped suburb that was soon to become its most prestigious. He also confided that as chief valuer, he did a great deal of work on President Kenyatta's properties, for which the president gave him a piece of land as a bonus. These and other properties, together with a consulting business, have provided Charles with income since his retirement in 1995.[25]

Other students have also drawn upon their knowledge or experience to take advantage of financial opportunities. Harrison, whose accounting firm serviced many Nairobi businesses and gave him knowledge of the city's financial needs, said there was a great demand for office space there. He partnered with a former Giakanja classmate who was in the construction business to buy old government office buildings that were for sale and then renovate them for resale. Harrison said, "Of course, this is very risky, but if you wait for a sure thing, then everyone will know about it and there will be no profit."[26]

Another student was a Nairobi City councilor for a number of years and deputy mayor. He was also a partner in the largest real estate company in Kenya. From his knowledge and experience in these areas, he knew there soon would be a demand for executive housing in Nairobi. When an opportunity came to purchase a run-down coffee farm just outside the city limits, he did so and developed a large subdivision for executive housing.[27]

While these are examples of significant wealth accumulation, they were not typical among most students. Nevertheless, many accumulated at least some wealth. Even the most financially modest among them would be considered rich by their younger colleagues, whose generation has not had these opportunities. Those students in banking careers had other opportunities for wealth accumulation because of employment benefits for loans available to them below the market rate.[28]

While there is great variation in the wealth accumulated among these students, especially between those who have established them-selves in Nairobi and those who lived elsewhere, almost all have signifi-cant financial assets. These assets began with savings from salaries that grew as they achieved promotions and seniority in their careers. Over time their net worth increased more from the profits earned through investments than from savings. But this accumulation of wealth is more than luck and good timing. Just as they had worked hard in school to pass well, they have been striving to develop their careers, studying privately to improve their qualifications and eligibility for promotions, and eventually to build financial security. All of them have had a financial plan, often starting out like Jesse, a mid-level government employee in Nakuru. Instead of using his government housing allowance to rent a house, he built one and paid off the mortgage with the monthly allow-ance. When he finally owned the house, he then used it as collateral for other business ventures.[29]

More ambitious plans were possible for people like Charles, who owned an engineering company in Nairobi. "Anytime we [he and his three partners] make a bit of money, I buy a plot of land here or a shamba [farm] there, anything that will help me for the future."[30] Many of these students who are anticipating retirement have already made plans for investing the lump sum they will receive as a pension. David, a systems analyst for a European company, planned to buy a dairy herd, placing them on the land he had previously purchased in the Rift Valley. He hoped to earn income from milk production equal to his monthly salary prior to retirement.[31] More modest plans include Stanley's use of his retirement payment to buy a vehicle for a taxi business that he hoped would provide a continuous income.[32]

While corruption has become endemic in Kenya, the degree to which it played a part in the students' financial lives is difficult to know. I never felt comfortable directly asking about corruption, but it did occasionally arise in my interviews. Jacob spoke earnestly and disapprovingly about the state of corruption in Kenya, saying that the kickbacks that went to contractors and politicians were the main cause for Kenya's lack of economic development.[33] He speculated that the atmosphere of greed that was modeled at the highest levels of government would not change until then-president Daniel arap Moi stepped down.[34] Erastus hinted at such high-level corruption when he told me that in his government position in the 1980s, he received a great deal of pressure from politicians and others. "I had to steer a tough course between doing what they wanted and doing what was ethically correct."[35] Francis told me that the most common corruption takes place when members of the public bribe government officers to reduce or eliminate such things as their income taxes and customs duties.[36] Harun implied that the reverse happens as well, when government officers solicit payment to smooth the way through complex and time-consuming regulations and procedures. He revealed that a former Giakanja classmate offered to fast track Harun's business through the ministry in which he worked for a "fee," which Harun refused to pay.[37]

I encountered two common examples of corruption while in Kenya. The first occurred when I was pulled over by the traffic police for speeding. While I was neither issued a ticket nor solicited for a bribe to avoid it, the policeman told my Kenyan passenger in Kiswahili that since I was a visitor, I would not have to pay for "tea." The second occasion involved renewing my Kenyan driving license. As I stood in line I noticed that in each case, while the payment given always exceeded the renewal fee, no change was ever given back. When I stepped up to pay with the exact amount of the stated fee, the clerk looked at me for an

extra moment and then accepted my money and issued my renewal certificate. In each case, had I been a Kenyan, I would most likely have had
to pay an extra amount that would have gone into the official's pocket.

Clearly corruption in Kenya is practiced on a petty to grand scale. I
would be naive to believe that none of my students have participated,
especially since there are many opportunities and participation is not
always voluntary. While corruption may well have been a factor in the
accumulation of wealth for some, other factors seem to be equally
plausible: the multiple opportunities to gather information on attractive
investments from one's network of friends and relatives, their professionally developed expertise in assessing the value of such information,
a degree of comfort with risk taking, and the rapid growth of Kenya's
economy during their wealth-building years. Each goes far to explain
their accumulation of wealth without the need to have done so through
corrupt practices.

Again it is worth noting that the extraordinary success of this first
postcolonial generation rests on a foundation only partially created
by them. Their hard work, determination, and academic achievement
did enable them not only to survive but also, in most cases, to excel
in Kenya's still largely colonially structured educational system. But
they were also fortunate to live in Central Province, where mission and
government schools were more numerous than almost anywhere else in
the colony. Then they entered the workforce under the very favorable
circumstances of an expanding economy and an exodus of expatriate
workers at the time of Kenya's independence. They had the good fortune
to be Gikuyu during the very time when that ethnic identity was favored
under the Gikuyu-dominated Kenyatta government. The confluence of
these extraordinary circumstances not only helps to explain how those
who excelled in school continued to do so in their careers, but also sheds
light on how those who did not do particularly well in school were still
able to find employment and build economically comfortable lives.
Such advantageous conditions are no longer present in Kenya, and
school-leavers now are acutely aware that there is no "desk job in
Nairobi" waiting for them. Teachers at Giakanja now relate that the
prospect of unemployment has also curtailed students' enthusiasm for
their studies.[38] The pursuit of excellence and striving to do one's best, so
apparent among the first postcolonial generation, is now less present in
secondary schools.[39]

The open door of opportunity that my students passed through has
now been firmly shut. From the mid-1960s until well into the 1980s,

Kenya's economy grew and jobs were plentiful. Since then, fewer positions are available even for students who have done well at school. The fact that young people now have a bleaker future was starkly revealed in a conversation with Peter, a young man I met who shines shoes outside one of Nairobi's tourist hotels. He had gone to secondary school and even scored high enough on his CSCE to go on to Forms 5 and 6. But in the seven years since then, he has had no permanent employment. Sometimes he has found work as a day laborer but mostly he shines shoes. Peter is not married, though he is nearly thirty years old. "I share a single room with others and have no savings," he said. "What do I have to give a wife?" His birth in the mid-1960s was at the very time when my students were beginning to leave Giakanja, but the contrast could not be greater. They, as members of the first postcolonial generation, were heading off to meaningful lives of abundant employment and middle-class lifestyle. Peter, as a member of the second postcolonial generation with equal education and fluent, idiomatic English, could only scrape out an existence in the informal sector as a shiner of shoes.[40]

But such hopelessness does not extend to most of my students' children, who are approximately in the same generation as Peter. Based on their privileged upbringings, their prospects for good employment and an economically comfortable life are high, as we will see in the next two chapters.

6

Personal Life in Elite Circles

In this chapter and the next, I will explore marriage and family for my cohort of former students. As we will see, their lives have been influenced by their cosmopolitan residence in Kenya's cities, especially Nairobi; their professional careers, often in multiethnic workplaces; and their comfortable lifestyle. Though their patterns of marriage and family life reveal some variability, they are significantly similar to each other and much of their lives will look familiar to urban, middle-class societies elsewhere. But what is marriage and family life like for those who remained in small, rural homogenous Gikuyu communities like the ones from which this cohort came? Residents of such communities are undoubtedly like the former playmates of my students who did not go to school, or were unable to remain in school, or did not pass their leaving exams well enough to advance in school. In an effort to compare the largely urban and middle-class family lives explored in chapters 6 and 7, I would like to set them against the many that still live in the rural Gikuyu heartland. There they are mainly engaged in small-scale agriculture, often in marginal economic circumstances that set the conditions of family life.

In the mid-1990s, anthropologist Neil Price studied such a community and his findings about family life give context to my cohort's changed lives. He found that the ideal marriage began with the process of bride wealth negotiation between the groom's father and his uncles, and the bride's father. When agreement was reached and the first payment made, the bride moved in with her husband and his family. Future payments would be made over a period of years at the birth of each child. However, this idealized pattern often collided with the much more common practice of the couple simply eloping without the consent of the bride's parents, usually to take up residence with the groom's family. Bride wealth negotiation was frequently delayed and only initiated when the groom was financially able to pay. In most cases the bride was pregnant when married as a means of proving her fertility, most particularly to produce a son.[1]

About one in five of the marriages in this rural community were polygynous, usually as a response to a first marriage that produced no sons. Most first wives support such a strategy to produce a son, as they similarly do when encouraging "a daughter of reproductive age to conceive out of marriage, with the resultant grandson(s) brought up as the couple's own son(s)."[2] In both cases first wives would be protecting themselves from the risk of divorce and, should their husband die before them, from losing the family land to his brothers, who would inherit it if there were no sons from the marriage. Legal adoption, though practiced in Nairobi, has never in this rural community been considered a solution to marriage without a son.

The spirits of ancestors, once a more active force, now play a diminished role in the lives of these rural Gikuyu families. Their main function now concerns the naming of children after their grandparents, which is done in the belief that when they die their spirits would be honored, even reincarnated into their grandchildren.[3] Community pressure generally has prevented parents from having fewer than four children (two sons, two daughters), since that is the minimum needed to "cover" the grandparents.

Price also discovered that witchcraft and sorcery were evident, especially in the way the community thought about family misfortune associated with fertility.[4] The death of one's child or one's miscarriage or barrenness was frequently attributed to those who were jealous of you, such as a girlfriend or co-wife. Such ways of thinking have also influenced the community's ideas about modern contraception and fertility control. It is strongly held that any attempt to limit fertility is not in the best interests of the family and could precipitate a curse from relatives. Such strong responses reveal the high value placed on children for their needed labor and eventually for their care of elderly parents, both essential for survival "in the harsh economic realities faced by the community."[5] Marriage and family life are closely circumscribed, then, by strategies to ensure survival and economic well-being. As we will see, such circumstances do not seem to be as constraining on the middle-class elite.

For some time after finishing secondary school or graduating from higher educational institutions, my students concentrated on establishing themselves in careers and building a comfortable lifestyle. But they also turned their attention to their personal lives, in particular to marrying and starting a family. Indeed, all of them married and had families without exception. Finding a wife and eventually raising children was both exciting and challenging for them, and they approached this era of their lives with the same combination of determination and hard work that characterized their earlier schooling and employment experiences. They considered themselves to be successful in their marriages but not so much in raising their children, who, because of their parents' material success, entered a privileged lifestyle so very different from the childhoods of their parents in the 1950s.

Marriage

Most of these students married within five or six years after leaving Giakanja, and some even sooner. Though unknown to me at the time, three were already married while students at Giakanja.[6] Unlike these classmates, Robert delayed marriage for some years because of the need to care for his siblings. His father, a forest fighter during the Emergency, had been killed, and his mother and four younger brothers and sisters were destitute: "I'd not thought of marriage because my first priority was to my brothers and sisters." Only after he had seen them through primary school did he consider marrying.[7] Two former students also married before they finished their education at the university, but this was unusual.[8] One wife commented to me that she wanted to marry her husband before they finished their postsecondary education, but he persuaded her to wait until they were both finished.[9] All the others waited until they had finished their education and had found employment. Francis, the last to marry at age 41, said that he had waited too long. Upon returning from his education in the Soviet Union in the early 1970s, his engineering career led to delays in marrying his girlfriend/ fiancée at the time. But finally, he said, "our wedding plans were at an advanced stage when, unfortunately, she passed away [in 1976]." Grief over her death and the loss of a missed opportunity prevented him from marrying for another eleven years.[10]

I asked each who they married and why. Almost everyone spoke without hesitation about marriage and family, though not necessarily at length. Some, like Sampson, were quite intentional about seeking a wife. Soon after he was posted to his home district of Nyeri as a prisons officer, he thought, "Now is the time to get a wife. I can't just keep running around without a wife." This was in 1971, three years after he joined the

Prisons Service. Sampson had an idea about whom he would marry: "I'd known her from primary school. She was right from my home area [and] she had just completed her secondary education and I decided before she was hooked by someone else I would take her."[11] Esther, his intended wife, had a brother who was a teacher at Nyeri, so Sampson befriended him in order to learn more about Esther and to have a connection to the family. Slowly he attempted to get to know her more directly too. "I'd see her over weekends [at her home] and at times we'd arrange to meet at [my parents'] home too." The relationship developed and Sampson finally asked her to be his wife:

> She said that she would think about it. I think she took me [to be] just like another suitor because there must have been other men, other boys, maybe better placed than me. I came to learn later there was even a headmaster who'd proposed to her long before me even when she was in school. . . . When she said she'd think about it I decided to use her brother who was a teacher and I became very friendly to him. Eventually the brother decided to marry and I became one of the best men. . . . I told her, next time it will be you and me. . . . Now she knew I was serious.

They were married the following April, a little less than one year after Sampson's arrival at Nyeri. Six months after the wedding, he was sent to Kitui to be the officer in charge of the prison there. He was so pleased to have married before going to Kitui. "There you can imagine, I may have married a Mkamba or a Giriama. [If that were the case] I don't know if I would have chosen the right girl. Even today, I tell everyone that my posting to Nyeri is the one that made my marriage work."[12]

Unlike Sampson, some of the students married women not from their home area but whom they met after they had left for higher education or work. Increasingly, though my students were introduced to a wider geographical segment of the country and a range of people beyond their acquaintance or knowledge, they nevertheless continued to seek out wives among women who were in the Gikuyu diaspora in the Rift Valley and beyond. Such was the case with Christopher, who said that while he was doing a field practicum at Elbergon Forest Station as part of his education at Egerton College he met his future wife at a prayer meeting. Though he did not know her family or the community from which she came, he was attracted to her and initiated a relationship. She was just finishing her secondary education at Nakuru High School and was visiting her parents, who lived at Elbergon. "I had a feeling towards her so when I returned to college and she went back to school, we started writing to each other. . . . We also visited each other even after she finished high school." They were married two years later after she had finished a postsecondary secretarial course and Christopher was in his first year of employment.[13] In each case, the man initiated the relationship. Charles stated, "The man has to take the lead." That was the case for him too. He said that he was visiting some friends at a teacher training college when he was introduced to his future wife. "It's in meetings like that where you meet people that you will find a wife."[14]

Duncan met his wife somewhat differently. He had just bought a piece of land at Ngong and spent his weekends clearing it in preparation for building a house there. A Maasai family lived nearby and as a neighbor, he introduced himself. As he explained, he had had many girlfriends in Nairobi where he worked but none that were serious. His neighbors had a daughter Diana, "who caught my eye. She became my wife about a year later."[15] Even though Gikuyu and Maasai have been neighbors for several centuries, trading goods, borrowing elements from each other's culture, and even settling disputes along frontier territory through intermarriage, Duncan's choice of a wife from another ethnic group was unusual among this cohort.[16] While they did volunteer that they often worked with and socialized with other ethnic groups, only one other student married a non-Gikuyu. It is not difficult to understand why this might be the case. Students who did not move away from the Nyeri area where they had grown up continued to live among a population that was overwhelmingly Gikuyu. But even for those who had moved elsewhere and lived among other ethnic groups, they still wanted to marry someone who spoke their language and who had been raised within the same cultural environment. That had certainly been the case for Sampson, who specifically sought a Gikuyu wife while he was posted at Nyeri.

From the woman's perspective, these courtship patterns appear somewhat differently. For Mary, she felt she was being rushed into marriage too quickly. She met her future husband George at a dance held at her nursing college. "When we were dancing, he asked me my name and where I had come from and so we realized that we had come from the same place. . . . After that he started writing to me and I started writing to him. . . . I had other boy friends and I was not serious with any. . . . I was just free and wanted to enjoy life as a young person." But George was more serious and pursued her. "He kept on following me. . . . I liked him because he was not drinking alcohol and was not smoking, but he pushed me very fast. . . . Finally he made me pregnant so I had no choice [but to marry him]."[17]

Though George did not address the issue of his wife's pregnancy before their marriage, two scholars who have studied Gikuyu marriage patterns have argued that such an occurrence was not uncommon, even in traditional Gikuyu marital history: "The notion that physical intimacy is part of the mate selection process has been retained from traditional practice."[18] Later they refer to the very time period when George and Mary were dating: "Of the women of our sample who were married in the 1960s, over 70 percent were pregnant before they moved in with their husbands."[19] Nevertheless, Mary's exclamation that she had to marry George because she was pregnant might reveal that she had accepted the Christian virtue of chastity before marriage, a teaching that had entered Gikuyu society through missionary teachings earlier in the century.

Two other wives had different experiences. Margaret said that she had known her future husband Samuel for a long time, starting when she was still in primary school and he was a student at Giakanja. "I used to go and visit my sister and Samuel was living with the father-in-law of my sister. . . . I remember he used to help me with some of the problems I had in math." Several years later she met him again at her secondary school. Samuel was there to visit his sister, and Margaret, as school prefect, showed him around. "He spent most of his time with me [and not his sister]. I talked a lot and he listened because he was interested." After he left, he wrote to her. But it was not until six years later, after Margaret had been teaching for some time and Samuel had finished his degree at Makerere University, that they began to meet frequently. Margaret had hoped for some time that Samuel would propose to her. When he did, they were married by the end of the year.[20]

Mary met her future husband Charles when she was still in school. "The first time for him to approach me as a lover was when he was in college and I was in Form 2, and although I was eighteen and I said yes, it did not seem serious to me. But by the time I reached Form 4, I had made up my mind that he was the one I would marry." When Charles's mother died a year later, Mary wanted to set the wedding immediately, reasoning that "I thought without a mother, the next person to comfort him should be the wife." But Charles counseled that they should wait until she finished her teacher training education.[21] From these illustrations it can be seen that, while men may have made the first move, women took an active part in courtship as well.

Once the couple agreed to marry, they were introduced to each other's parents. According to Charles, "in our tradition we don't bring every girl home."[22] Ephantus added that the man usually brings the woman home first to meet his parents; if they approve, then he proposes to her and they visit her parents.[23] This procedure may be the ideal, but most of these students used the exchange of family visits to help them determine whether they should go forward with the relationship. This was certainly the case with Joseph and Jane. Jane agreed to a visit by Joseph to her family home at Nyeri when she was back from Nairobi to see her parents. While Jane thought this was just a visit from one of her Nairobi friends, Joseph was more serious about their relationship and was hoping to make a good impression on her parents. When Joseph arrived, Jane's father immediately greeted him by his family name. Apparently Joseph bore a striking resemblance to his father, who had been a popular subchief of the area until he was assassinated during the Emergency fifteen years earlier.

Jane related what happened next: "Now my [future] husband didn't sit with me, he sat with my father and they had a lot to talk about since my father had been a subchief too. . . . They talked and became friends. So when I was serving him food he said, 'I know your father and I'm here to stay. . . . I have already passed the test.'" To confirm Joseph's claim, Jane's father startled her with this statement as Joseph was leaving: "If this is the man you are going to go with, you have my blessings."[24] Joseph went away very pleased. Though he had not anticipated it, he had made a connection with Jane's family that was vitally important in gaining their approval for marriage to their daughter. According to Joseph, "Because they had known my father, they felt at home with me. I was not a total stranger. When somebody comes from another district and they want to settle here, no one knows their roots. But when they know your family, and even know your clan and all that, then they will be with you."[25]

Clearly Joseph is articulating the long-practiced and, perhaps, still ideal pattern of proposing marriage to someone from your area where the parents know you. But as we have seen with Christopher and other students, this pattern is no longer universal and perhaps in decline. When Joseph invited Jane to his house, his mother knew that this was an important meeting because she was the first woman Joseph had invited home. "She cooked a special meal and my mother treated her specially. . . . Afterward, Jane said she really liked my mother."[26] Rather than confirming the seriousness of their relationship by visiting each other's homes as Gikuyu tradition suggested, this case in reverse order helped Jane move forward in realizing that she was serious about Joseph and wished to marry him.

Charles had been a regular visitor in the home of his future wife Mary. He was from the same area and was also a friend of Mary's brother. But when it came time to introduce him to her parents as their future son-in-law, Mary's mother said that she had known for three years that Charles would marry her daughter. She had never told her husband this, however, and he was very surprised to hear the news. "I had to write it out in a note to him," Mary said, "because he could not believe that this regular visitor to his house was going to marry me. 'Have you thought about it for long?' [he asked] and he was surprised to hear that I had been doing so for many years." As surprised as Mary's father was, he wholeheartedly supported the marriage and he and Charles have become very good friends.[27] This seems to be a case of mothers being more intuitive about the lives of their children than fathers, a trait that appears in many cultures.

From the above accounts, it can be seen that parents were clearly helpful to their sons in choosing a wife. They were supportive and instructive about the process of mate selection, but they did not actually choose a wife for him. In the words of Worthman and Whiting, "Marriages were not arranged; rather they were based on the mutual consent of partners."[28] Mutual consent was not a modern development either. In the past, Gikuyu young men and women chose their marriage partners as well. Following a period of social instruction, which culminated with their circumcision, they participated in several years of social life highlighted with frequent evening dances. It was during this period of dancing, feasting, and intimacy that the mutual identification of spouses took place. Once the selection was made, the couple would seek the approval of their parents. But if they did not approve and withheld the bride wealth payment, the son could choose to pay it himself, usually by raiding Maasai for cattle.[29] In contemporary times, classrooms, workplaces, and church activities, among other things, have provided opportunities for young people to identify possible mates, just as traditional dances had done in the past. Parents' consent is desired but even less crucial than in the past, since their role of providing the bride wealth payment has passed increasingly to their sons.[30]

Once the couple has chosen to marry and have informed the groom's parents of their intention, then the marriage plans can move forward. Since Sampson was the first son in his family to marry, he had not witnessed marriage preparations before. He consulted his parents about what to do next after they had consented to the marriage. "[My Father] told me, go and look for money but for a start I must have at least a she-goat and a kid. Those are the ones you present to the girl's parents for acceptance."[31] These gifts provided an opportunity for the parents and other close relatives in both families to meet and get to know each other.

Many of the students volunteered that they paid bride wealth as part of their marriage traditions. This information confirms recent scholarship by Bert Adams and Edward Mburugu, who argue that this custom is still widely practiced among Gikuyu.[32] Discussions about bride wealth usually took place between the parents. Daniel said that in the past the whole of the groom's extended family contributed to the bride wealth sent to the bride's family, but these days the groom himself is mostly responsible for the payment (now converted from animals to cash) because of his earning potential, and it goes directly to the bride's parents. Daniel remembers his father-in-law telling him: "I have spent so much on this girl's education and you are not taking her from me until I have been given something,"[33] suggesting that bride wealth payment was a business affair in which the bride's family sought to drive a hard bargain for their profit.

This idea was reinforced by Edmondo Cavicchi's research from the 1970s, which reported that Gikuyu generally believed that bride wealth was too high.[34] But even though Cavicchi wrote about the very time period when these students were marrying, none of them complained about their bride wealth payments. Jane said that her husband Joseph expected to pay more because she came from a wealthy family. "But my father just asked him for the basics: a goat, some blankets for my mother and a rope (I don't know, I think that it was given traditionally to carry firewood) and 3,000 shillings which he gave much later."[35] Joseph revealed to me that he thought he would have to pay 10,000 shillings, a common sum in the 1970s for an educated and professionally employed wife.[36]

Daniel said that when the bride wealth for his wife was finally settled, his father-in-law was very fair. "He was not very strict on that, they were very soft. . . . He is a very good *mzee* [elder]. He made it very easy for me."[37] Charles also had very good relations with his in-laws right from the very beginning of his marriage. They live near each other, and according to Charles's wife, he frequently helps his aging father-in-law much like a son would.[38] Margaret dates the good relations between her husband's family and hers from the time of the bride wealth negotiations as well. Because her uncles had killed their brother (her father) as a punishment for being employed on a European farm during the Emergency (apparently a political taboo during this rebellion to some Gikuyu), Margaret's mother did not want to involve them even though their participation in the marriage of their niece would normally have taken place. Instead, Margaret's uncles on her mother's side of the family negotiated the bride wealth payment and took part in other wedding preparations with the groom's family. She credits the smooth running of the marriage arrangements to the tolerance of her husband's family for these irregular procedures. The two families have been close ever since.[39] Though not all the students chose to talk about the bride wealth arrangements with their in-laws, many remember it as amiable and often the beginning of friendly relations between the two families. Their wives also related these times to me as pleasurable. Their parents treated their future son-in-law and his family with respect and friendship. Perhaps they were preparing the way for their daughter to smoothly enter another family, rather than insisting on a high bride wealth payment, which could have been an impediment to her future happiness.

Once the bride wealth agreement was made, the families gathered to celebrate the marriage of their children. Harun said that it was common for the bride's parents to host this celebration. "They invited the extended family on both sides so that they get to know each other and to eat and drink. . . . The main feature of the traditional wedding ceremony was the cutting of the leg of the goat and when you pass it to your wife-to-be and she takes it, traditionally she has become your wife."[40] For Harun and his wife Helen, and for many of the other students, this traditional family ceremony preceded their church wedding. Other students said that they just had a civil ceremony the next day in the DC's office. Sometimes this was a decision of convenience, as in the case of Joseph and his wife Jane. Joseph remembers that just when they had planned to marry, Jane was notified that she was to be posted as a nurse to a hospital located in the remote and very dry district of Kitui, but they both wanted to continue to live together in Eldoret, where Joseph was working. They hurriedly called a few friends together and were married at the DC's office. Interestingly, Jane remembered the circumstances of their hurried wedding somewhat differently. She noted that indeed it was her posting to Kitui that prompted the timing of the wedding, but only because of her fear of snakes, which thrived in Kitui. "I really fear snakes more than anything, even seeing a picture of it, I will scream. So I told Joseph, if you are ever going to marry me, now is the time because I knew only the marriage would give me a transfer [elsewhere]."[41]

Only one student, Amos, has taken a second wife.[42] Other students reported this to me long before I interviewed Amos. They were strongly disapproving and said that his mother, a staunch Christian (his father was dead), was mortified when she heard of it.[43] Amos, however, has said to me that while his mother initially resisted, she eventually accepted his decision and led the family delegation that brought the bride wealth to the new wife's parents. He also acknowledged that only a few of his friends and his professional colleagues in government have been supportive. But he maintained that formally marrying another wife is the most honest way to represent yourself to society: "There are a lot of friends who have got one wife, but I know and everyone knows that they have got many mistresses out there and that is worse. . . . I know of friends of mine who have even bought cars and houses for their mistresses. That means that they divert resources from their families, sometimes even leaving them suffering, but when they go to church and meet their friends, they are known to have only one wife, but that is not how they are behaving." Such deceit was not for him: "I would rather come out in the open and say 'Here we are and life continues.'" Amos stated that both of his marriages have been successful because he provides for each family equally. Amos's mother is as friendly with his second wife and children as with the first. There is visiting and friendly relations between the two wives as well, though his second family lives with him in Nairobi, while his first wife and his unmarried children live on his farm at Embu, about seventy-five miles away.[44]

Only four of the ninety students have experienced the death of a spouse or a divorce. Two spouses have died from cancer, and my students have remarried and begun a second family in each case. Two others have divorced. One of them, Alex, said that he was not yet married in 1979 when he received notice from the Ministry of Foreign Affairs, where he was an accountant, that he would soon be posted to Kenya's embassy in Ottawa. He felt that he should marry before he departed to Canada and did so quickly since he knew he would most likely be gone for at least four years. But five years later, upon his return to Kenya in 1985 without any children, he and his wife divorced. Alex cited that being childless "and other reasons" brought on the divorce. He has since remarried and had a family.[45] Charles and his wife divorced after about ten years of marriage, which had produced five children. Charles did not discuss the reasons for the divorce, though he has raised the children, and according to one of his daughters, they have infrequently seen their mother.[46]

Children

After marriage, all of the students started families. Most of them had come from large families themselves. Peter's parents had sixteen children,[47] and those students from polygynous households often had even more siblings.[48] But these students generally had fewer children than did their parents.[49] Of the sixty-one students who volunteered information about their children, twenty-five stated that they had four children. Another twenty-five divided almost equally between having three (12) or five (13). Only two families had fewer than two children. The largest family belonged to Amos, though his nine children were divided between his two wives.[50] Three of the students had twins;[51] in one family, there were two sets.[52] All the students said that having fewer children than was typical during their parents' generation was necessary because of the cost of supporting and educating them in independent Kenya.

Many of the students said that they discussed with their wives the number of children they wanted and then practiced birth control to achieve the desired number. However, several students revealed that they had one more child than planned, the last one being a "surprise."[53] They reported that according to Gikuyu tradition, you named your sons after their paternal and maternal grandfathers and your daughters after each grandmother. The ideal family identified by almost everyone was composed of four children, two boys and two girls. But this ideal was not always achieved since the husband's parents are chosen first in this naming tradition. Sometimes tension arose between husband and wife about whether to have additional children in order to name them after the wife's parents. For instance, if a family had set a goal of four children and three sons and a daughter or three daughters and a son have already been born, then usually the wife advocated for another child, hoping that it would be the right gender so as to name her remaining father or mother.

At Joseph's insistence, he and his wife Jane settled on having just two children, and in time a son and a daughter were born. But Jane told me, "After a while, I realized that with only two children, I would never be able to name my parents, and my mother kept asking me, when was she going to be named. My sisters and brother all had sons and no daughters so my mother felt that if she was to be "born" [among her grand-children], it would have to be up to me." Jane found it difficult to tell her mother that she and Joseph had decided to limit their family to only two children, even though she would have liked to have more. Finally, after her mother had pressed her a number of times about having another child, she told her that they must all sit down together and discuss it. "My mother didn't want to discuss this with my husband because she was a shy person, but she agreed. So we all gathered and she said, 'You people have to reconsider that I have to be born.' So I told my husband I have named your parents now I have to name mine." Joseph changed his mind as a result of this discussion and a third child was eventually born; everyone was happy that it was a girl. Jane's mother died contentedly shortly afterward.[54]

Stanley and his wife had seven children, though they had planned on having fewer. Their first child, a son, died only a few years after he was born. Stanley said the clan elders insisted that the next son be named after Stanley's father again since the first son had died so young. But this decision caused a problem between Stanley and his wife. "A kind of disagreement arose. . . . My wife insisted that we continue having children until we get one for her father. . . . That's the time we started having girls. The second was a girl, third a girl, fourth a girl, and the fifth a boy. He was named after my father again. The sixth was a girl and seventh a boy. He is our last born. After we named her father, we stopped, finally."[55]

Stanley attributes the cause for his large family to the clan elders' decision, though from his demeanor during the interview he seemed to agree with them. Perhaps living as he did in the Gikuyu heartland of rural Nyeri, both he and his wife felt more strongly about honoring the naming tradition and following clan instructions. But not everyone was guided by the naming tradition in determining family size. Joyce had to coax her husband James into having more than one child. She told me that he had been so traumatized by the poverty experienced after the murder of his father during the Emergency, he now felt that one child was all that he could adequately care for. They eventually had three children, all daughters, and did not consider having more even though neither his father nor hers was named.[56] Francis was the most direct about whether to honor the naming tradition by having more children. He told me that he would not have wanted more than four children even if it meant that not each of his or his wife's parents were named.[57]

The raising of children has changed during these students' generation. Essays about family life that the students wrote for me at Giakanja
were filled with images of harsh discipline by their fathers. Esther, a
friend of one of the students and about the same age, told me that in the
past the father's role was supposed to be harsh toward the children. "If a
child misbehaved while the father was away, you'd hear the mother say,
'Let your father come, you'll see what's going to happen.'" She said that
was the case among her friends and certainly in her own life, too. Now
when she thinks of her father, she remembers the discipline the most.
"He was keen on discipline. If we did something wrong he had a whip
he kept and you were whipped. When I look back into my childhood, I
remember that whip. It was long, maybe it was an animal tail. . . . He
beat us, me and my sisters; I remember we organized to throw it away."[58]
Students frequently told me that because of their mistakes and shortcomings, fathers were always beating them, tying them up, or even
locking them in a room and denying them food. In contrast, mothers
were depicted as nurturing and soothing parents.

Yet my students' parenting has significantly changed from that of
their fathers. Of the wives interviewed, all have said that they and their
husbands have collaborated in raising the children. Mary told me that
she and her husband Charles decided together that they would send
their children to Nyeri Primary School, a former European-only school,
because of the fine facilities and multiethnic atmosphere. Later when
Mary went to the United Kingdom for two years to complete an education degree at Leeds University, Charles cared for the children as a single
parent. She told me, "They are so close to their dad. You can see him
giving them money to go to town and watch a movie and then come
back and narrate it to him. They are very free with him and comfortable.
I don't think there is anything they can't discuss with him."[59]

Margaret said that she and Samuel have raised their children
together as well. This decision was tested in 1976, when Samuel was
hired for a position in Kitale more than a hundred miles from their farm
at South Kinangop. As a result they decided that Margaret and the
three children should stay on the farm so she could manage it. But after
a few months, Margaret related, "My husband could not stay alone
without us, so we left the farm and shifted to Kitale."[60] Samuel did not
like being separated from his family.

Joseph enjoyed participating with his wife in the raising of his children too, but his career in government sometimes prevented him from

doing so. After finishing a master's degree in agricultural finance, he was promoted and posted to Kisumu, where he had to travel away from home for at least one week each month. It was a new dimension to his career and it brought some distress between him and his wife. "I didn't like to travel so much," he confessed to me, "because I didn't want to lose my wife. . . . My main desire was being home with my family, not just my wife but also my two children." When an opportunity came to switch to another career, he took it in part because he did not have to travel.[61] His wife Jane told me that from the very beginning of their marriage they had talked frankly to each other about all aspects of their life together. "I have told my [oldest] daughter that a husband should be able to talk to his wife about more than financial topics. It is for you and him to talk about everything." She and Joseph got into a routine of taking a walk together every evening and then using that time to talk. "We have walked in every town that we've lived in. . . . We knew where each house was because we used to walk every evening. This time that we spent together has put us very close."[62] Joseph said that when he wanted to build a country home at Nyeri to which the family could go on weekends for relaxation, he made sure that his wife and his youngest daughter Faith, who was still at home, had a part in the planning and decision making "so it would be their home too."[63] When I was given a tour of the completed house, he proudly pointed out that all the light fixtures had been chosen by his daughter.

These students often have had a relationship with their children that is quite different from what they experienced with their own parents when they were growing up in the 1940s and 1950s. Whereas their parents, especially their fathers, were seen as disciplinarians and emotionally distant, they have strived to be closer and friendlier with their children and to take an active part in all areas of their upbringing and to be partners with their wives in doing so.

A partial explanation for this change in parenting style may be found in the historical migratory patterns of Gikuyu labor. From the very beginning of Kenya's colonial existence, the British intentionally created a migratory labor system that for significant periods of time each year drew Gikuyu (especially men) to work on settler farms, government projects, and other forms of employment, including their own entrepreneurial pursuits.[64] Force and the need to pay an annual tax in cash were the factors that caused fathers to be absent from home. This long-established labor pattern was still in place, and even exacerbated by a population increase, landlessness, and Mau Mau detentions, when these students' parents were raising their families. Through their absence, fathers (and sometimes mothers) had fewer opportunities to parent or even to know their children very well. This migratory labor pattern has been largely absent from the adult lives of this cohort. With only a few exceptions, their employment options have enabled them to live with their families uninterrupted throughout the year. Of course as the examples below reveal, they also wanted, and considered it part of their natural responsibility, to take an active part in raising their children.

Parenting styles might be determined by new challenges from their children too. Richard related his parenting philosophy in this way: "So many of the issues [with our children] these days have to be tackled by discussion. I find that even today, my old man can still dictate to me, but I cannot dictate to my kids. . . . If parents force their point of view on their children, they will act very negatively. . . . I have to give them a kind of leeway, not like it used to be in the old days."[65] Many of the students found that they could not necessarily use their parents as a guide for successfully parenting their own children.

Charles and his wife Rose are bringing up four children in Nairobi ages twelve to twenty-three. He stated that he had to give his children a great deal more direction than was necessary for him to receive from his parents while growing up in rural Nyeri. "You've got to use a bit of pressure, not actually using a real 'iron fist,' but sometimes not far from that. You must keep your children near [to you] and make sure they get interested in something for themselves."[66] Charles seemed confident in his parenting and had high praise for his children, but other classmates of his expressed frustrations with raising their children. John and his wife are both secondary school teachers who have enjoyed their careers but have had to frequently live apart because they were posted to schools in different areas. He told me that his father had to live apart from his family while John was growing up as well. He remembers that he saw his father only at Christmas and perhaps a few other times each year. While he is able to be with his family each weekend, he wonders if his three young children are experiencing the loneliness he felt for his father and what this condition might lead to in their development.[67]

Joseph's concerns about his relationship with his children runs even deeper. When he was seven years old, the British colonial government detained his father for his involvement in the Mau Mau Rebellion. Joseph did not see his father again until he was fourteen, and then only briefly, since he died shortly after his release. Joseph related how his father's long absence during detention and his early death had adversely influenced his relationship with his own children: "I have a problem with my children. I don't know what to tell them at times. . . . Now I believe it is because I didn't have some fatherly love. . . . I think that I missed something in my life. I really don't know how to be a father. About what topics should I talk to my children? They are not free with me and I also don't always feel like talking to them."[68] Although parenting his own children has been made more difficult because of the lack of a father role model while he was growing up, Joseph was not unique. About 25 percent of my students grew up without the guidance from their fathers (and sometimes even from mothers), who were detained for long periods of time during the Mau Mau Rebellion. Several of these students can still recite the actual date when their parents were detained and released; though young at the time, the loss of their parent has been burned deep into their memories.

The financial success my students have enjoyed has also influenced their parenting. James, a successful sales representative, told me that his father's death during the Emergency plunged the family into great poverty. James vowed that his own family would never suffer from material want as he did; as a result, he has indulged his three daughters.[69] His wife is even more forthright in describing his parenting: "He over-does it at times. He'll give them everything they ask for and even what they don't ask for. . . . He had a very difficult childhood and that's why he likes to be comfortable now. . . . He believes you should enjoy yourself and not save money in banks which you might never use."[70] Joseph also admits to giving his family great luxury. He knows that he has brought up his children "with a silver spoon in their mouth . . . because I didn't want them to go through what I went through. . . . I came to Giakanja without shoes . . . and I have had hunger and it is painful. I have slept hungry."[71]

A few parents have understood that it may not be in their children's best interests to shield them too completely from the realities of life and smooth out all the rough spots that confront them. Erastus and his wife have purposely sent their two sons to India for their university education. They want them to experience their early adulthood in a developing world culture similar to Kenya rather than university life in Great Britain or the United States.[72] Other parents have insisted that their children pay for at least part of their private post-secondary training in an effort to teach them the value of education.[73] Even some parents who plan to take their children into the family business first require them to make their own way. Jacob said that his children have received very good educations but have no experience of being on their own. As a result, though he hopes to provide the capital for a family business that will eventually be operated by his children, it is too soon to begin that enterprise. He told me, "First, they need to mature and get financial discipline. If they can show me they can manage their salaries for a while, then they will be able to manage bigger money in the future."[74] But such a rational perspective on parental indulgence of their children was tempered by a degree of extravagance, such as when children often continued to live at home or were provided with a monthly allowance long after they had left university or professional training.

Many in this cohort have said to me that the younger generation was immature and lacked ambition. One confided that his two older daughters had everything they ever wanted, including loving parents, a luxurious home, and a first-class education; in other words, they had all of the advantages he never had. Still they had dropped out of their professional studies, had not sought employment, and seemed only to want to have a good time with their friends.[75] Another was equally frank with me about his disappointment with his children. The older three had stayed on in Britain to work after finishing their education there, but they were only marking time and not progressing. "They are good, they have a brain, but they don't want to apply it. They don't want to exact themselves. They don't seem to have any ambition." His youngest son, who was in Form 4 and still lived at home, also frustrated his parents. "I'm having a lot of problems with my [youngest] son because he has fallen into wrong company and peer group pressure; they want to drink, smoke and try all sorts of things. . . . He is very irresponsible and I talk to him, my wife talks to him. . . . Sometimes we cane [beat] him just to see whether we can instill some discipline in him." I have heard this type of story from others too, but usually not with the insight of this father. "I suppose young fellows [like my son] who just like to take life easy look around themselves and see that they are living in a nice house, they have a nice car and are eating well. They can't see why they should have to struggle because as far as they are concerned, life will always be like that. . . . They can't visualize life without us [rich parents]."[76]

Without doubt there are sharp differences between my students' adolescent years and those of their children. Whereas my students as children of the Mau Mau era grew up under circumstances of physical deprivation, fractured families, and delayed education, their children have experienced none of this. Rather, their lives have been lived during times of economic and political stability, cushioned by attentive parents, and given unparalleled opportunity at all levels of education. Yet within these contrasts lie surprising parallels between the two generations. The values instilled in my students by their parents focused on education as the pathway to a better future. Discipline, focus, and hard work, the values that had enabled the parents to survive the rigors of the late colonial period, were now passed on to the students who refashioned them into the tools for success in their educations and careers. Now as parents themselves, the students have instilled the values and perspectives in their children that will lead to successful futures too.

My students correctly discerned that the fundamental value of the modern world was inclusiveness—one must be able to relate to all groups in society. Their own parents had acknowledged this value when they took their children to school in the 1950s, knowing that they would be taught English. The students mastered the language in secondary schools like Giakanja and in time the concept behind it—that English was the central means of relating to the world. Many students then took the extraordinary step of appropriating English to become the language of the home and family, simultaneously setting in motion the assurance of their children's fluency and the diminishing of their Gikuyu language facility and their Gikuyu ethnic identity. The parents' lack of fear of this loss of ethnicity has led their children to embrace a broader identity by thinking of themselves as Kenyan. While this process is clearly visible in Nairobi, it is also functioning to some extent wherever students are raising their families, especially outside of the Gikuyu heartland.

Unlike their parents, who received little or no career advice, the children of the students have been the recipients of abundant planning for the future. Indeed, after the value of inclusiveness, preparation for the future has been the underlying value that parents have passed on to their children. They sent them on to the best schools they could afford and encouraged their children to excel in these educationally superior environments. Careful choice of universities followed, including sending them abroad to India and Great Britain, and some even to the United States, for graduate studies. These choices were made in light of the career paths jointly identified with the children as the most promising in Kenya's future or in an anticipated family business. Above all, this parental tutelage prompted self-awareness among their children of how to prepare themselves for meaningful careers and secure financial futures.

All the students have lived their adult lives in the world of science-driven efficiency, record-keeping administration, and evidence-based decision making (i.e., the modern world). This world has become largely secular for the students and, by extension, for their children. As a result I found little evidence that Christianity was integral to their lives. It is true that some are devout believers and have instructed their children in Christian principles and behavior, even guiding their music and television-viewing choices.[77] Others, like William, prompted by a sense of Christian responsibility, have served their church and community throughout their lives.[78] Some have been "born again," a term used by Evangelical Christians to describe their conversion.[79] And a few have hinted that their prosperity and comfortable lifestyle has been a reward for their piety. Christianity, in this sense, has penetrated the culture. But as Michael told me, "Though Christianity is popular and many people go to church, they are not committed."[80] This comment suggests that Christianity had become an element of culture for his generation but not necessarily a set of religious principles that carefully guided their lives. Rather, it is the principles of the modern world that have influenced them even more. They believe in the value of education, now applied equally to all their children regardless of gender. Hard work, planning, and inclusiveness are also seen as the pathway to a modern life. Even in the case of Amos, the only polygynist among them, their repugnance over his taking a second wife was because it was not modern.[81] Similarly, though corruption in Kenyan society was not a topic that most students felt comfortable discussing with me, when it did come up it was always criticized because it promoted inefficiency, curtailed development, or gave Kenya a bad reputation.[82] In other words, neither infraction was condemned because it was not Christian. It is this largely secular world fashioned by their parents that is being inherited by the next generation. Chapter 7 will focus more explicitly on the future, exploring the joys and struggles experienced by both parents and children as they grapple to understand each other in the context of preparing for and safeguarding the next generation.

7

Reflections on the Next Generation

Generational conflict is not unique to the tensions arising between this cohort of former students and their children. Youth have frequently challenged their parents' generation; indeed, the very structure of past African societies seems to reflect tension between the generations. John Iliffe recognized this condition when he claimed that "conflict between the male generations [has been] one of the most dynamic and enduring forces of African history."[1]

Colonialism gave a new dimension to the conflict between generations with the arrival of capitalism and wage labor, Christianity and Western education, and city life. As always, the junior generation was ever alert to renegotiating their status with their seniors, and they identified colonial rule and its attributes as a set of opportunities to do just that. Becoming a Christian, gaining a mission education, earning wages, and living on a settler farm or in the city enabled young people to gain access to wealth and new knowledge that was not regulated or monopolized by the elders. Burgess identified these new opportunities available to juniors as "an exit option from years of servitude to their seniors."[2]

The challenge to elders by young people eventually drew the attention of the colonial government, which "worried over the potential emergence of an urban crowd of materialistic consumption-oriented youth." They reasoned that a challenge to elders could lead to doubt about the legitimacy of the colonial rule. The fact that in the 1950s young people took up arms against the British in the Mau Mau Rebellion in greater numbers than their seniors reveals the accuracy of their concern.[3]

Of course the youth of the colonial era were the parents' generation of my cohort of former students. As we have seen, when they began their lives as young professionals in Nairobi and elsewhere, they continued the drive for autonomy begun by their parents' generation: moving away from their rural Gikuyu community and its direct ethnic influence, raising their children in a nuclear style family, and adopting English as the family language. Now, as we will see in this chapter, their children have become the young urban professionals of the next generation and have set about securing further autonomy for themselves and by doing so have again triggered the criticism of the elder generation.

The promise of a golden future, which I heard Kenyans joyously express to each other during their independence celebrations in 1963, have largely been realized by the first postcolonial generation. This generation has developed careers and families and built bright futures for themselves, as previous chapters have revealed. But what about their children, the next generation? They are now reaching their adulthood during very different times. How are they likely to fare in the Kenya of the twenty-first century, where the abundant jobs and economic opportunities of their parents' generation are now much less available? They have lived the good life as children of elites. Will they have the self-discipline and determination as adults to do as well as their parents have done? What are the lives of the next generation going to be like?

Generational Conflict

One place to start in answering these questions is to explore the conflict that has arisen between the generations to which my students and their children belong. This conflict centers on the hard work, ambition, and striving for a better life among the former cohort as they grew up and on their assessment that the younger generation now lack these qualities. According to the older cohort, their childhood was consumed with surviving the cruelty, anxiety, and poverty created by British colonial rule and the Mau Mau Rebellion. During their adolescent years they labored to master their studies, first in primary and then in secondary school, all the while with only the most meager financial, material, and even emotional support available to them. Nevertheless they persevered and succeeded by discipline, hard work, and sacrifice to obtain good educations and eventually good jobs. Over the years, by their careful management they have saved, invested, and created wealth for their family. According to their parents, the younger generation has not suffered or even been inconvenienced in their lives but has been cocooned in luxury, their every want met. In response, they do not express their thanks but take their comfortable lives for granted or even claim them as their right. The younger generation, according to their parents, is far less ambitious, lacks focus to their lives, except for enjoyment and easy living, and seems less well positioned to contribute to society in their adulthood. In the minds of the cohort, the misery of the poverty they experienced in their youth has now been replaced by the misery of plenty, which their children's generation now experience.

But the younger generation see themselves and their future lives differently. Though I was able to interview only seven grown children of my students, their narratives bear a remarkable similarity.[4] They all acknowledged that while growing up they had not experienced a life of poverty as their parents did. Several told me that they knew they came from rich families and that the lifestyle they enjoyed would have been considered luxurious by their parents at the same age and by many of their own peers at school or university. They said that this was a circumstance over which they had no control; they simply were born into families with the resources to support such luxury.[5] However, they did feel that they worked hard to pass school exams well and to obtain good educations, even though they have benefited from some of Kenya's best educational institutions at their parents' expense. Salome noted that a number of her peers who were raised in urban middle- or upper-class families like hers were not very responsible about their food, money, and time. But she did not behave like this because she was taught by her parents to be a responsible person.[6] She and others also said that because employment was now scarce in Kenya, they had to be very careful about planning their courses of study at the university and identifying useful career-entry skills. They talked about the importance of using their school holidays for such things as learning to drive a car, acquiring computer literacy, being tutored in a foreign language, and obtaining career advisement.[7] Such careful and particular career preparation was in stark contrast to the more unfocused experience of their fathers' generation. Their fathers often chose careers and launched themselves into their first jobs without any clear direction, preparation, or anticipated outcome. Though their sons and daughters know that they stand a good chance of securing employment because of their privileged educations and their parents' contacts, they do not seem to be taking this completely for granted and are working hard to prepare themselves to compete well for the jobs that do exist.

My students' children and their generation are also uniquely suited to participate in the multiethnic society developing in Kenya. They have mostly been raised in urban areas inhabited by other races and ethnicities. This multiethnic environment was most evident in their schooling: Salome was sent to Hospital Hill Primary, as were her older brothers and sisters. For eight years prior to secondary school, she mixed with all the races and ethnic groups in Nairobi. Katherine and her siblings attended Nyeri Primary School, a former Europeans-only school during the colonial era but later open to all groups. Salome and Katherine, as well as others of their generation who attended the many all-race schools now available in Kenya, got to know many people with different lifestyles and perspectives. They made friends across racial and ethnic lines. Many of her generation echoed what Katherine told me, "I can relate to anyone now."[8] Such schools also offered English language instruction by native speakers so that now Salome, Katherine, and many of their generation speak fluent, unaccented English. These urban children have also acquired a similar fluency in Kiswahili. Their university educations have continued to introduce them to many different kinds of people. All of them told me that they felt most comfortable around other urban-raised students regardless of their ethnicity.

As the younger generation filled out their urban lives with multiethnic experiences, their Gikuyu ethnic identities were diluted. While the early lives of their parents had evolved entirely in the environment of the Gikuyu heartland, the children have been less surrounded by Gikuyu culture. Returning to the Gikuyu rural areas where their fathers were raised has often become an alien experience for the younger generation. Salome remembers going to her grandmother's house at Nyeri for Christmas celebrations when she was young. "You know, it's only the older people who enjoyed [themselves]. They were drinking, slaughtering goats. There was nothing for me to do; I didn't like it. I felt like I had to go there out of respect."[9] Even facility with the Gikuyu language has become limited for the younger generation.[10] English was frequently the language of the home as these children grew up and, at least in Nairobi, it seemed to have replaced Gikuyu as the vernacular. Of course, it was this cohort and their generation that have enabled younger people to acquire their multiethnic experiences and language abilities. They have encouraged identification with the country as a whole, a Kenyanization of their identity.

Only in Mombasa at Kenya's coast, with its ancient Swahili and Muslim culture, did I hear some of this cohort's concern about the decline of their children's Gikuyu identity. They considered sending them "up country" to the Gikuyu heartland for their secondary educations or even leaving the coast themselves at retirement and resettling at Nyeri. But there was also the realization that the coast had become their home and the place where their life-long friends now lived. They did not really know anyone any longer at Nyeri; it would be an alien place to them as much as it would be to their children.[11] Generally speaking, their multicultural experiences and educations, as well as diminished Gikuyu identity, have empowered the younger generation to carry forward the building of a Kenyan society. Katherine gives voice to this generational transition, "in the future, our generation will change tribalism, and discrimination. . . . There is beauty in our past [heritage] but there is no future in such beliefs."[12] For Katherine and others of her generation, the promise of a nontribal and discrimination-free future lies with the development of a multicultural society, a process that she believes has already begun.

But is a diminished sense of ethnic identity a realistic possibility for Kenya anytime soon? It is true that many of these young people have spent their adolescent years, and their schooling and university education in elite institutions, in the cosmopolitan environments of Nairobi or other Kenyan cities, even outside Kenya for some. For all, these were multiethnic experiences. In such environments it would be easy and even necessary to form friendships across ethnic boundaries and ultimately to identify oneself as sharing affinities with a common social class (i.e., composed of the children of Kenya's elite). Perhaps such environments and the social alliances that accompanied them led to a diminishment of Gikuyu consciousness. But there are a number of factors that mitigate this tendency. First, the relatives of their parents' generation are all Gikuyu, as are many of their parents' friends and associates.[13] This is the very network of people that their parents drew upon to help smooth the way for their children with such things as scholarships (abroad), jobs, promotions, bank loans, retail discounts, etc. Second, to the extent that these children of elites form a social class unto themselves, much of that class itself is composed of Gikuyu. The fact that a large percentage of Kenya's elite is composed of Gikuyu has caused resentment among other ethnic groups. That development may well have sharpened these young peoples' awareness of their Gikuyu identity.[14]

What then will be the role of ethnicity in Kenyan society for the next generation? Clearly we must not undervalue the fact that the daily lives of this young generation have existed in a multicultural context and will continue to do so as they enter the urban workforce. This generation can expect to be taking jobs far from home where they will continue to have contact across ethnic lines, much as they did in their boarding schools and at university. In time this contact will invariably lead to an increasing incidence of multiethnic friendships and marriages. Neal Sobania suggested that under these circumstances a shift had taken place, "away from kinship and ethnic groups and to the nuclear family."[15] According to this new pattern, parents and their children are being guided less by their ethnic heritage and more by their interpretation of the society in which they now live. Perhaps it can be said more accurately that such identities are taking place on a continuum. At one end, in the ethnic heartlands of the country like Central Province for the Gikuyu, language, culture, friendship, and marriage are more driven by kinship and ethnicity. But increasingly, young people in these heartlands are seeking out educational and employment opportunities elsewhere in Kenya, as was the pattern for my students and now especially for their children. In these cases, moving across the continuum, kinship and ethnicity come to play a lesser role in their everyday lives and the perspectives they hold more generally about society.

But this multicultural society is not likely to fully develop until the ethnic dimensions of Kenyan politics diminish. This element of Kenyan life was visible in my conversations with my students and their friends. Though sometimes guarded in their comments, all spoke of their longing for the return of a Gikuyu president after the death in 1978 of Jomo Kenyatta. It did not matter whether they lived in the rural Gikuyu heartland or the cosmopolitan and multiethnic cities of Kenya, all my students thought that a Gikuyu would do a better job than the Kalenjin president, Daniel arap Moi. Some even suggested that a Gikuyu should perpetually be president in recognition, according to their point of view, of the definitive role that Gikuyu played in liberating the country from British colonial rule through the Mau Mau Rebellion.

Finally, the younger generation does not seem to put as much value on the family as their parents have done. Whereas their parents married shortly after finishing their educations and began families quickly thereafter, their children expressed some ambivalence about following this pattern. Some of the young women I interviewed were cautious about marriage because they first wanted to pursue a career. Unlike their mothers' generation, which had only three career choices—teaching, nursing, or secretarial work—these young women saw every career area open to them. They wanted to live an independent life and have their own money. A daughter said to me, "I've got too much to do to think about marriage now." She had her career sights set on being a counselor, "to help others with their inner turmoils."[16] Another young woman wanted to open a clinic in Nairobi to treat mental problems suffered by children, and she was making plans for graduate study in psychology. But she also said that marriage did not appeal to her, that she thought marriage would make her sad.[17] She would consider having a child at some time in the future but would not marry the father.

The fact that marriage would not be a happy state of affairs was either stated or implied by each young woman I interviewed. Even the two high school students said that they would maybe have a child but would certainly not marry the father, because men were irresponsible.[18] Esther, a friend to several of my students' grown children, had actually implemented the plan that the high school students were contemplating. After finishing a university degree in accounting, she had built a solid career by working for a succession of large companies in Kenya and eventually landed a high position with the United Nations Africa Office in Nairobi. She told me that though she was not keen on marriage, she had three children by the same man but had not married him. They had all lived together as a family for several periods of time in the past, but she had not pursued marriage with him because he was not a responsible person in her estimation. Esther admitted that being a single mother was difficult for her and her children, who were sometimes harassed at school by their peers "for not having a father."[19] But to her such difficulties were more bearable than a bad marriage.

It was nearly impossible to assess the marriages of my former students. I caught glimpses of family life during interviews with family members, and I did get to know a few of these students and their families well, but those were the exceptions. Most of my interviews took place only with the student and many were held away from the home. For this majority I had only their self-reports about marriage.[20] From this limited knowledge, it was difficult to fully explain why their grown children had little interest in marriage. Esther told me that there were many unhappy marriages in Kenya in spite of the low divorce rate, which she attributed to peoples' fear of what others would think if they divorced. Several parents did confide to me that they worried about their daughters' future marriage. They implied that there were many men who would not make good husbands. One mother said that the only suitable husband for her daughter was a practicing Christian, though she acknowledged that being a good Christian might not guarantee that one would also be a good husband.[21] Another mother related a strategy that she had heard about that called for betrothing one's daughter to a likely partner when both were still children. Then the families would train the children to be good partners, perhaps a decade or more before they married.[22] Such an extreme strategy may have indicated the poor state of many Kenyan marriages (or at least peoples' perceptions of such) and that married couples would try anything to protect their children from bad marriages. Perhaps the children who stated that they had no interest in marriage were simply implementing their own strategy to avoid a bad marriage.

Much of this talk about having little interest in marriage might also reflect the greater interest of these young women in career development, further education, professional employment, and a desire for autonomy at this point in their lives. With such issues on their minds, they might more accurately be delaying marriage and family rather than abandoning them. They rightly understand that their educations at elite institutions would qualify them for good jobs, and this, together with the professional connections of their parents and the safety net they provided, would enable these young women to set aside the economic necessity of marrying in ways that their mothers and grandmothers were not able to. The next generation may also feel that they need time to consider the new parameters of married life; they anticipate that it will contain much uncharted territory.

I caught a glimpse of the dynamics of this new territory when I sold my car to a young couple at the end of my research period in Kenya. They were representative of the next generation in age, education, and economic independence. They were also Gikuyu. I noticed right away that each took an equal part in the negotiations over price. When it appeared that they would not be able to pay what I wanted for the car, they both stepped out of the room to confer; this took some time and I could occasionally hear raised voices. Finally the husband returned and then the wife, with more of her money, to close the deal. In the conversation afterward, they revealed that the plan had been to each contribute an equal amount toward the purchase price and then share the car fifty-fifty. But when they were unable to meet my price through equal contributions (the husband had run out of money), the wife paid the greater share and negotiated the new understanding that she would have greater use of the car for work, something that her husband had wanted for himself.

Clearly a significant change has taken place among the young regarding marriage. This change is related to the growing economic independence and functional autonomy that women have achieved in recent decades, largely through education. Though the wives of my students were all educated themselves, generally it was not to the same degree as their husbands, and it was their husbands and not they who achieved the higher positions in the private sector or government. That discrepancy in education and the attendant dependence on one's husband is less likely to happen in the next generation because parents have taken great pride in educating their sons and daughters equally. The ideal family size, now expressed as two sons and two daughters, represents a significant reduction from the previous generation and has contributed to the goal of equal education for all children. Generally this means that many of my students' children received or expected to receive a university education. Such educations may well enable women to compete as the financial equals of their husbands. For Esther, her economic independence enabled her to go much further, and she decided not to marry the father of her children at all. My research does not reveal other cases such as Esther's, although several previously mentioned daughters forecast that while they might well choose to have a child, it would not necessarily mean they would marry the father. This attitude toward delaying or even a reluctance to marry at all may not have resulted from a disagreeable relationship with their fathers or even from acrimony they observed between their parents. They may simply have realized that they did not want to duplicate the lives of their mothers, whom they assessed as not being the financial and interpersonal equals of their fathers.

The attitude of these young women toward marriage can also be interpreted against the wider backdrop of Kenyan women of all classes striving for greater financial independence from their husbands than in the past. Sobania stated that women who work outside the home are increasingly doing so to support themselves and their children, too, rather than expecting their husbands to do so. They want to be known and honored by the community for their contributions to society as writers, scholars, soldiers, journalists, etc. and not just as wives or even as mothers.[23] The daughters of my students appeared to reflect this perspective on their lives as well.

Preserving the Next Generation

My students not only had a head start over many other Kenyans in their education, with its attendant career development and wealth accumulation, but they also passed on this advantage to their children. The majority of them have also been residents of Central Province or Nairobi, the most privileged district. The education expert Fantu Cheru described the elite Nairobi schools with their foreign teachers in this way: "In the city of Nairobi, non-citizens make up 83 percent of the qualified teachers in unaided schools. This is an indication that a high proportion of the private elite schools are concentrated in Nairobi."[24] No rural, spartan day-school education like their fathers experienced for these children! And if my students lived in a less-privileged district in Kenya, where education was deemed inadequate, they sent their children to elite schools in Nairobi with high pass rates and close access to the university and to good careers. It is interesting to note that none of the students sent their children to Giakanja for their secondary education. Though in the past it never compared with the elite schools of Central Province or Nairobi, it was still considered a good school in the area, and in less privileged districts, its facilities and teaching staff would be considered excellent. But now in its decline, when parents have the option of sending their children to the best schools in the country as many of my students do, then those children of parents without that financial capability are marginalized to schools like Giakanja and many that are much worse.

My students were well aware of how their privileged position would help build bright futures for their children. When asked about what the future held for them, they focused on the economic strategies that would enhance the future well-being of their children. A generation ago, their own parents encouraged them to study hard at school so that they could pass their exams and complete a secondary school education. The parents and children sacrificed to pay the school fees to achieve that end. In the 1960s and 1970s most of Kenya's secondary school graduates were rewarded for their achievement with white-collar jobs in the expanding civil service and private sector. Those students with additional professional certificates or university degrees entered the white-collar workforce at higher levels, although every one of these students secured excellent wage-paying employment.

The employment landscape had changed for their children. Nahashan succinctly captured the difference when he told me: "My children will have a harder time than me in making their living. There are no white-collar jobs in government or the private sector."[25] But as bleak as this sounded, it did not mean that the next generation could not earn a living. Just as the previous generation had set a course for their children to follow with their education, these students have a strategy that could bring success to their children, too. One part of this strategy was for their children to have the best education available in Kenya and abroad. Whereas only about 50 percent of my students earned postsecondary diplomas or degrees themselves, almost all of their children have earned university degrees, some at the master's level.[26] With such education and their parents' influence, some children would secure employment in the remaining white-collar jobs available, especially in professional and technical fields. But for most of the younger generation, it would not be public- or private-sector employment but, rather, self-employment that would be the focus of their careers.

Owning one's own business was not new to Gikuyu. White-collar employment had not been available to these students' parents either, because in the colonial era that type of work had been reserved for Europeans and Indians. As a result, Gikuyu had become entrepreneurs. Some of my students told of fathers who owned butcheries or transport companies or were builders and suppliers or shopkeepers. The row of shops adjacent to Giakanja School were all owned and operated by local people. In reference to this entrepreneurial activity, I recall hearing white settlers in the area call Gikuyu the Jews of East Africa. However, all but a few of my students had eschewed going into business when public- and private-sector white-collar jobs were plentiful. Now with that avenue of employment mostly unavailable to their children, self-employment again became an attractive alternative. This process had already begun. For instance, when Stanley retired from a thirty-year career, he invested his lump-sum retirement check to purchase a shop at Gachatha, a rural community outside of Nyeri where he lived. He also purchased a van, which he will use as a *matatu*, a rural taxi, to transport people to and from Nyeri. His wife and four sons, all of whom had finished secondary school, were partners in the business. When I spoke to him, both businesses were doing well.[27] Richard, who had spent his life selling insurance in Nairobi, now had his own agency. He had absorbed his oldest son into the business and planned to do the same with his other children after each had finished their university education.[28]

Wilson explained to me that self-employment should not be considered second-best to working for government or a private company. He had worked as a civil servant for the first fifteen years after leaving Giakanja. Since then he had slowly built up a successful transport business in Nyeri. He started on a small scale, first with a second-hand parts store, and then he added a truck to transport his parts. Ten years later, as I sat in his office hearing an account of his life, he told me that he had become quite successful and had been able to send his seven children to good schools. The two oldest were presently receiving their university education in the United States. Wilson told me that Kenya was passing through a transition: "We are shifting from that regimen of thinking that one can only make some money if he fights and joins for the jobs. [Now] it's the informal sector that is absorbing most of the employable people." He went on to tell me that the informal sector involves agriculture as it always has but much more. "Now an educated person can be a better farmer, even a livestock farmer, or he can be a better mechanic, and especially a small retail trader. . . . Most of the small businesses are now being run by educated people."[29] Wilson said that he raised his children to understand that they should expect to make their living through self-employment. The two who are at U.S. universities would be absorbed into his transport business upon their return; when the others were finished with their education, they might seek their own self-employment or be put into family businesses that would develop in the future.

Erastus and his wife undertook the most ambitious family business venture. When his retirement from banking was still several years away, they began to grow flowers on the land around their Ngong home for export. With just a couple of employees they had slowly developed about ten acres of land, on which they experimented in growing a number of flowers, especially carnations, which each morning would be cut, graded, and driven to the Nairobi airport for overnight shipment to Europe. Having mastered this business on a small scale, they expanded with the purchase of land in the Rift Valley for growing roses, the most difficult, but also the most profitable, segment of the flower business. The conditions for growing and harvesting roses must be carefully controlled or the flowers will not meet the high grading standards of the Amsterdam Auction, their sales destination. A great deal more capital is necessary to grow roses since they must be raised inside protective plastic "green houses." But roses command a high price and so there is the promise of great profit. Erastus told me that since his sons have between them an MBA and a law degree, they are likely to play important roles in the business. His two daughters, though still teenagers in high school, may enter the business with their spouses at sometime in the future as well.[30]

While a few of my students have actually launched their family businesses, most of them are still talking about it as a future venture. Most have not yet retired from their careers and their children have not yet finished their educations. But as each example above makes clear, developing a family business could become a reality because they have the resources to make it possible. For instance, many have invested in land both in Nyeri and elsewhere in the country. Some land would be suitable for farming; other land would be used for rental housing or as an asset to secure business loans or sold outright for capital. Many also bring such expertise as accounting, marketing, and computer-based skills to their businesses, as well as a network of contacts. Several also said that there was much they could learn about business from Asians who have been entrepreneurs in Kenya since the beginning of the twentieth century. "We are now going Asian," as one of them told me. He meant that just as Asian business owners were known for their good management with everyone in the family pulling together and pooling their talents for success, Gikuyu should start small, keeping the business in the family and training family members for new areas of responsibility as the need arises.[31]

While almost everyone expressed interest in starting a family business as a way to secure their children's future in a time when little employment was available, some raised questions about whether such ventures could be successful.[32] Would their children have the discipline to learn to make good decisions? Would they be able to postpone their material gratification so that the businesses would grow? And most fundamentally, even if they were up to the task of being adept business people, could the Kenyan economy support a nation of small businesses? If everyone were selling goods and services, would there be sufficient buyers?

Finally, not all of my students had sufficient resources to establish a family business that could support their children. Several told me stories similar to that of Stephen. He recently retired to his small farm after a career as a low-level civil servant. He and his wife raise their own food and sell the tea they harvest from their small plot for cash. Though they did not have much, Stephen told me that he and his wife would be confident about their financial future if it were not for the fact that none of their eight grown children had a job. He and his wife may have to support their children on their small farm, and they are fearful that the resources may not be sufficient for them to do so.[33]

But having raised some caution in predicting a positive future for their children, most of my students remain confident about themselves and their children's future, and I do not think that such confidence is misplaced. As the first generation to reach adulthood in postcolonial Kenya, they have been perfectly placed to attain the best jobs, achieve the highest promotions, and earn the best salaries. During their childhood of poverty in the late colonial era, they were forced to grow up fast, to learn self-discipline and the merits of hard work and patience; these have been just the right attributes to successfully manage their new wealth and financial power. While few of these students have earned fortunes, most of them have attained significant economic resources, and a few of them even occupy the top rungs of Kenya's economic ladder.

As previous chapters have revealed, the decade following Kenya's independence, to which my students and the cohort of elites belonged, were exceptional times no longer present for the next generation. The exception to this reversal of circumstance was the group composed of children of the elite. Unlike most of their contemporaries, these children nurtured in the English language from a young age have had the door opened for them to the best schools, from primary on up to university level, including those abroad. Such schools with their challenging curricula have provided not only a superior education but also given them a maturity and confidence that will enable them to compete well for the few professional positions now available in Kenya. Their parents' guidance and resources also make self-employment a realistic venture for them. The exceptional times now ended for most of their generation still remain available to them. They have inherited an elite status from their parents and this position will be sufficient to shield and protect them from the economic uncertainty of present times. The poverty and hardship experienced by my students during their childhoods, and now present for many in Kenya, will not befall their families in the next generation.

When I began this research project into my former students' lives, I wondered what had become of them and how their lives had been shaped by education. Some have argued that "these new elites have used their education as a means of political domination. . . . These elites make sure that their power is never threatened because they deny the poor the necessary knowledge . . . to advance society."[34] Others criticize African elites for succumbing to the influence of Western cultural imperialism. According to one scholar, "Africans are narcotized with Western values and norms . . . , transformed into western beings" through the socializing process of acquiring their education.[35] Both portray African elites as disempowered pawns caught in the machinations of the West, bereft of direction and goals and having no will of their own. The primary critique of these ideas is that in seeking to include the entire continent in their analysis, such a broad field of inquiry often leads to lack of depth. As one reviewer stated, "Lack of scope and contextualization leads to problematic over-generalization."[36]

The cure for overgeneralization is a more detailed scholarship that recognizes the complexity of African experience. The narrative and analysis of my former students' lives has been my attempt to provide a window into the patterns and nuances of their lives, especially what has transpired as a result of their education. In so doing we have explored their perseverance as young boys over the hardships of Mau Mau and their struggles to become educated, the culmination of which led to a CSC and its companion eligibility to higher education for some and to professional careers for all. As young men at Giakanja, they came to understand for themselves the link between a Western-style education and a successful future, a concept first introduced to them by their parents. In their adult lives, we have explored their career development and financial growth, their marriage and family life, and ultimately their concerns for securing a bright future for their children. What I found and what has moved me throughout this study is the profound understanding of the breadth and depth of the individuality of their lives and how together they have formed Kenya's first postcolonial elite.

Appendix

Cohort Profiles

The profiles below represent approximately 10 percent of my former students. I have included them to reveal how their life patterns bear much similarity and yet are noticeably different, each life with its own trajectory.

David e (b. 1947): born in Rift Valley, the oldest son of uneducated parents (father b. 1922, mother b. 1924) who worked as squatters on white-settler farm. David's mother first of father's six wives (marriages: 1945, 1946, 1948, 1956, 1964, 1970). This mother detained; father, wives and children repatriated to Central Province and housed in Emergency village near Giakanja. Began primary education during Emergency, finished 1962, and admitted to Giakanja class II 1963–66. Finished second in class (Div. I CSC 1966). A level completed at Kenyatta College, then started career at a national bank; left after one year to join East African Railways because they offered a computer training course in Great Britain. Remained at East African Railways (Kenya R.R. after 1977) as principle systems analyst until 1980, when he shifted to British American Tobacco in the private sector for higher wages and better benefits. Took early retirement in 1994 to farm in the Rift Valley with father and siblings on land that they had previously worked as squatters. Married 1970 (three sons, two daughters), all receiving education (two with university degrees, rest still in school). Investment in Rift Valley land on which he plans to build a large dairy business will enable him to educate his children to university level and enjoy a comfortable lifestyle.

Dickson (b. 1947): primary-school-educated father (b. 1908, d. 1966) and uneducated mother (b. 1920), who was first of four wives, had six children (four girls, two boys), all educated (one Std. 8, one Form 2, two Form 4, one university). Family was exempt from being forced to Emergency village because father was

147

headman of local community. Did very well on Std. 4 and 8 leaving exams, was admitted to Giakanja class II 1963–66 (Div. I CSC 1966). Attended A level at a national school, then at Makerere University 1969–72, earning a BEd (English, history, education). Taught at three teacher training colleges, rising to position of principle lecturer at Kagumo College in his home area. Married musician/music teacher in 1978; four children (three boys, one girl) all presently in school (kindergarten through Form 4). His plans are for each to receive university education. Will retire at age 55 with government pension and income from rents on buildings he owns.

Esau (b. 1942): parents with no education (father b. 1906, mother b. 1910), who married in 1928; his mother was his father's second of three wives. Father worked in the Rift Valley as a migrant laborer. Esau and twin sister (d. 1987) had five other siblings (four brothers, one sister); the oldest two brothers went to the forest in 1952, later surrendered and were detained for rest of Emergency. Esau and rest of family forced into Emergency village, where his education, begun in 1950, stopped. Mother and children were destitute, and his loyalist relatives neglected them and would not pay his school fees. Resumed education in 1959, his older employed brother paid fees. Finished elementary school in 1963 as twenty-one-year-old and admitted to class III at Giakanja, 1964–67 (Div. III CSC 1967). Went to teacher training college and has worked as teacher and later headmaster in various schools in Nyeri town and area. Married nurse in 1974; four children (three boys, one girl), the first girl and boy are twins. All are being educated: the oldest are at university and the youngest still in secondary school. Esau identifies himself as a Christian and became a licensed clergyman in 1987, assisting part-time in area churches while continuing as an employed educator.

Frederick (b. 1945): primary-school-educated parents (father b. 1905, mother b. 1915). Married 1932, seven children (six survived: four girls, two boys). Frederick, second youngest and most educated (4 Std. 8, 1 O level, 1 A level). Family moved to Emergency village, where sister died and parents forced to help dig fifty-mile security trench around Aberdare Mountains. After Emergency, repeated Std. 8 leaving exam twice to improve score; admitted to Giakanja class II, 1963–66 (Div. II CSC 1966). Completed A level; employed after completing technology course by SOK, 1969–81; partner in private survey firm, 1981–91; has own business since 1991. Married in 1970 to woman whose parents were killed during Mau Mau; four children (three boys, one girl), oldest are educated and working, youngest still in school. Wife died of cancer in 1992; Frederick raising youngest two children.

James b (b. 1945): Parents (father b. 1914, mother b. 1921) educated at Church of Scotland Mission. Father became a primary school teacher. Married in the

Church in 1943 and have been parents to eight children (seven survived: five girls, two boys), all but one educated through secondary school (two at Form 6). They are church elders. James attended primary and intermediate schools of the Presbyterian Church of East Africa and was admitted to Giakanja's class II, 1963–66 (Div. II CSC 1966). Has spent entire career as a government civil servant: Office of the President, 1967–75; National Assembly, 1975–81; Ministry of Education, 1981–89; and Ministry of Tourism and Wildlife, 1989–96. Married in a church wedding in 1972 to woman educated to Form 4; have been active in the Church ever since. Parents to four children (three boys, one girl) born 1971–81. All are educated and working. James credits the investment conscious-ness of his parents as the impetus for his own investments, which include his own house (paid for with government housing allowance), another house and commercial property (which he rents out), undeveloped plots near Nairobi, and agricultural land in the Rift Valley, Mweiga, and near Giakanja inherited from his father.

Richard c (b. 1946): uneducated parents (father b. ca. 1900, d. 1950; mother b. ca. 1900, d. 1982) married 1920, eight children (five girls, three boys). In 1930s, parents joined Gikuyu independent church and sent all children to indepen-dent schools, except Richard, who started school after independent schools were closed by government in 1952. When Senior Chief Nderi was murdered by Mau Mau, many people left community for forest to begin rebellion. But brother (b. 1930) joined Home Guard to protect family since father was dead. Richard started at Home Guard–protected school in 1956, passed leaving exams, and admitted to Giakanja class III, 1964–67 (Div. III CSC 1967). Joined insurance company in 1968; over the years shifted to other insurance companies to learn the business and in 1990 opened own agency. Married 1978, parents to five children (one boy, four girls), all in school. Richard's goal is to educate all to university level, either in Kenya or abroad.

Simon (b. 1947): primary-school-educated parents (father b. 1915, mother b. 1924). Father became primary school teacher and eventually headmaster; was detained 1952–60. Maternal grandfather became Home Guard to protect his daughter and grandchildren. Simon did exceptionally well in his Std. 4 and 8 leaving exams, scoring highest in his school, but failed to get a place in secondary school because his father had been detained. Was admitted to Giakanja only after grandfather spoke to provincial education official about Simon's high test scores. Joined class I, 1962–65 (Div. I CSC 1965). When Simon was admitted to a national school for A level, life was made tough for him again (by the European headmaster) because of father's detention. After completing A levels, he went to University of Nairobi, graduating in 1971. Since then, he has been a civil servant, posted for ten years to rural areas, where he worked in district and provincial administration, receiving regular promotions to provincial commissioner level.

Posted to Nairobi in 1981, he married and has occupied increasingly responsible positions in the Ministry of Health and Ministry of Finance, rising eventually to be an undersecretary in the Treasury Department, a senior position in the civil service that only one other Giakanja student has achieved.

Titus (b. 1945): the oldest of his father (b. 1925) and mother's (b. 1925) eight children. Parents with only basic literacy, but seven of the eight children were educated (one to Std. 5, six to Form 4), with Titus paying school fees for last five siblings and helping all get jobs in 1970s. Father was detained 1954–56, and together with whole community had to pay fine for Mau Mau murder of Senior Chief Nderi. Father married second wife in 1964 (two more children), one year before Titus finished secondary school at Giakanja (Div. II CSC 1965). Titus's first job was teaching in a private school before he was admitted to Kenyatta Teacher Training College, which he left after one term to join local branch of a national bank as a clerk in 1966. For next thirty years, he worked in many branches, steadily rising in rank, and completed a diploma in banking in 1980. By 1996 he occupied a senior position at the bank's Nairobi headquarters. Titus is married with six children (three boys, three girls), all of whom are educated (two A level, two university, two in primary). Titus owns his house in a Nairobi housing estate and a second one, in which his oldest son lives; some rural land, where he has cows and some coffee; and a small plot in Nyeri town.

Notes

Preface

1. John Iliffe, *Africans: The History of a Continent*, 2nd ed. (Cambridge: Cambridge University Press, 2007), 251.

2. Grace Bunyi, "Constructing Elites in Kenya: Implications for Classroom Language Practices in Africa," in *Discourse and Education*, 2nd ed., Encyclopedia of Language and Education 3, edited by Marilyn Martin-Jones, Anne-Marie De Mejía, and Nancy H. Hornberger (New York: Springer, 2008), 147.

3. Magnus O. Bassey, "Higher Education and the Rise of Early Political Elites in Africa," *Review of Higher Education in Africa* 1, no. 1 (2009): 31–32.

4. Ibid., 31.

Introduction

1. My memory has been aided by the following document: "Orientation Course—T.E.A. Wave III: August 1963, Royal College, Nairobi," Ed/2/18319, KNA.

2. I never kept a journal during my time at Giakanja, a circumstance for which I now have much regret. As a result, though I had many conversations with students as I have described, I can recall few details.

3. All of these provisions are set out in the contract that I signed upon arrival in Nairobi. "TEA Postings," Ed/2/17617, KNA. My 1963 group was not required to sign the Official Secrets Act nor pass a Kiswahili language exam, as earlier TEA groups had done. Ed/2/7409, KNA.

4. Heidi Gengenbach, "Truth-Telling and the Politics of Women's Life History Research in Africa: A Reply to Kirk Hoppe," *International Journal of African Historical Studies* 27, no. 3 (1994): 624.

5. Jean Davison, *Voices from Mutira: Change in the Lives of Rural Gikuyu Women, 1910–1995*, 2nd ed. (Boulder, Colo.: Lynne Rienner, 1996); Leonard Plotnicov, *Strangers to the City: Urban Man in Jos, Nigeria* (Pittsburgh: University of Pittsburgh Press, 1967). Of those not interviewed, two were known to have died, one lived abroad, another was mentally ill, several others lived in inaccessible parts of the country, and the remainder I simply could not locate.

6. I wish to thank an anonymous reviewer of my manuscript for this phrase.

7. Leroy Vail and Landeg White, *Power and the Praise Poem: Southern African Voices in History* (London: James Curry, 1991), 222–27.

8. Elizabeth Tonkin, *Narrating Our Pasts: The Social Construction of Oral History* (Cambridge: Cambridge University Press, 1993), 3.

9. Lawrence Stone, "Prosopography," *Daedalus* 100, no. 1 (Winter 1971): 46.

10. K. S. B. Keats-Rohan, "Prosopography and Computing: A Marriage Made in Heaven?" *History and Computing* 12, no. 1 (2000): 2.

11. K. S. B. Keats-Rohan, "Biography, Identity and Names: Understanding the Pursuit of the Individual in Prosopography," in *Prosopography Approaches and Applications: A Handbook*, edited by K. S. B. Keats-Rohan (Oxford: University of Oxford, 2007), 143–44, http://prosopography.modhist.ox.ac.uk/images/06%20 KKR.pdf.pdf. For a list of works on prosopography, see "Select Bibliography of Works Relating to Prosopography," Modern History Research Unit, University of Oxford, http://prosopography.modhist.ox.ac.uk/bibliography.htm.

12. Susan Geiger, "Tanganyikan Nationalism as 'Women's Work': Life Histories, Collective Biography and Changing Historiography," *Journal of African History* 37 (1996): 465–78; ibid., 477.

Chapter 1. Late Colonial Childhoods

1. Captain F. D. Lugard, *The Rise of our East African Empire: Early Efforts in Nyasaland and Uganda*, vol. 1 (Edinburgh: Blackwood, 1893), 327.

2. There are a number of accounts of colonial rule in Kenya; perhaps the best is Bruce Berman and John Lonsdale, *Unhappy Valley: Conflict in Kenya & Africa*, book 2, *Violence & Ethnicity* (London: James Currey, 1992).

3. Bruce Berman, *Control and Crisis in Colonial Kenya: The Dialectic of Domination* (London: James Currey, 1990), 56–60.

4. Gavin Kitching, *Class and Economic Change in Kenya: The Making of an African Petite Bourgeoisie* (New Haven, Conn.: Yale University Press, 1980), chap. 6.

5. Interview, Peter a, Nairobi, 13 February 1996.

6. Interview, Jacob, Nairobi, 21 February 1996.

7. David Sandgren, *Christianity and the Kikuyu: Religious Divisions and Social Conflict* (New York: Peter Lang, 2000), chap. 2.

8. J. E. Otiende, S. P. Wamahiu, and A. M. Karugu, *Education and Development in Kenya: A Historical Perspective* (Nairobi: Oxford University Press, 1992), 46.

9. John Anderson, *The Struggle for the School* (London: Longmans, 1970), 136.

10. Ibid., 138.

11. Sandgren, *Christianity and the Kĩkuyu*, chap. 2.

12. A very readable synthesis of this interpretation can be found in Wunyabari O. Maloba, *Mau Mau and Kenya: An Analysis of a Peasant Revolt* (Oxford: James Currey, 1998).

13. John Lonsdale, "The Moral Economy of Mau Mau: Wealth, Poverty and Civic Virtue in Kikuyu Political Thought," in Bruce Berman and John Lonsdale, *Unhappy Valley*, book 2, *Violence & Ethnicity* (Oxford: James Currey, 1992), 265–504, esp. 461–68.

14. Ibid., 462.

15. Greet Kershaw, *Mau Mau from Below* (Oxford: James Currey, 1997), 227, 324.

16. Derek Peterson, *Creative Writing: Translation, Bookkeeping, and the Work of Imagination in Colonial Kenya* (Portsmouth, N.H.: Heinemann Books, 2004).

17. Ibid., 191–93.

18. Ibid., 197.

19. Ibid., 209–11.

20. Daniel Branch, *Defeating Mau Mau, Creating Kenya: Counterinsurgency, Civil War, and Decolonization* (New York: Cambridge University Press, 2009).

21. For example, see Derek Peterson's review in *The Journal of Imperial and Commonwealth History* 38, no. 2 (2000): 337–39.

22. Interview, Alexander, Nairobi, 17 November 1995.

23. The most likely date for this event was 26 July 1952, when Kenyatta spoke at Nyeri. E. Mutonya, "Mau Mau chairman," unpublished manuscript, n.d., seen at the KNA, Nairobi. For a text of the speech see Government of Great Britain, *Historical Survey of the Origins and Growth of Mau Mau* [Corfield Report], Cmnd. 1030, London, 1960, Appendix F.

24. Jomo Kenyatta, *Facing Mount Kenya* (London: Secker and Warburg, 1938).

25. Interview, James, Nairobi, 30 January 1996.

26. Interviews, Francis a, Nairobi, 22 February 1996; Peter b, Nyeri, 26 February 1996.

27. The total number of repatriates was estimated to be 100,000. Tabitha Kanogo, *Squatters and the Roots of Mau Mau, 1904–1963* (London: James Currey, 1987), 138.

28. Interviews, Peter a, Nairobi, 13 February 1996; David a, Njoro, 15 February 1996.

29. Interview, David a, Njoro, 15 February 1996.

30. Interview, Joseph a, Mombasa, 12 April 1996.

31. Interview, Erastus, Nairobi, 5 December 1995.

32. Caroline Elkins, *Imperial Reckoning: The Untold Story of Britain's Gulag in*

Kenya (New York: Henry Holt and Co., 2005). I have consulted Elkins's publication, esp. chap. 6, for my information on detention camps.

33. For a succinct discussion of Mau Mau oaths, see Maloba, *Mau Mau and Kenya*, 102–7. Maloba stated that Mau Mau oaths can be divided into three types, the first of which was widely administered to Gikuyu as an oath of unity. The second and third types were generally given to forest fighters. For an example of the unity oath, see Donald L. Barnett and Karari Njama, *Mau Mau from Within: Autobiography and Analysis of Kenya's Peasant Revolt* (New York: Modern Reader, 1966), 118–9.

34. Interview, Jacob, Nairobi, 21 February 1996.

35. Elkins, *Imperial Reckoning*, 235.

36. C. D. Monthly Report, 6 December 1955, CD/AB/1/8/32, KNA.

37. C. D. Monthly Report, August 1955, CD/AB/15/61, KNA.

38. C. D. Monthly Report, December 1955, CD/AB/4/74, KNA.

39. Elkins, *Imperial Reckoning*, 244.

40. Interview, David a, Njoro, 15 February 1996.

41. Interview, Newton, Nyeri, 21 March 1996.

42. Evelyn Baring, Governor, Colony and Protectorate of Kenya, "The Closure of Independent Schools," 14 November 1952, MAC/KEN/35/4, KNA.

43. Advisory Committee on Education in Colonies, Kenya Independent Schools, 8 March 1940, Arthur Creech Jones Papers, Mss. Brit. Emp. s. 332, Box 37/2, RH.

44. Interviews, Daniel, Nyeri, 4 March 1996; Richard c, Nairobi, 14 March 1996; Douglas, Nyeri, 21 March 1996.

45. Nyeri District Annual Report 1952, PC/CP/VQ/16/89, KNA.

46. Care-Takers Association for African Closed Schools to Governor of Kenya, 12 February 1953, MAC/KEN/35/3, KNA.

47. "Annual Appeal to the Public by Parents of Children in Closed Schools," n.d., Care-Takers Association for African Closed Schools, 1953, MAC/KEN/35/3, KNA.

48. Nyeri District Annual Report 1952, PC/CP/VQ/16/89, KNA.

49. Interviews, Jesse, Nakuru, 15 February 1996; Duncan, Nyeri, 12 March 1996.

50. Nyeri DEB, 1948–55, Ed/2/13274, KNA.

51. Interviews, Daniel, Nyeri, 4 March 1996; Richard c, Nairobi, 14 March 1996; Douglas, Nyeri, 21 March 1996.

52. H. G. [Home Guard] Posts, Memorandum, n.d., KEM [Kikuyu Embu Meru] Guards, VQ/1/5, Folio 194c, KNA.

53. Interview, Joseph b, Nairobi, 28 February 1996.

54. Interview, Esau, Nyeri, 13 March 1996.

55. *East African Standard*, 18 May 1954.

56. C. D. Report Nyeri District, July 1957, CD/AB/1/4/71, KNA.

57. Interviews, Joseph c, Nairobi, 16 and 21 November 1995; Alexander, Nairobi, 17 November 1995; Peter a, Nairobi, 13 February 1996.

58. B. E. Kipkorir, "The Alliance High School and Origins of the Elite: 1926–1962" (PhD diss., University of Cambridge, 1969), 331.

59. Interview, Stanley a, Gachatha, 17 March 1996.

60. Interview, James a, Nairobi, 10 November 1995.

61. Interview, Harun, Nairobi, 31 October 1995.

62. Interview, Jonas, Nairobi, 20 February 1996.

63. Interview, Dickson, Gatitu, 12 March 1996.

64. Interview, Joseph c, Nairobi, 16 and 21 November 1995.

65. Interviews, Charles a, Nairobi, 5 April 1996; Joseph c, Nairobi, 16 and 21 November 1995.

66. Interview, Peter a, Nairobi, 13 February 1996.

67. Interview, James a, Nairobi, 10 November 1995.

68. Interview, Wilson b, Wamagana, 11 March 1996.

69. Interview, Joseph a, Mombasa, 12 April 1996. The Batuni or second oath was administered to Mau Mau fighters and directed them to use violence against the enemies of Mau Mau, including loyalists. "Bringing in the head of an enemy" was encouraged; perhaps this accounts for the murdered headmaster's missing head. Barnett and Njama, *Mau Mau from Within*, 131.

70. Interview, David a, Njoro, 15 February 1996.

71. Interview, Nahashan, Nairobi, 14 February 1996.

72. Ibid.

73. Interview, Amos, Nairobi, 21 February 1996.

74. Interview, Jacob, Nairobi, 21 February 1996.

75. Interview, Dickson, Gatitu, 12 March 1996.

76. Interview, Amos, Nairobi, 21 February 1996.

77. Interview, Joseph c, Nairobi, 16 and 21 November 1995.

78. Interview, Dickson, Gatitu, 12 March 1996.

79. Interview, Michael b, Nairobi, 17 November 1995.

80. Interview, James a, Nairobi, 10 November 1995.

81. Ngugi wa Thiong'o's novel *A Grain of Wheat* contains a vivid passage of such required meetings. *A Grain of Wheat*, rev. ed. (New York: Heinemann, 1986), 118–21.

82. J. M. Kariuki reported in his memoir that, upon returning home from detention at this time, "the bitter antagonism between loyalists and detainees" might even have led to violence. *Mau Mau Detainee* (London: Oxford University Press, 1963), 148.

83. Elkins, *Imperial Reckoning*, 270.

Chapter 2. Entering Secondary Education

1. O. W. Furley and T. Watson, *A History of Education in East Africa* (London: Nok Publications, 1977), 246–50.

2. *Harambee* is a Swahili word meaning "self-help."

3. J. E. Anderson, "The Kenya Education Commission Report: An African

View of Educational Planning," *Comparative Education Review* 19, no. 2 (1965): 205–6.

4. Jerry B. Olson, "Secondary Schools and Elites in Kenya: A Comparison Study of Students in 1961 and 1968," *Comparative Education Review* 16, no. 1 (1972): 46–47.

5. For example, see Kenneth King, "Development and Education in Narok District of Kenya: The Pastoral Maasai and Their Neighbors," *African Affairs* 71, no. 285 (1972): 394. King's research reveals that primary school places were often filled by other ethnic groups. I remember hearing from a TEA colleague who taught in Narok Secondary School that there were always at least some Gikuyu in his classes.

6. David Court, "The Education System as a Response to Inequality in Tanzania and Kenya," *Journal of Modern African Studies* 14, no. 4 (1976): 661–90. Several other scholars have written on the Harambee Movement: see especially John Anderson, "Self Help and Independency: The Political Implications of a Continuing Tradition in African Education in Kenya," *African Affairs* 70, no. 278 (1971); Kilemi Mwiria, "Kenya's Harambee Secondary School Movement: The Contradictions of Public Policy," *Comparative Education Review* 34, no. 3 (1990): 350–68; and Edmond J. Keller, "Development Policy and the Evaluation of Community Self-Help: The Harambee School Movement in Kenya," *Studies in Comparative International Development* 18, no. 4 (1983): 57.

7. Court, "The Education System as a Response to Inequality," 680–81.

8. Mwiria, "Kenya's Harambee Secondary Schools Movement," 355.

9. Keller, "Development Policy and the Evaluation of Self-Help," 61–63.

10. Ibid., 63.

11. According to Keller, 84 percent of all Harambee schools were rated D, whereas only 7 percent of government schools received that low score (ibid. 66).

12. Court, "The Education System as a Response to Inequality," 689.

13. Daniel N. Sifuna, "Diversified Secondary Education: A Comparative Survey of Kenya and Tanzania," *Geneve-Afrique* 28, no. 2 (1990): 97–99.

14. Ibid., 102.

15. Nyeri District Annual Report, 1956, DC/Nyeri 1/1, KNA.

16. Nyeri District Annual Report, 1958, DC/Nyeri 1/1, KNA.

17. I have had to extrapolate from 1959 statistics to arrive at this figure. Nyeri District Annual Report, 1959, DC/Nyeri 1/1, KNA.

18. Interviews, Alex, Nairobi, 17 November 1995; Joshua, Nyeri, 25 November 1995; Stanley b, Nyeri, 26 November 1995; David c, Nairobi, 1 December 1995; Peter a, Nairobi, 21 March 1996.

19. Interview, Joseph c, Nairobi, 16 November 1995.

20. Interview, Stanley b, Nyeri, 26 November 1995.

21. Interview, Joseph d, Nairobi, 29 November 1995.

22. Interview, David c, Nairobi, 1 December 1995.

23. Ed/2/17358, KNA.

24. Iliffe, *Africans*, 230.

25. Anderson, *The Struggle for the School*, 118–22; Sandgren, *Christianity and the Kikuyu*, chap. 2.

26. Interview, Beatrice, Nyeri, 22 April 1996.

27. Interview, John a, Nairobi, 4 April 1996.

28. Ibid. He also supported the Tom Mboya airlift to the United States, a scheme to send Kenyans abroad for their university education. In 1960, fifty students from Nyeri District qualified to participate but each had to contribute 1000 shillings. Although a small amount compared with the years of free education abroad, it was beyond the means of every candidate. In desperation, the DO authorized the temporary allocation of 50,000 shillings from the Nyeri African District Council budget to be reimbursed later by free-will contributions from the entire district. Little if anything was ever collected, and his superiors threatened to deduct the amount from his salary. Anderson, *The Struggle for the School*, 140; interview, David f, Kabete, 4 April 1996.

29. Interview, Beatrice, Nyeri, 22 April 1996.

30. Interview, John a, Nairobi, 4 April 1996.

31. Victor H. Skiles, ICA Representative, to R. G. Ngala, Ministry of Education, 3 July 1961, Ed/2/68 "AID Schemes," KNA.

32. P.S. File Minute, 21 July 1961, Ed/2/68 "AID Schemes," KNA.

33. During my tenure at Giakanja, I heard repeated speculation that Giakanja was to have been a boarding school but ultimately the building budget had been halved to build two day schools instead. However, I found no evidence that the U.S. government was ever interested in building a boarding school at Giakanja.

34. Nyeri District Standing Orders, DC/Nyeri 7/2, Minute 119, KNA; interview, Walter, Nyeri, 16 March 1996.

35. Interview, Julius, Giakanja, 9 April 1996.

36. Interview, Walter, Nyeri, 16 March 1996.

37. Ibid.

38. Interview, Julius, Giakanja, 9 April 1996.

39. Ibid.

40. Interview, Samuel a, Nakuru, 2 December 1996.

41. Interview, Stanley b, Nyeri, 26 November 1995.

42. Interview, Johnson, Nyeri, 8 November 1995.

43. Interview, Dickson, Gatitu, 12 March 1996.

44. Interview, Samuel b, Nyeri, 26 November 1995.

45. Ibid.

46. Interview, James a, 10 November 1995.

47. Interview, Samuel b, Nyeri, 26 November 1995.

48. Interview, James a, 10 November 1995.

49. Ibid.

50. Ibid.

51. Interview: Cyrus, Nyeri, 26 February 1996.
52. Frederick Cooper, *Africa since 1940: The Past of the Present* (Cambridge: Cambridge University Press, 2002), 111.
53. Interview, David b, Nairobi, 1 December 1995.

Chapter 3. Confronting the Cambridge Exams

1. Kevin M. Lillis, "Processes of Secondary Curriculum Innovation in Kenya," *Comparative Education Review* 29, no. 1 (1985): 86–87. See "A Colonial Curriculum in Independent Kenya" later in this chapter for comments on how failing to Africanize the curriculum has led to negative outcomes for students.
2. Court, "The Educational System as a Response to Inequality," 682.
3. David Koff and George von der Muhll, "Political Socialization in Kenya and Tanzania—A Comparative Analysis," *Journal of Modern African Studies* 5, no. 1 (1967): 33–35.
4. Ibid., 36–39.
5. Interview, David a, Njoro, 15 February 1996.
6. Interview, Harrison, Nairobi, 17 November 1995.
7. Interview, Kihumba, Nairobi, 19 March 1996.
8. Interviews, David d, Nyeri, 22 November 1995; James b, Nairobi, 30 January 1996; Joseph a, Mombasa, 12 April 1996. Several years later, however, such sensibilities seem to have disappeared when these same students reported that they would have happily gone to the Catholic high school at Nyeri rather than to Giakanja.
9. Interviews, James a, Nairobi, 10 November 1995; Amos, Nairobi, 21 February 1996; Esau, Nyeri, 13 March 1996; James b, Nairobi, 30 January 1996.
10. Interview, Simon, Nairobi, 29 January 1996. Four years later, Simon earned the highest CSCE score in his Giakanja class too.
11. Interview, Stanley a, Gachatha, 17 March 1996.
12. Interview, Cyrus, Nyeri, 26 February 1996.
13. Interview, Joseph c, Nairobi, 21 November 1995.
14. Interview, David c, Nairobi, 1 December 1995.
15. Interview, Stanley a, Gachatha, 17 March 1996.
16. Interview, Samuel a, Nakuru, 2 December 1995. At the end of their second year, Samuel dropped out of secondary school and enrolled in a nearby teacher training college for primary school teachers.
17. Interview, Stanley a, Gachatha, 17 March 1996.
18. Interview, Titus, Nairobi, 31 January 1996.
19. The eight subjects were English language, English literature, religious knowledge, history, geography, mathematics, biology, and physics with chemistry.
20. "Revision" is a British English term for "review."

21. All teachers maintained an archive of past questions and often perused them to identify how frequently certain topics appeared on the exam. I had copies of past exams dating back to 1956.

22. *East African History Notebook*, Peace Corps Project, 1967, introduction, mimeo.

23. E. B. Castle, *Growing Up in East Africa* (London: Oxford University Press, 1966), 219.

24. Ibid.

25. They reasoned that since there was no oral section to the Cambridge English Exam, these speech drills could not be related to exam preparation.

26. Interview, Charles b, Kerugoya, 20 April 1996.

27. Gordon D. Morgan, *Practices, Problems and Issues in East African Education* (Privately printed, 1968), 127.

28. The Kenya Ministry of Education alerted history teachers to this problem in a memo based on student answers to the 1963 Exam by stating: "One of two major weaknesses . . . was not answering the exact question. [The students] fail to do well by going outside the question and supplying all the information he knew on a certain topic regardless of its relevance. His answer may have dealt with the topic concerned but not the actual question itself." *Teaching Techniques and Classroom Activities*, Government of Kenya, 1964, RG 67, B 10, no. 8, Special Collections, Milbank Memorial Library, Teachers College, Columbia University.

29. Morgan, *Practices, Problems and Issues*, 127.

30. Interview, Kihumba, Nairobi, 19 March 1996.

31. Interview, David c, Nairobi, 1 December 1996. Students revealed in their interviews, however, that it took them a whole term to get used to my American accent, during which time they had to "break their ears" to understand me.

32. Interview, Charles b, Kerugoya, 20 April 1996. Another student told me that when he taught for two terms at a Harambee school while waiting to go to university, the school drew a larger number of talented students than usual because they identified the newly arrived Peace Corps volunteer as a superior teacher.

33. The British term *invigilate* is used for the activity of watching over students as they take exams. It was serious business, for as an invigilator I had to sign a document each day testifying that the packet containing the question papers for exams scheduled that day was sealed when it came out of the headmaster's safe, and at the end of each day, that I had sealed and returned the students' answers to the headmaster's safe. Exam questions were to be kept secret until the very moment the exam took place. As an invigilator, it was my responsibility to make sure that this happened. Breaking these rules was a punishable offense under Kenya's criminal code.

34. Interview, Michael a, Nakuru, 3 December 1995.

35. Interview, David c, Nairobi, 1 December 1995.

36. Ibid.

37. Ibid.

38. Only those who passed were listed.

39. Interview, Daniel, Nyeri, 4 March 1996.

40. Ibid.

41. There were three failures in 1965 and 1967 and one in 1966.

42. The headmaster was well acquainted with this established and respected school at Embu, where he had served as a teacher for a decade and was acting headmaster just before he was posted to Giakanja at the beginning of 1964.

43. Interview, Harun, Nairobi, 4 February 1996.

44. Interview, William a, Nairobi, 6 December 1995. Kagumo High School was the school with the most prestige in the area. All Giakanja students would like to have gone there.

45. The national pass rate for 1965, 1966, and 1967 was as follows: 71.9 percent, 74.9 percent, 77.9 percent. *East African Standard*, 15 February 1966, 16 February 1967, 17 February 1968. Giakanja's pass rate for each of these years was 89 percent, 96 percent, and 91 percent.

46. Headmaster Giakanja Secondary School, personal communication, 24 February 1996.

47. Interview, Ephantus, Nyeri, 3 March 1996. The clerk of a county council is the chief executive officer whose job it is to implement the decisions of the elected officials. It is comparable to an American city manager.

48. Less known among his classmates is the accomplishment of Nahashan. He earned a Division III school certificate in 1967 and then took his A level privately, scoring high enough to be admitted to university. After earning his degree, he entered the civil service and rose to senior personnel officer.

49. Interview, Joseph c, Nairobi, 16 November 1995.

Chapter 4. Making a Career

1. H. C. A. Somerset, "Educational Aspirations of Forth-Form Pupils in Kenya," in *Education, Society and Development: New Perspectives from Kenya*, edited by David Court and Dharam P. Ghai (Nairobi: Oxford University Press, 1974), 99.

2. Ibid.

3. Emil R. Rado, "The Relevance of Education for Employment," in *Education, Society and Development: New Perspectives from Kenya*, edited by David Court and Dharam P. Ghai (Nairobi: Oxford University Press, 1974), 37–38.

4. The project tracked the higher education and employment history of 3,179 boys drawn from twenty-two secondary schools in Kenya. Peter Kabiru Kinyanjui, "Education, Training and Employment of Secondary School Leavers in Kenya," *Education in Eastern Africa* 2, no 1 (1971): 3–21.

5. Ibid., 14–18.

6. Ibid., 19–20.

7. Government of Kenya, *High-Level Manpower Requirements and Resources in Kenya, 1964–1970* (Nairobi: Government Printer, 1965), ii–iii.

8. Kinyanjui, "Education, Training and Employment," 4.

9. Government of Kenya, *High-Level Manpower Requirements*, iii.

10. Government of Kenya, Sessional Paper No. 10, *African Socialism and Its Application to Planning in Kenya* (Nairobi: Government Printer, 1965); Government of Kenya, *Kenyanization of Personnel in the Private Sector* (Nairobi: Government Printer, 1967), 1.

11. Ibid.

12. Ibid., 4.

13. Just about the time in 1967 that this government memorandum was issued, I was approached by the Ministry of Education with the offer of a ten-year contract as a teacher and administrator in remote, newly opened government day schools. They had found that with abundant jobs available elsewhere, Kenyans did not want such remote postings. I declined since I had already made plans to leave Kenya and begin my graduate studies.

14. Interview, Churchill, Nairobi, 18 May 1996.

15. Government of Kenya, *Choosing a Career*, Vocational Guidance Pamphlet No. 1 (Nairobi: Government Printer, 1965), para. 15.

16. Ibid.

17. Interview, Charles a, Nairobi, 5 April 1996.

18. Interview, Philip, Nairobi, 6 December 1995.

19. For half of my four-year residence at Giakanja, two other members of the teaching staff were young, inexperienced Americans who were not likely to have been any more able than I to advise students about careers.

20. Interview, David d, Nyeri, 22 November 1995.

21. Interview, Kihumba, Nairobi, 19 March 1996.

22. Interviews, David d, 22 December 1995; Stanley b, Nyeri, 26 November 1995; Charles f, Karatina, 8 April 1996.

23. Interview, Stanley b, 26 November 1995.

24. Interview, Joseph a, Mombasa, 12 April 1996.

25. Interview, David e, Nairobi, 12 February 1996.

26. Interview, Jacob, Nairobi, 21 February 1996.

27. Ibid.

28. "Tarmacking" is the local idiom for job hunting. Since the blacktop material used for making roads is called tarmac in Kenya, it is similar to the American expression of "pounding the pavement" for a job.

29. Interview, Robert, Mombasa, 13 April 1996.

30. Interview, Alex, Nairobi, 17 November 1995.

31. John Cameron, *The Development of Education in East Africa* (New York: Teachers College Press, 1968), appendix A, "Salary Scales and Teacher Categories," 135.

32. Interview, Titus, Nairobi, 13 November 1995. Titus is the oldest of eight children and felt responsible for them. If he stayed in the three-year S1 course, his siblings might not have been able to find alternative funding for their school fees during that time. In the 1960s, 7 shillings = $1.00.

33. Interview, Joseph b, Nairobi, 28 February 1996.

34. Interview, Kihumba, Nairobi, 19 March 1996.

35. Ibid.

36. Interview, Jonas, Nairobi, 20 February 1996.

37. Interview, Erastus, Nairobi, 5 December 1995.

38. Interview, Charles b, Kerugoya, 20 April 1996. The headmaster confided to me in a 1996 interview that he had always regretted not retaking his university exams after failing them in 1951. Perhaps this explains, at least in part, why he so encouraged his students to continue their educations, including their university degrees.

39. Interview, Michael a, Nairobi, 3 December 1995.

40. Interview, Richard b, Nairobi, 14 March 1996.

41. Ibid.

42. Interview, Samuel a, Nakuru, 11 February 1996.

43. Interview, Charles b, Kerugoya, 20 April 1996.

44. Interview, Dickson, Gatitu, 12 March 1996.

45. Interview, Charles b, Kerugoya, 20 April 1996.

46. Interview, Francis a, Nairobi, 22 February 1996. Francis came from a politically aware family, too, and this might have influenced his decision. His father had been a member of the Kikuyu Central Association and active in the Gikuyu Independent Church movement; he was also a friend of Kenyatta.

47. Unless otherwise noted, the material in this section on the Soviet Union all comes from the interview with Francis a (Nairobi, 22 February 1996).

48. Two students later returned to the university to complete master's degrees and one a doctorate, all in Europe or the United States.

49. Interview, Charles b, Kerugoya, 20 April 1996.

50. Interview, Erastus, Nairobi, 5 December 1995.

51. He had completed his senior secondary education (A level) in one year instead of two.

52. Interview, Harrison, Nairobi, 17 November 1995.

53. Interview, Charles c, Nairobi, 11 April 1996.

54. Each of the three classes I researched had initially divided themselves in employment equally between the public and private sectors.

55. Interview, Michael b, Nairobi, 17 November 1995.

56. Interview, Erastus, Nairobi, 5 December 1995.

57. Interview, Stanley a, Gachatha, 17 March 1996.

58. David Himbara, *Kenyan Capitalists, the State, and Development* (Boulder, Colo.: Lynne Rienner, 1994), 1–13.

59. Ibid., 8.

60. David Himbara, "Myths and Realities of Kenyan Capitalism," *Journal of Modern African Studies* 31, no. 1 (1993): 107.

61. This dream had often been expressed in autobiographical essays assigned in my Giakanja English classes.

62. Interview, Charles b, Kerugoya, 20 April 1996.

63. Interview, Amos, Nairobi, 21 February 1996.

64. Interview, Jesse, Nakuru, 15 January 1996.

65. I remember seeing him bolt from the laboratory after attempting a science paper and throwing himself on the ground in frustration. It was the last trial exam paper that he attempted.

66. Interview, Alex, Nairobi, 17 November 1995.

67. Interview, Nicholas, Nyeri, 10 April 1996.

68. One earns a credit if the exam score falls in the 3–6 grading range.

69. Interview, Richard a, Nairobi, 25 March 1996.

70. Interviews, Daniel, Nyeri, 4 March 1996; Ephantus, Nyeri, 3 March 1996.

71. Interview, Titus, Nairobi, 13 November 1995.

72. Interview, Joseph d, Nairobi, 29 November 1995.

73. Interview, Titus, Nairobi, 13 November 1995.

74. Jack Bloom, "The Economic Crisis in Kenya: Class and Ethnic Conflict," *Insurgent Sociologist* 13, no. 1/2 (Summer/Fall 1985): 96.

75. Ibid., 101.

76. Interview, William b, Nyeri, 24 November 1995.

Chapter 5. Entering an Economic Elite

1. Sandgren, *Christianity and the Kikuyu*, 37.

2. Peterson, *Creative Writing*, 55.

3. Ibid.

4. David K. Leonard, *African Successes: Four Managers of Kenyan Rural Development* (Los Angeles: University of California Press, 1991), 34.

5. Kitching, *Class and Economic Change in Kenya*, 297–311.

6. Interview, Joseph a, Mombasa, 12 April 1996.

7. Unless otherwise stated, I have been guided in the paragraphs that follow by Todd J. Moss, *African Development: Making Sense of the Issues and Actors* (Boulder, Colo.: Lynne Rienner, 2007), especially chap. 1, "The Complexities and Uncertainties of Development" and chap. 6, "Africa's Slow-Growth Puzzle."

8. Ibid., 91.

9. Frederick Cooper reminds us that such "gate-keeper states," as he calls them, were also designed to enrich the gate-keepers, generally recognized as the political elite of the country. *Africa since 1940*, 5.

10. For a full explanation of dependency theory applied to Kenya, see

Colin Leys, *Underdevelopment in Kenya: The Political Economy of Neo-colonialism* (Berkeley: University of California Press, 1975).

11. William Ochieng', "Independent Kenya, 1963-1986," in *A Modern History of Kenya 1895-1980*, edited by William Ochieng' (Nairobi: Evans Brothers, 1989), 209-14. See also Himbara, "Myths and Realities," 93-107. Himbara reminds us that some of Kenya's capitalists were of Asian origin.

12. Moss, *African Development*, 91.

13. Fantu Cheru, *Dependence, Underdevelopment and Unemployment in Kenya* (London: University Press of America, 1987), 61-67.

14. Interview, Stanley b, Nyeri, 16 October 1995.

15. Interviews, Harun, Nairobi, 31 October 1995; Joseph c, Nairobi, 16 November 1995; Michael b, Nairobi, 17 November 1995; Francis b, Nairobi, 7 February 1996.

16. Several former students have said that while they would never sell their land, it is worth several million shillings now and continuing to increase in value.

17. Interview, Joseph a, Mombasa, 12 April 1996.

18. Interview, Jesse, Nakuru, 15 February 1996.

19. Interview, Christopher, Nakuru, 3 December 1995.

20. Interview, Joshua, Nyeri, 25 November 1995; Ibid.

21. Interviews, Wilson, Nyeri, 24 November 1995; Charles e, Nyeri, 17 March 1996; William b, Nyeri, 24 November 1995.

22. Interviews, Erastus, Nairobi, 5 December 1995; Samuel a, Nakuru, 2 December 1995 and 11 February 1996.

23. Interviews, Erastus, Nairobi, 11 November 1995 and 5 December 1995. During the year 1995-96, Erastus developed recently purchased land near Nyahurura in the Rift Valley into a flower farm. His intention was to grow flowers, especially roses, which would be picked and shipped overnight for sale the next morning in Europe. More recently, having survived the 1997 terrorist bombing in Nairobi, which nearly leveled his bank (which was located next to the American Embassy), he has retired to his Rift Valley flower farm. Private communication, April 1998.

24. Interviews, David e, 12 February 1996; Duncan, Nairobi, 13 February 1996.

25. Interview, Charles a, Nairobi, 5 April 1996.

26. Interview, Harrison, Nairobi, 17 November 1995.

27. Interviews, Harun, Nairobi, 31 October 1995 and 4 February 1996.

28. Interview, Stanley a, Gachatha, 17 March 1996. 3 percent for a car loan, 2 percent for a house loan, and 5 percent for a farm land loan were typical rates for bank employee, whereas everyone else paid 25-30 percent for the same loans.

29. Interview, Jesse, Nakuru, 15 February 1996.

30. Interview, Charles c, Nairobi, 11 April 1996.

31. Interview, David e, Nairobi, 12 February 1996.

32. Interview, Stanley a, Gachatha, 17 March 1996.

33. Interview, Jacob, Nairobi, 21 February 1996. It is worth noting that the world economist Jeffrey Sachs does not link corruption with lack of development as closely as does Jacob. Sachs states that "the focus on corruption and governance is exaggerated, and seriously overstates the casual role of corruption and poor governance in Africa's laggard growth performance." Rather, Sachs argues, "Africa shows absolutely no tendency to be more or less corrupt than other countries at the same income level." In his opinion, adverse geography and deficient infrastructure are the culprits of slower growth. *The End of Poverty: Economic Possibilities for Our Time* (New York: Penguin, 2005), 312-14.

34. Mwai Kibaki, the new president elected in 2002, has been implicated in corruption as well. Michela Wrong: *It's Our Turn to Eat: The Story of a Kenyan Whistle-Blower* (New York: Harper, 2009).

35. Interview, Erastus, Nairobi, 5 December 1995.

36. Interview, Francis a, Nairobi, 22 February 1996.

37. Interview, Harun, Nairobi, 4 February, 1996.

38. Jane Karuiru, Giakanja physics instructor, personal communication, 13 March 1996. Claudia Buchmann reports that primary school enrollments have stagnated too, signaling to her that "Kenyans are losing faith in the value of schooling." "The State and Schooling in Kenya: Historical Developments and Current Challenges," *Africa Today* 46, no. 1 (1999): 112-13.

39. Giakanja's school certificate scores had begun to decline in the late 1980s. By 1995 they had plummeted to the point where none of the 150 students taking the exam scored well enough to go on to further education or to secure good employment. The current headmaster suggested that past concentration on athletics (Giakanja had been National Volleyball Champions), a failed experiment with coeducation, and administrative mismanagement accounted for its poor academic record, all of which he was now changing. Headmaster Giakanja Secondary School, personal communication, 8 November 1995.

40. The conversation took place on 21 October 1995. In a paper about Nairobi shoeshiners written thirteen years earlier, the authors lauded the industriousness of these informal sector entrepreneurs, although no mention is made of their living conditions or their limited prospects for marriage and family. Walter Elkan, T. C. I. Ryan, and J. T. Mukui, "The Economics of Shoeshining in Nairobi," *African Affairs* 81 (1982): 247-56.

Chapter 6. Personal Life in Elite Circles

1. Neil Price, "The Changing Value of Children among the Kikuyu of Central Province, Kenya," *Africa: Journal of the International African Institute* 66, no. 3 (1996): 417-19.

2. Ibid., 421.

3. The formula used is that the first son will be named after the paternal grandfather, the first daughter after the maternal grandmother, etc. If there are more than two sons and two daughters, then the naming continues to the parents' brothers and sisters, starting with the oldest. Ibid., 422–23.

4. Ibid., 423–24.

5. Ibid., 426.

6. Interviews, Titus, Nairobi, 31 January 1996; Matthew, Nyeri, 18 March 1996; Steven, Nyeri, 23 April 1996. Each had impregnated a woman whom he married but did not live with until he had finished secondary school. For one, this happened while he was in Form 1; the other two were in Form 4. Each has remained with his wife and had other children over the years.

7. Interview, Robert, Mombasa, 15 April 1996.

8. Interviews, Harun, Nairobi, 31 October 1995; Erastus, Nairobi, 5 December 1995.

9. Interview, Margaret, Nakuru, 16 February 1996

10. Interview, Francis a, Nairobi, 22 February 1996.

11. Interview, Sampson, Nairobi, 29 March 1996.

12. Ibid.

13. Interview, Christopher, Nakuru, 3 December 1995.

14. Interview, Charles e, Nyeri, 17 March 1996.

15. Interview, Duncan, Nairobi, 13 February 1996. As Duncan revealed, this was an interethnic marriage.

16. For more information about historical relationships between Gikuyu and Maasai, see the following: Ian Parker, "Strange Misunderstood Relationship," *East African Magazine*, http://www.theeastafrican.co.ke/magazine/-/434746/509930/-/item/0/-/d99cxiz/-/index.html (accessed 22 March 2010); William Lawren, "Masai and Kikuyu: An Historical Analysis of Cultural Transmission," *Journal of African History* 9, no. 4 (1968): 571–83.

17. Interview, Mary b, Kerugoya, 25 April 1996.

18. Carol M. Worthman and John W. M. Whiting, "Social Change in Adolescent Sexual Behavior, Mate Selection and Premarital Pregnancy Rates in a Kikuyu Community," *Ethos* 15, no. 2 (1987): 157.

19. Ibid., 158.

20. Interview, Margaret, Nakuru, 16 February 1996.

21. Interview, Charles f, Karatina, 16 February 1996.

22. Interview, Charles e, Nyeri, 17 March 1996.

23. Interviews, Ephantus, Nyeri, 3 March 1996; Daniel, Nyeri, 4 March 1996.

24. Interview, Joseph c, Nairobi, 21 November 1995.

25. Ibid.

26. Ibid.

27. Interview, Charles f, Karatina, 8 April 1996.

28. Worthman and Whiting, "Social Change," 150.

29. Ibid., 151, 158.

30. Ibid., 159.

31. Interview, Sampson, Nairobi, 29 March 1996.

32. Bert N. Adams and Edward Mburugu, "Kikuyu Bride Wealth and Polygyny Today," *Journal of Comparative Family Studies* 25, no. 2 (1994): 159–66. Bride wealth is defined by the authors as "the money and goods paid from the groom's family to that of the bride."

33. Interview, Daniel, Nyeri, 4 March 1996.

34. Edmondo Cavicchi, *Problems of Change in Kikuyu Tribal Society* (Bologna: EMI, 1977), 47, cited in Adams and Mburugu, "Kikuyu Bride Wealth," 160.

35. Interview, Daniel, Nyeri, 4 March 1996.

36. Interview, Joseph c, Nairobi, 21 November 1995.

37. Interview, Daniel, Nyeri, 4 March 1996.

38. Interview, Charles f, Karatina, 8 April 1996.

39. Interview, Margaret, Nakuru, 16 February 1996.

40. Interview, Harun, Nairobi, 4 February 1996.

41. Interviews, Joseph c, Nairobi, 16 November 1995; Jane, Nairobi, 29 February 1996.

42. With regard to polygyny, my students as a group are not representative of other Gikuyu of approximately their age. Research conducted in 1990 reveals that while polygyny is declining, about 15 percent of both rural and urban 30–40-year-old Gikuyu men still are polygynous or intend to practice polygyny. Adams and Mburugu, "Kikuyu Bride Wealth," 163.

43. Interview, James b, Nairobi, 30 January 1996.

44. Interview, Amos, Nairobi, 21 February 1996. I was not able to interview either of Amos's wives, although I met his second wife and their children.

45. Interview, Alex, Nairobi, 17 November 1995.

46. Interviews, Charles a, Nairobi, 5 April 1996; Salome, Nairobi, 4 February 1996.

47. Interview, Peter b, Nyeri, 26 February 1996.

48. Interview, Peter a, Nairobi, 13 February 1996. The average number of children in same mother–same father families was 6.9.

49. The average number of children in the students' families was 4.3.

50. Interview, Amos, Nairobi, 21 February 1996.

51. Interview, Samuel a, Nakuru, 2 December 1995.

52. Interview, George, Kerugoya, 20 April 1996.

53. Interviews, Duncan, Wamagana, 12 March 1996; Charles b, Kerugoya, 20 April 1996.

54. Interview, Jane, Nairobi, 29 February 1996.

55. Interview, Stanley b, Nyeri, 26 November 1995.

56. Interview, Joyce, Nairobi, 8 March 1996.

57. Interview, Francis b, Nairobi, 7 February 1996.

58. Interview, Esther, Nairobi, 10 March 1996.

59. Interview, Mary a, Karatina, 8 April 1996.

60. Interview, Margaret, Nakuru, 16 February 1996.

61. Interview, Joseph c, Nairobi, 21 November 1995.

62. Interview, Jane, Nairobi, 29 February 1996.

63. Interview, Joseph c, Nairobi, 21 November 1995.

64. The creation of such migratory labor trends was not unique to Kenya but was also found among many colonial economies on the continent. For an excellent introductory account of colonially created economies in Africa, see Iliffe, *Africans*, chap. 10.

65. Interview, Richard b, Nairobi, 14 March 1996.

66. Interview, Charles c, Nairobi, 11 April 1996.

67. Interview, John b, Kiganjo, 24 April 1996.

68. Interview, Joseph b, Nairobi, 28 February 1996.

69. Interview, James a, Nairobi, 10 November 1995.

70. Interview, Joyce, Nairobi, 8 March 1996.

71. Interview, Joseph d, Nairobi 19 November 1995.

72. Interview, Erastus, Nairobi, 5 December 1995.

73. Interview, Jonas, Nairobi, 20 February 1996.

74. Interview, Jacob, Nairobi, 21 February 1996.

75. Interview, Kihumba, Nairobi, 19 March 1996.

76. Interview, Charles c, Nairobi, 11 April 1996.

77. Interviews, Christopher, Nakuru, 3 December 1995; Francis b, Nairobi, 7 February 1996.

78. Interview, William b, Nyeri, 24 November 1995.

79. Interview, Erastus, Nairobi, 5 December 1995.

80. Interview, Michael a, Nakuru, 3 December 1995.

81. Interview, James b, Nairobi, 30 January 1996.

82. Interviews, Titus, Nairobi, 13 November 1995; Francis a, Nairobi, 22 February 1996.

Chapter 7. Reflections on the Next Generation

1. Iliffe, *Africans*, 95, as discussed in Thomas Burgess, "Introduction to Youth and Citizenship in East Africa," *Africa Today* 51, no. 3 (2005): ix.

2. Burgess, "Youth and Citizenship in East Africa," xii.

3. Ibid., xiv–xv.

4. All the interviews took place in the home of their parents, among children either at home on school holidays from secondary school (2), from university (2), or waiting to go to graduate school (3).

5. Interviews, Salome, Nairobi, 4 February 1996; Becky, Nakuru, 16 February 1996.

6. Interview, Salome, Nairobi, 4 February 1996.

7. Interview, Katherine, Karatina, 8 April 1996.

8. Interviews, Salome, Nairobi, 4 February 1996; Katherine, Karatina, 8 April 1996.

9. Interview, Salome, Nairobi, 4 February 1996.

10. Salome's grandmother was present on the day I interviewed her and came to greet me since I had previously met her when I was her son's teacher at Giakanja. She confided in me that young people had changed a great deal from earlier generations, especially in their inability to speak good Gikuyu. She told me that she could hardly understand her grandchildren.

11. Interview, Robert, Mombasa, 13 April 1996.

12. Interview, Katherine, Karatina, 8 April 1996.

13. At the fiftieth birthday celebration of a former student, attended by sixty to seventy friends and relatives, I was the only non-Gikuyu guest present.

14. This resentment exploded into violent attacks against Gikuyu during the 2007 Kenya Election Crisis. See Human Rights Watch, http://www.hrw .org/en/news/2008/01/03/kenya-review-elections-needed-end-violence, for a summary of these happenings.

15. Neal Sobania, *Culture and Customs of Kenya* (Westport, Connecticut: Greenwood Press, 2003), 156.

16. Interview, Becky, Nakuru, 16 February 1996.

17. Interview, Salome, Nairobi, 4 February 1996.

18. Interview, Emily and Salome, Kerugoya, 25 April 1996.

19. Interview, Esther, Nairobi, 10 March 1996. Esther instructed her children to tell their peers that they have a father; he just does not live with them.

20. Interviews, Joseph d, Nairobi, 29 November 1995; Erastus, Nairobi, 5 December 1995. One student did tell me that the hardships he experienced at Giakanja have made him a better husband. Just as he had to work hard to overcome the problems of life at a day school, so also he has worked hard to be a good husband. Another student told me that he and his wife had problems early in their marriage but worked hard to overcome them and have succeeded in doing so. None of the other students talked about their relationship with their spouse as a process of hard work or problem solving.

21. Interview, Mary b, Kerugoya, 25 April 1996.

22. Interview, Jane, Nairobi, 29 February 1996.

23. Sobania, *Culture and Customs of Kenya*, 156–57.

24. Ibid., 68

25. Interview, Nahashan, Nyeri, 14 February 1996.

26. These students are enormously proud of being able to educate their children at the best schools, often to advanced levels. From the most "well off" to the least, all of them were eager to tell me about their children's education, bragging, as many of them did, that all had university degrees. When asked, What has been your greatest achievement?, almost all answered, "I have educated all of my children."

27. Interview, Stanley a, Gachatha, 17 March 1996.

28. Interview, Richard c, Nairobi, 14 March 1996.

29. Interview, Wilson, Nyeri, 24 November 1995.

30. Interview, Erastus, Nairobi, 5 December 1995.

31. Interview, David e, Nairobi, 12 February 1996. See also Vincent Cable, "The Asians of Kenya," *African Affairs* 68, no. 272 (1969): 218–31.

32. Interviews, Jacob, Nairobi, 21 February 1996; William a, Nairobi, 6 December 1995; Richard c, Nairobi, 14 March 1996.

33. Interview, Stephen, Othaya, 23 April 1996.

34. Magnus O. Bassey, *Western Education and Political Domination in Africa: A Study in Critical and Dialogical Pedagogy* (Westport, Connecticut: Bergin & Garvey, 1999), 3.

35. G. K. Kieh, "The Roots of Western Influence in Africa: An Analysis of the Conditioning Process," *Social Science Journal* 29, no. 1 (1992): 3.

36. Adam Meyer, Review of *Western Education and Political Domination in Africa: A Study in Critical and Dialogical Pedagogy*, by Magnus O. Bassey (Westport, Conn.: Bergin & Garvey, 1999) in *African Studies Quarterly* 2, no. 2 (Summer 2000), http://web.africa.ufl.edu/asq/v4/vi2.htm (accessed 13 May 2010).

BIBLIOGRAPHY

Primary Sources

INTERVIEWS

I conducted my interviews between October 1995 and April 1996. They were primarily with former students and their families, though I also interviewed people associated with the planning and building of Giakanja, the secondary school that these students attended 1962–67 and at which I taught 1963–7. I began my interviews at Nyeri, the area closest to the school, and then proceeded to other parts of the country, though I frequently backtracked among all these areas as I located new people to interview. When completed, the interviews reveal the following geographic distribution: Nyeri District, 29; Nairobi District, 38; Rift Valley, 7; Mombasa, 2; Other, 21. See the appendix in this book for a selection of short biographies of some of the interviewees. Following is a complete list of interviews:

Agatha, Nyeri, 3 March 1996
Alexander, Nairobi, 17 November 1995
Amos, Nairobi, 21 February 1996
Anna and Susan, Giakanja, 16 March 1996
Beatrice, Nyeri, 22 April 1996
Becky, Nakuru, 16 February 1996
Benson, Nairobi, 7 December 1995
Charles a, Nairobi, 5 April 1996
Charles b, Kerugoya, 20 April 1996
Charles c, Nairobi, 11 April 1996
Charles d, Nyeri, 17 March 1996
Charles e, Kiganjo, 22 March 1996
Charles f, Karatina, 8 April 1996

Charles g, Nyeri, 23 November 1995
Charles h, Mahiga, 24 April 1996
Christopher, Nakuru, 3 December 1995
Churchill, Nairobi, 18 May 1996
Cornelius, Giakanja, 13 March 1996
Cyrus, Nyeri, 4 March 1996
Daniel, Nyeri, 4 March 1996
David a, Njoro, 15 February 1996
David b, Kabete, 4 April 1996
David c, Nairobi, 1 December 1995
David d, Nyeri, 22 November 1995
David e, Nairobi, 12 February 1996
Dickson, Nyeri, 12 March 1996
Douglas, Nyeri, 21 March 1996
Duncan, Nairobi, 13 February 1996
Edward, Nyeri, 22 March 1996
Emily and Salome, Kerugoya, 25 April 1996
Ephantus, Nyeri, 3 March 1996
Erastus, Nairobi, 5 December 1995
Esau, Nyeri, 13 March 1996
Esther, Thika, 10 March 1996
Eunice, Ruringu, 24 April 1996
Francis a, Nairobi, 22 February 1996
Francis b, Nairobi, 7 February 1996
Frederick, Nyeri, 25 February 1996
George, Kerugoya, 20 April 1996
Harrison, Nairobi, 17 November 1995
Harun, Nairobi, 31 October 1995, 4 February 1996
Helen, Nairobi, 4 February 1996
Jacob, Nairobi, 21 February 1996
James a, Nairobi, 10 November 1995
James b, Nairobi, 30 January 1996
Jane, Nairobi, 19 February 1996
Jesse, Nakuru, 15 February 1996
Joan, Nyeri, 19 April 1996
John a, Nairobi, 4 April 1996
John b, Kiganjo, 24 April 1996
Jonas, Nairobi, 20 February 1996
Joseph a, Mombasa, 12 April 1996
Joseph b, Nairobi, 28 February 1996
Joseph c, Nairobi, 16, 21 November 1995
Joseph d, Nairobi, 29 November 1995

Joshua, Nyeri, 25 November 1995
Joyce, Nairobi, 8 March 1996
Julius, Giakanja, 9 April 1996
Katherine, Karatina, 8 April 1996
Kihumba Nairobi, 19 March 1996
Margaret, Nakuru, 16 February 1996
Mary a, Karatina, 8 April 1996
Mary b, Kerugoya, 25 April 1996
Mathenge, Giakanja, 13 March 1996
Matthew, Nyeri, 18 March 1996
Michael a, Nakuru, 3 December 1995
Michael b, Nairobi, 17 November 1995
Millicent, Ihururu, 4 March 1996
Nahashan, Nairobi, 14 February 1996
Nancy, Nyeri, 16 March 1996
Newton, Nyeri, 21 March 1996
Nicholas, Nyeri, 10 April 1996
Patricia. Langata, 6 April 1996
Paul, Nyeri, 26 February 1996
Penina, Gachatha, 24 April 1996
Peter a, Nairobi, 13 February 1996
Peter b, Nyeri, 26 February 1996
Philip, Nairobi, 6 December 1995
Richard a, Nairobi, 25 March 1996
Richard b, Nairobi, 14 March 1996
Richard c, Nairobi, 14 March 1996
Robert, Mombasa, 13 April 1996
Salome, Nairobi, 4 February 1996
Sampson, Nairobi, 29 March 1996
Samuel a, Nakuru, 2 December 1995, 11 February 1996
Samuel b, Nyeri, 26 November 1995
Samuel c, Nyeri, 27 February 1996
Samuel d, Nyeri, 19 April 1996
Simon, Nairobi, 29 January 1996
Stanley a, Nyeri, 17 March 1996
Stanley b, Nyeri, 26 November 1995
Steven, Othaya, 23 April 1996
Titus, Nairobi, 31 January 1996
Walter, Nyeri, 16 March 1996
William a, Nairobi, 6 December 1995
William b, Nyeri, 24 November 1995
Wilson, Nyeri, 24 November 1995

ARCHIVES

Kenya National Archives (KNA)
    The following deposits at KNA were consulted:
        CD/AB   Community Development
        DC/Nyeri   District Commissioner, Nyeri
        Ed/2   Ministry of Education, Deposit 2
        MAC/KEN   Murumbi Africa Collection
        PC/CP   Provincial Commissioner, Central Province
        VP   District Commissioner, Nyeri
        VQ   Provincial Commissioner, Central Province
Rhodes House Library, Oxford (RH)
    Mss. Brit. Emp s. 332 Arthur Creech Jones Papers
    Mss. Afr. S, 2100 Thomas Askwith Correspondence

OFFICIAL PUBLICATIONS

Government of Great Britain. *Historical Survey of the Origins and Growth of Mau Mau.* [Corfield Report.] Cmnd. 1030. London, 1960.

Government of Kenya. *African Socialism and Its Application in Kenya.* Sessional Paper No. 10. Nairobi, 1965.

———. *Choosing a Career.* Vocational Guidance Pamphlet No. 1. Nairobi, 1965.

———. *High-level Manpower Requirements and Resources in Kenya 1964–1970.* Nairobi, 1965.

———. *Kenyanization of Personnel in the Private Sector.* Nairobi, 1967.

Secondary Sources

BOOKS AND ARTICLES

Adams, Bert N., and Edward Mburugu. "Kikuyu Bride Wealth and Polygyny Today." *Journal of Comparative Family Studies* 25, no. 2 (1994): 159–66.

Anderson, J. E. "The Kenya Education Commission Report: An African View of Educational Planning." *Comparative Education Review* 19, no. 2 (1965): 201–7.

Anderson, John. "Self Help and Independency: The Political Implications of a Continuing Tradition in African Education in Kenya." *African Affairs* 70, no. 278 (1971): 9–22.

———. *The Struggle for the School.* London: Longmans, 1970.

Barnett, Donald L., and Karari Njama. *Mau Mau from Within: Autobiography and Analysis of Kenya's Peasant Revolt.* New York: Modern Reader, 1966.

Bassey, Magnus O. "Higher Education and the Rise of Early Political Elites in Africa." *Review of Higher Education in Africa* 1, no. 1 (2009): 30–38.

————. *Western Education and Political Domination in Africa: A Study in Critical and Dialogical Pedagogy*. Westport, Conn.: Bergin & Garvey, 1999.

Berman, Bruce. *Control and Crisis in Colonial Kenya: The Dialectic of Domination*. London: James Currey, 1990.

Berman, Bruce, and John Lonsdale. *Unhappy Valley: Conflict in Kenya & Africa*. Book 2, *Violence & Ethnicity*. London: James Currey, 1992.

Bloom, Jack. "The Economic Crisis in Kenya: Class and Ethnic Conflict." *Insurgent Sociologist* 13, no. 1/2 (Summer/Fall 1985): 93–103.

Branch, Daniel. *Defeating Mau Mau, Creating Kenya: Counterinsurgency, Civil War, and Decolonization*. New York: Cambridge University Press, 2009.

————. "The Enemy Within: Loyalists and the War Against Mau Mau in Kenya." *Journal of African History* 48 (2007): 291–315.

Buchmann, Claudia. "The State and Schooling in Kenya: Historical Developments and Current Challenges." *Africa Today* 46, no. 1 (1999): 95–117.

Bunyi, Grace. "Constructing Elites in Kenya: Implications for Classroom Language Practices in Africa." In *Discourse and Education*, 2nd ed., edited by Marilyn Martin-Jones, Anne-Marie De Mejía, and Nancy H. Hornberger, 147–57. Encyclopedia of Language and Education 3. New York: Springer, 2008.

Burgess, Thomas. "Introduction to Youth and Citizenship in East Africa." *Africa Today* 51, no. 3 (2005): vii–xxiv.

Cable, Vincent. "The Asians of Kenya." *African Affairs* 68, no. 272 (July 1969): 218–31.

Cameron, John. *The Development of Education in East Africa*. New York: Teacher's College Press, 1968.

Castle, E. B. *Growing Up in East Africa*. London: Oxford University Press, 1966.

Cavicchi, Edmondo. *Problems of Change in Kikuyu Tribal Society*. Bologna: EMI, 1977.

Cheru, Fantu. *Dependence, Underdevelopment and Unemployment in Kenya*. London: University Press of America, 1987.

Cooper, Frederick. *Africa since 1940: The Past of the Present*. Cambridge: Cambridge University Press, 2002.

Court, David. "The Education System as a Response to Inequality in Tanzania and Kenya." *Journal of Modern African Studies* 14, no. 4 (1976): 661–90.

Davison, Jean. *Voices from Mutira: Change in the Lives of Rural Gikuyu Women, 1910–1995*. 2nd ed. Boulder, Colo.: Lynn Rienner, 1996.

Elkan, Walter, T. C. I. Ryan, and J. T. Mukui. "The Economics of Shoe Shining in Nairobi." *African Affairs* 81 (1982): 247–56.

Elkins, Caroline. *Imperial Reckoning: The Untold Story of Britain's Gulag in Kenya*. New York: Henry Holt and Co., 2005.

Furley, O. W., and T. Watson. *A History of Education in East Africa*. London: Nok Publications, 1978.

Geiger, Susan. "Tanganyikan Nationalism as 'Women's Work': Life Histories,

Collective Biography and Changing Historiography." *Journal of African History* 37 (1996): 465–78.

Gengenbach, Heidi. "Truth-Telling and the Politics of Women's Life History Research in Africa: A Reply to Kirk Hoppe." *International Journal of African Historical Studies* 27, no. 3 (1994): 619–27.

Himbara, David. *Kenyan Capitalists, the State, and Development*. Boulder, Colo.: Lynne Rienner, 1994.

———. "Myths and Realities of Kenyan Capitalism." *Journal of Modern African Studies* 31, no. 1 (1993): 93–107.

Iliffe, John. *Africans: The History of a Continent*. 2nd ed. Cambridge: Cambridge University Press, 2007.

Kanogo, Tabitha. *Squatters and the Roots of Mau Mau, 1904–1963*. London: James Currey, 1987.

Kariuki, J. M. *Mau Mau Detainee*. London: Oxford University Press, 1963.

Keats-Rohan, K. S. B. "Biography, Identity and Names: Understanding the Pursuit of the Individual in Prosopography." In *Prosopography Approaches and Applications: A Handbook*, edited by K. S. B. Keats-Rohan, 139–81. Oxford: University of Oxford, 2007. http://prosopography.modhist.ox.ac.uk/images/06%20KKR.pdf.pdf (accessed 23 September 2010).

———. "Prosopography and Computing: A Marriage Made in Heaven?" *History and Computing* 12, no. 1 (2000): 1–11.

Keller, Edmond J. "Development Policy and the Evaluation of Community Self-Help: The Harambee School Movement in Kenya." *Studies in Comparative International Development* 18, no. 4 (1983): 55–75.

Kenyatta, Jomo. *Facing Mount Kenya*. London: Secker and Warburg, 1938.

Kershaw, Greet. *Mau Mau from Below*. Oxford: James Currey, 1997.

Kieh, G. K. "The Roots of Western Influence in Africa: An Analysis of the Conditioning Process." *Social Science Journal* 29, no. 1 (1992): 7–19.

King, Kenneth. "Development and Education in Narok District of Kenya: The Pastoral Maasai and Their Neighbors." *African Affairs* 71, no. 285 (1972): 389–407.

Kinyanjui, Peter Kabiru. "Education, Training and Employment of Secondary School Leavers in Kenya." *Education in Eastern Africa* 2, no 1 (1971): 3–21.

Kipkorir, B. E. "The Alliance High School and Origins of the Elite: 1926–1962." PhD diss., University of Cambridge, 1969.

Kitching, Gavin. *Class and Economic Change in Kenya: The Making of an African Petite-Bourgeoisie*. New Haven, Conn.: Yale University Press, 1980.

Koff, David, and George von der Muhll. "Political Socialization in Kenya and Tanzania—A Comparative Analysis." *Journal of Modern African Studies* 5, no. 1 (1967): 13–51.

Lawren, William. "Masai and Kikuyu: An Historical Analysis of Cultural Transmission." *Journal of African History* 9, no. 4 (1968): 571–83.

Leonard, David K. *African Successes: Four Managers of Kenyan Rural Development*. Los Angeles: University of California Press, 1991.

Leys, Colin. *Underdevelopment in Kenya: The Political Economy of Neo-colonialism.* Berkeley: University of California Press, 1975.

Lillis, Kevin M. "Processes of Secondary Curriculum Innovation in Kenya." *Comparative Education Review* 29, no. 1 (1985): 80–96.

Lonsdale, John. "The Moral Economy of Mau Mau: Wealth, Poverty and Civic Virtue in Kikuyu Political Thought." In Bruce Berman and John Lonsdale, *Unhappy Valley: Conflict in Kenya & Africa*, book 2, *Violence & Ethnicity*, 265–504. Oxford: James Currey, 1992.

Lugard, Captain F. D. *The Rise of our East African Empire: Early Efforts in Nyasaland and Uganda.* Vol. 1. Edinburgh: Blackwood, 1893.

Maloba, Wunyabari O. *Mau Mau and Kenya: An Analysis of a Peasant Revolt.* Oxford: James Currey, 1998.

Morgan, Gordon D. *Practices, Problems and Issues in East African Education.* Privately printed, 1968.

Moss, Todd J. *African Development: Making Sense of the Issues and Actors.* Boulder, Colo.: Lynne Rienner, 2007.

Mwiria, Kilemi. "Kenya's Harambee Secondary School Movement: The Contradictions of Public Policy." *Comparative Education Review* 34, no. 3 (1990): 350–68.

Ochieng', William. "Independent Kenya, 1963–1986." In *A Modern History of Kenya, 1895–1980*, edited by William Ochieng', 209–14. Nairobi: Evans Brothers, 1989.

Olson, Jerry B. "Secondary Schools and Elites in Kenya: A Comparison Study of Students in 1961 and 1968." *Comparative Education Review* 16, no. 1 (1972): 44–53.

Otiende, J. E., S. P. Wamahiu, and A. M. Karugu. *Education and Development in Kenya: A Historical Perspective.* Nairobi: Oxford University Press, 1992.

Peterson, Derek. *Creative Writing: Translation, Bookkeeping, and the Work of Imagination in Colonial Kenya.* Portsmouth, N.H.: Heinemann Books, 2004.

———. Review of *Defeating Mau Mau, Creating Kenya: Counterinsurgency, Civil War, and Decolonization* by Daniel Branch (New York: Cambridge University Press, 2009). *Journal of Imperial and Commonwealth History* 38, no. 2 (2000): 337–39.

Plotnicov, Leonard. *Strangers to the City: Urban Man in Jos, Nigeria.* Pittsburgh: University of Pittsburgh Press, 1967.

Price, Neil. "The Changing Value of Children among the Kikuyu of Central Province, Kenya." *Africa: Journal of the International African Institute* 66, no. 3 (1996): 411–36.

Rado, Emil R. "The Relevance of Education for Employment." In *Education, Society and Development: New Perspectives from Kenya*, edited by David Court and Dharam P. Ghai, 29–46. Nairobi: Oxford University Press, 1974.

Sachs, Jeffrey. *The End of Poverty: Economic Possibilities for Our Time.* New York: Penguin, 2005.

Sandgren, David. *Christianity and the Kikuyu: Religious Divisions and Social Conflict.* New York: Peter Lang, 1989.

Sifuna, Daniel N. "Diversified Secondary Education: A Comparative Survey of Kenya and Tanzania." *Geneve-Afrique* 28, no. 2 (1990): 95–103.

Sobania, Neal. *Culture and Customs of Kenya.* Westport, Conn.: Greenwood Press, 2003.

Somerset, H. C. A. "Educational Aspirations of Forth-Form Pupils in Kenya." In *Education, Society and Development: New Perspectives from Kenya,* edited by David Court and Dharam P. Ghai, 149–84. Nairobi: Oxford University Press, 1974.

Stone, Lawrence. "Prosopography." *Daedalus* 100, no. 1 (Winter 1971): 46–79.

Thiong'o, Ngugi wa. *A Grain of Wheat.* Rev. ed. New York: Heinemann, 1986.

Tonkin, Elizabeth. *Narrating Our Pasts: The Social Construction of Oral History.* Cambridge: Cambridge University Press, 1993.

Vail, Leroy, and Landeg White. *Power and the Praise Poem: Southern African Voices in History.* London: James Curry, 1991.

Worthman, Carol M., and John W. M. Whiting. "Social Change in Adolescent Sexual Behavior, Mate Selection and Premarital Pregnancy Rates in a Kikuyu Community." *Ethos* 15, no. 2 (June 1987): 145–65.

Wrong, Michela. *It's Our Turn to Eat: The Story of a Kenyan Whistle-Blower.* New York: Harper, 2009.

ELECTRONIC SOURCES

Human Rights Watch. "Kenya: Review of Elections Needed to End Violence." http://www.hrw.org/en/news/2008/01/03/kenya-review-elections-needed-end-violence (accessed 23 March 2010).

Meyer, Adam. Review of *Western Education and Political Domination in Africa: A Study in Critical and Dialogical Pedagogy* by Magnus O. Bassey (Westport, Conn.: Bergin & Garvey, 1999). *African Studies Quarterly* 2, no. 2 (Summer 2000). http://web.africa.ufl.edu/asq/v4/vi2.htm (accessed 13 May 2010).

Parker, Ian. "Strange Misunderstood Relationship." *East African Magazine* (2009). http://www.theeastafrican.co.ke/magazine/-/434746/509930/-/item/0/-/d99cxiz/-/index.html (accessed 22 March 2010).

"Select Bibliography of Works Relating to Prosopography." Modern History Research Unit, University of Oxford. http://prosopography.modhist.ox.ac.uk/bibliography.htm (accessed 14 September 2010).

INDEX

Page numbers in italics indicate illustrations and captions.

179

AFRICA AND THE DIASPORA
History, Politics, Culture

SERIES EDITORS

Thomas Spear
David Henige
Michael Schatzberg

Spirit, Structure, and Flesh:
Gendered Experiences in African Instituted Churches among the Yoruba of Nigeria
Deidre Helen Crumbley

A Hill among a Thousand:
Transformations and Ruptures in Rural Rwanda
Danielle de Lame

Defeat Is the Only Bad News:
Rwanda under Musinga, 1897–1931
Alison Liebhafsky Des Forges; edited by David Newbury

Power in Colonial Africa:
Conflict and Discourse in Lesotho, 1870–1960
Elizabeth A. Eldredge

Nachituti's Gift:
Economy, Society, and Environment in Central Africa
David M. Gordon

Intermediaries, Interpreters, and Clerks:
African Employees in the Making of Colonial Africa
Edited by Benjamin N. Lawrance, Emily Lynn Osborn, and
Richard L. Roberts